FINDING MY WAY HOME

FINDING MY WAY HOME

A Christian Life in Communist China

NETTIE MA *with Kenneth Chatlos*

Smyth & Helwys Publishing, Inc.
6316 Peake Road
Macon, Georgia 31210-3960
1-800-747-3016

The paper used in this publication meets the minimum requirements of
American National Standard for Information Sciences—
Permanence of Paper for Printed Library Materials.
ANSI Z39.48–1984. (alk. paper)

Library of Congress Cataloging-in-Publication Data

Ma, Nettie, 1942-
Finding my way home : a Christian life in communist China
by Nettie Ma with Kenneth Chatlos.
p. cm.
ISBN 1-57312-431-1 (alk. paper)
1. Ma, Nettie, 1942-
2. Christian biography–China
3. Christian biography–United States
I. Chatlos, Kenneth, 1941-
II. Title.
BS1725.M2A3 2004
275.1'082'092–dc22

2004004010

Table of Contents

Preface vii
Introduction ix
Prologue xi

1. Exiles in the Interior, *1942–1945* 1
2. Life During Our Civil War, *1945–1949* 11
3. Education and Re-education, *1949–1953* 17
4. New Directions in School, *1953–1961* 29
5. A Communist College Education, *1961–1965* 47
6. A Budding Romance Amidst the Great Proletarian Cultural Revolution, *1965–1966* 59
7. On the Road for the Revolution, *1967–1968* 73
8. Re-education on a Military Farm in Rural Jiangsu, *1968–1970* 93
9. Political Realities and the Birth of a Child, *1970–1974* 117
10. The Last Train, *1974–1980* 131
11. Open Door to the United States, *1980–1984* 147
12. "A Time to Sow, a Time to Weep," *1984–1986* 173
13. Adoption or Expatriation, *1986–1990* 191
14. Green Pastures, *1990–1991* 213

Epilogue: Comfortably at Home 223
Notes 225

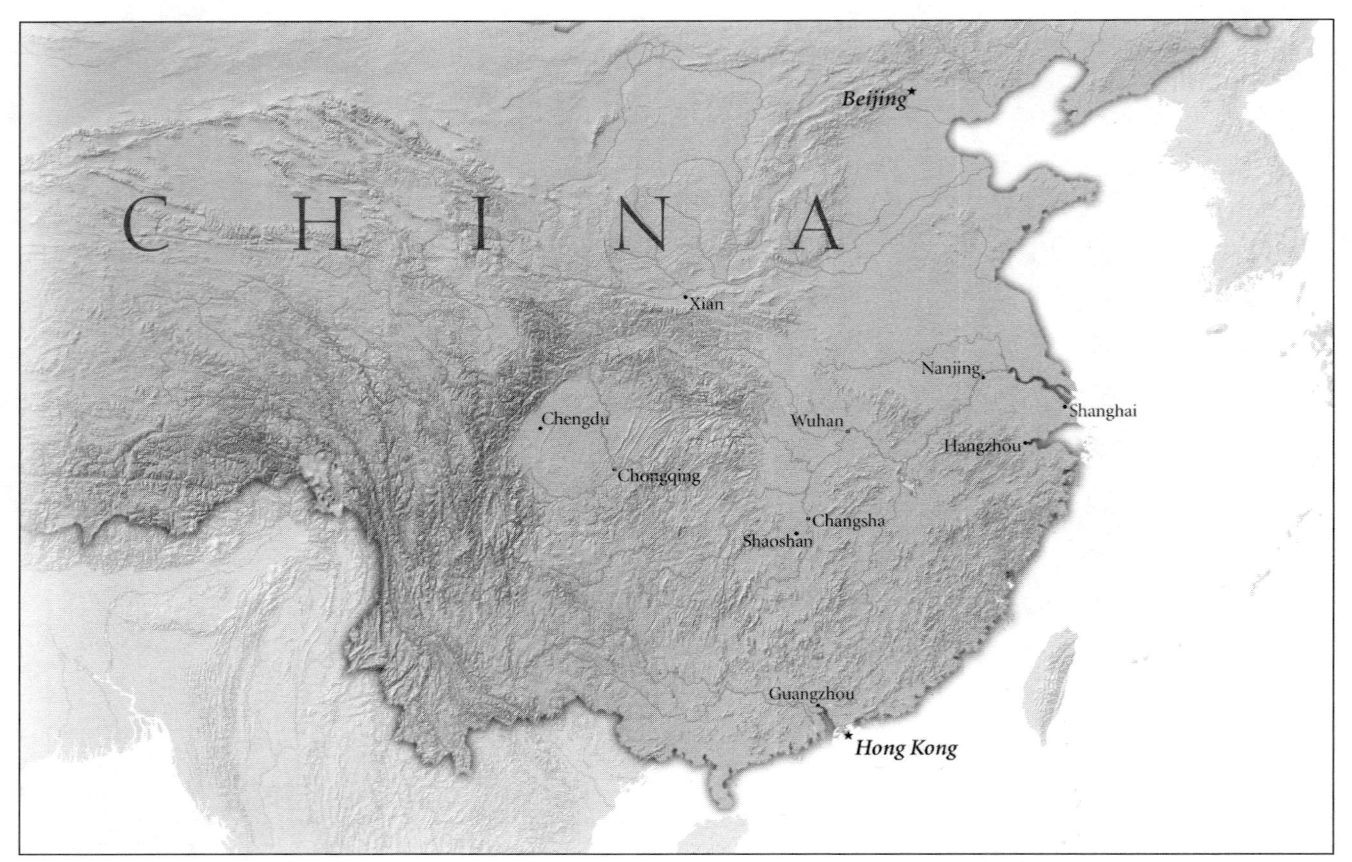
CHINA
Beijing
Xian
Nanjing
Shanghai
Chengdu
Wuhan
Hangzhou
Chongqing
Changsha
Shaoshan
Guangzhou
Hong Kong

Preface

Our colleagues, friends, and families have encouraged us as we have told them bits and pieces of Nettie's story. We could not begin to name them all here. Still, we offer our special thanks to a few people. Paul and Harriet Smock, Lucy O'Neill, and Ken's wife Phyllis have followed our work with interest. John Young, Director of Curry Library at William Jewell College, has helped out on computer questions. Mary Xu, Nettie's daughter, prepared the map and assisted with the pictures.

Ma Geshun knows his daughter Nettie's story firsthand; she has repeatedly phoned him in Shanghai to check on particulars in "their story." Daniel Bays, Professor of History at Calvin College, and Deborah Chasteen, Professor of Communication at William Jewell College, read the entire manuscript, corrected mistakes, and offered suggestions. Our book is better because of their counsel. The problems that remain are of our own doing.

Friends who read Nettie's story might ask how she persevered. Her answer to their question rings clear: "God's grace and strength, which I have often found in the company of friends, have made it possible for me to find my way home and to tell you about my journey."

Introduction

When I was a young girl, my parents warned me never to record my story with black ink on white paper. Their political experiences in Chairman Mao's China had taught them the dangers of such candor and openness. Chinese people from my generation speak guardedly about the grand and terrible events that have defined our lives for the past seven decades. We have survived war with Japan, our own civil war, Mao's "new order," re-education, brainwashing, imprisonment, Tiananmen Square, and more. Indeed, we have witnessed so many crises that the extraordinary has become ordinary. If I could have ignored or escaped these "ordinary events," I might have enjoyed permanent safety and security in my native Shanghai. Too often, however, escape has proved impossible. Too often, then, I have traveled on an extraordinary journey as I have tried to find my way home.

The path of my life has been far from straight and smooth. More often than not, the hills have been steep and long, and the valleys have been deep and rough. But when I have looked up, God has given me eyes to see. The tiny sparrows sing from the trees and the wildflowers decorate the way; the sunrise gladdens my heart and the moon's soft glow calms my soul. Such treasures, hidden among painful thorns and soul-destroying dangers, have paved my daily path for as long as I can remember.

My parents' cautions served me well in my homeland. But now that I have moved to the United States and have become an American citizen, now that I have found my way home, I remember the words of the Preacher, who wrote that "for everything there is a season, and a time for every matter under heaven; . . . a time to keep silent, and a time to speak." Now it is a time to speak and to write, especially for my two dear daughters, Lana and Mary. Now I must record my story for them.

Prologue

Between 1912 and 1942, China witnessed thirty years of intermittent conflict and permanent disorder. China's child emperor, Henry Puyi, abdicated in February 1912. A major revolution had broken out four months earlier. Within a decade, regional warlords had replaced China's central government. In the southeast, Sun Zhongshan (Sun Yat-sen) established his Nationalist Party, also known as the Guomindang (GMD). There, he formed an alliance with the Chinese Communist Party (CCP) and trained an army. When Sun died in 1925, Jiang Jieshi (Chiang Kai-shek) took over the leadership of the GMD. By 1928, Jiang gained control of much of southern China, established a new government at Nanjing, and turned on his Communist allies. Three years later, the Communists fled from rural Jiangxi and marched north, some 6,000 miles, and set up their base in Shanxi.

The Nationalists and the Communists understood something of China's vulnerability when, in 1931, Japan annexed Manchuria. Five years later, Jiang agreed to a United Front with the CCP, now led by Chairman Mao Zedong, also known as Mao Tse-tung. Together, they would fight the common enemy. The Japanese armies moved quickly. They attacked Beijing in July 1937 and captured Nanjing the following December. Jiang fled his capital and established his new headquarters to the west, in Sichuan. Four years later, Japan brought the United States into China's war when they bombed Pearl Harbor. Unfortunately, this brought no quick relief to China . . .or to the lives of the family of Nettie Ma.

My family witnessed and participated in the "re-formations" of China. Their story begins before the 1912 abdication of the boy-emperor Puyi and extends well beyond the 1949 Communist victory in our Civil War.[1] For the most part, they lived during these troubled years in or near Shanghai and Nanjing. Here, on our east coast, Christian missionaries from the West influenced my family in profound ways. Indeed, both of my grandfathers and my maternal great-grandfather founded and pastored churches. Although my family, men and women alike, undoubtedly knew about Mao Zedong's and Jiang Jieshi's political and military battles, they steered clear of politics. Even so, my family, through their lives and ministries, occasionally came into contact with high-level politicians. Unlike our own politicians, the Japanese, who invaded our country in 1937, could not be avoided. Unless, of course, one took my father's course and retreated to the interior of China. I will tell my own story—it begins in 1942—soon enough and in great detail. But before I get on to that, the subject of this book, I must reflect briefly on my parents and grandparents. Their stories, which reach back for half a century and more, enveloped and enriched my own past and future, even on those early occasions when I could not be present to witness what they experienced.

Sheng Youngpao, my maternal grandfather, became a wealthy man while he worked as the senior accountant for the Presbyterian Publishing House in Shanghai. During these days, he periodically visited the church that Shi Ziping, my great-grandfather, pastored. There, in Shi's church, he met Nettie Moomau, an American Protestant missionary who had left Los Angeles to minister among the Chinese.[2] In time, Sheng embraced the Christian faith and offered all that he had to God. No longer satisfied with an accountant's career, he turned to the ministry. As he prepared for this calling, he applied his considerable gifts and energies to school, where, among other things, he mastered the Hebrew language. After he graduated, he built and pastored a church in Shanghai.

Shi Lizhen, my maternal grandmother, knew from experience the Chinese custom that led many parents to bind their little girls' feet. After a while, this binding created unnaturally small, misshaped feet. Understandably, adult women, victims of this custom, walked with difficulty on their "lily feet"; strangely, adult men, suitors of such women, found their walk sexually attractive. In time, however, her parents realized that as a Christian family they should allow their daughter's feet to grow naturally. So they took off the wrappings, but not soon enough to avoid minor injury. Grandmother took on multiple responsibilities when she married Pastor Sheng. She bore him seven children, managed the household, taught school, and assisted her husband and Miss Nettie in their work.[3] Auntie Bessie, one of Grandma's daughters and also a bookkeeper, cautioned her mother about being excessively generous. It did no good. If someone was short of money, or if another needed a shirt, Grandma, hardly a wealthy woman, came to the rescue. She also entertained regularly on Sundays, occasions when she set up three or four extra tables for the guests who filled her home.[4]

In the early days, Grandpa Sheng and Miss Nettie (occasionally accompanied by Grandma Shi) engaged in evangelism and church planting in small communities close to Shanghai. They walked from village to village, preaching, translating, and caring for their parishioners. The deacons from these little churches served both their Shanghai visitors and their local brothers and sisters well. In time, Grandpa sent some of these men off to school for further study. Soon after my mother's birth, Grandma Shi began her own itinerant ministry in these same villages. She too would tell her people about Jesus. The injury that she had sustained from having her feet bound made this walking difficult, especially when she made her way down the country roads. Most of the time that Grandmother was gone, my mother stayed with a cousin who served as Mama's wet nurse. On one particular occasion when Grandma took her little girl on a preaching trip, her poor baby got head lice. The remedy was simple yet dramatic: they shaved her head. Poor baby, her beautiful hair all gone, bald. She cried and cried and cried.

Grandma taught math at the McTyeire girls' high school. A few of her pupils, girls whose parents she knew from their Shanghai Church, were people with important connections to GMD.

God spoke through Scripture with certainty and power to each of my grandparents. Grandpa loved to quote his favorite biblical passage, "I have fought the good fight, I have finished the race, I have kept the faith" (1 Tim 4:7), a challenging text he had read thousands of times from its frame up on his bedroom wall. Grandma, when she looked up on her bedroom wall, saw her favorite passage: "forgetting what lies behind and straining forward to what lies ahead, I press on toward the goal for the prize of the upward call of God in Christ Jesus" (Phil 3:13-14). This framed text written in calligraphy reminded her of God's strength and expectations. In the difficulties of life, Grandmother may have exceeded her husband when it came to courage and endurance. When she faced hardship, she always knew that there would be a way to cope, for she also knew that God never burdens people with loads they cannot bear.[5]

Ma Shaorui, my paternal grandfather, was born in Little Horse Village in the province of Shanxi. His mother died when he was three; his father died two years later. That left him at the mercy of his uncle, who stole the property that his nephew should have inherited. At age thirteen, Shaorui ran away from home and joined a church in Xian. He hoped that his new American friend, a man affiliated with the China Inland Mission, would help him in regaining his property. While the missionary could not assist my grandfather in this matter, he did help him with his education. The missionary hired a Chinese tutor to teach the young boy the Chinese classics.

This missionary soon recognized his charge's brilliance and sent him east for further study. Fifteen days later, Shaorui showed up in Shanghai. His association with the China Inland Mission in Xian probably helped him secure a position with their Shanghai Office. He learned English from these missionaries and again sought their assistance in suing his relatives for stealing his heritage. Amid his legal controversy, however, he embraced the Christian faith, forgave his relatives, and abandoned his suit.

Thereafter, my grandfather attended a revival at Mother Lawler's Shanghai church, a place known also as "The Four Corners." At this revival he witnessed Christian love and a remarkable healing.[6] In time, he was ordained in Shanghai as a Christian minister. At that point, he adopted "Nathan" as his English name. This reflected his hopes that he would be able to pattern his life after the Old Testament prophet, a man who had had enough courage to confront King David about his notorious sins.

Chen Ciai, my paternal grandmother, lost her mother when she was a young girl in the city of Beihai in Guangdong Province.[7] Later, when her father remarried, he sent his daughter to the Shanghai Door of Hope Orphan Home. "Mother Lawler," a missionary at the home, gave her new little girl the English name of "Grace."[8] Nathan Ma worked at this same orphanage. There, Mother Lawler served as the matchmaker for Grace and Nathan, who were married in Shanghai around the year 1912. Both of the newlyweds understood only too well the difficulties orphans face. Thereafter, they moved to Nanjing and, although poor themselves, started a church. In time, Grandma bore Grandpa five children.[9]

At some point between 1912 and 1920, a lawyer showed up at the front door of the house where my grandparents lived. He presented Grandma Grace with a large sum of money (more than 300 silver dollars) that her parents had left as her inheritance. My grandparents decided to use this money to build a church and to start an industrial school for orphan girls. Before they started these grand projects, they returned to Shanghai, where they studied lace-making and other arts and crafts. After this training, they started both the church and the "Sincerity Industrial School for Girls." There, they taught arts and crafts to the seven to eight orphan girls who wandered in. Grandma prepared the meals and took care of other routine tasks at the school; she also taught her girls such handwork as knitting and sock-making.

Miss Sharp, an American missionary, became the first person to sell products from my grandparents' school. Indeed, she did so well at this that they bought her a special rickshaw that enabled her to sell and deliver her goods more easily. Among other things, she helped my grandparents export their products to the West. Within a year's time, they took on an additional twenty girls. But even with this increase in workers, they failed to keep up with the demand for their goods. So they invited their Nanjing neighbors to take on piecework.[10]

The 1920 struggles among the warlords and between the CCP and the GMD changed considerably after Jiang Jieshi's Northern Expedition from his southern base close by Guangzhou. By 1928, Jiang had outmaneuvered his enemies and assumed the presidency of the National Government; now, he resided in Nanjing. When his domestic servants got sick, Jiang's housekeeper frequently invited my grandfather to the President's home to pray for their recovery. On one morning at about 5 A.M., the car of H. H. Kong, China's Minister of the Treasury and the husband of Song Ailing,[11] showed up outside my grandparent's home. They asked my grandfather to come with them and pray for David, Kong's son. Grandpa returned with these people and, like the apostles, prayed in Jesus' name that the boy would be healed. David's fever abated immediately. Soon thereafter, my grandfather received an anonymous gift.

My grandparents used that gift to buy a larger piece of property where they moved the school and built a new church. This church, located by the Yangzi River, was an oasis for missionaries for many years.[12] In 1928, a famine in Shandong Province made people so desperate that they sold their children. Some good parents took in seventy such girls with hopes of bringing them to the Nanjing School. Along the way, bandits surrounded the group. Fortunately, one girl recognized the bandit leader as her uncle and secured the prisoners' release when she told him about their destination. After they arrived in Nanjing, the school housed more than 100 orphan girls. In the 1932 famine in Shanxi, desperate people resorted to eating the bark off trees; many of these people died. During this crisis, Grandpa returned home, his first visit in thirty years, and picked up sixty additional orphans. At this point my grandparents opened their orphanage, now called the "Sincerity Industrial School," to boys.[13] They also began producing such different goods as cotton, gauze, goat's milk, books, and pamphlets.

My grandparents taught their girls a wide range of subjects, including arts and crafts, the Bible, literature, patriotism, music, and cooking. The age level of the girls ranged from kindergarten through middle school. Their graduates, skilled and attractive women, had no trouble finding husbands. One married the mayor of Nanjing City. Many married college professors, medical doctors, and pastors. Others went on to serve as workers in today's China.[14] Some now live in the United States.

Many churches invited my grandfather to preach and to conduct revivals. On one such occasion, he was scheduled for meetings at a remote country location. Rather than walk, he rented a donkey.[15] As he headed toward his destination, Grandpa sang hymns while the donkey did the work. When he—Grandpa, not the donkey—got thirsty, he stopped and bought cucumbers from a farmer. Afterward, he couldn't see the farmer anywhere; in the end, Grandpa took this unusual episode to be God's special provision for God's servant's needs. Grandpa went as far as Inner Mongolia on these legendary trips; sometimes he traveled by camel.

My grandfather became a world traveler, when, in 1947, Assembly of God churches in Florida and Alabama invited him to the United States to preach. When he stepped up to the pulpit, he spoke out forcefully against the hypocrisy that prevents white Christians from loving their "colored"[16] brothers and sisters. "Why," he questioned, "must Negroes sit on the back of your buses?" "I remind you," he remarked, "that we Chinese are not white people." In order to demonstrate his point, he would sometimes walk to the back of a bus and sit with these second-class citizens. His conclusion was clear: "God loves all people, no matter what their skin color." In short, although whites had invited Grandfather to preach to them, he never hesitated to speak forthrightly about their sins. In this, he resembled Nathan, the Old Testament prophet whose name he had taken so many years ago. Later, the Assembly of God denomination recognized[17] Grandpa Ma as the "Bishop of China." During these days, the Communists, less receptive to Christian correction, would put my paternal grandparents to the test.

My mother, Sheng Lude, was born in Shanghai in 1912. Her English name "Ruth" reflects in a small way her Christian heritage. Lude chose to attend the Jinhai Normal School (in Suzhou City and Jiangsu Province) rather than go to a more traditional high school. She hoped to teach and understood well the advantages of her getting an education at Jinhai, a famous kindergarten training school.

Many outside the family rightly described Lude as a beautiful woman. For a Chinese woman, she stood tall and slim.[18] On one occasion, a photographer whom she had hired to take her picture secretly kept one of these photos and displayed it in his window. When my mother's sister-in-law passed by the man's shop, she recognized the mystery woman. Afterward, she spoke out in anger about the photographer's failure to secure permission to display the photograph; soon, the man took the photo out of his window. More important than this, Mother's friends looked beyond external features and thus understood her interior beauty. Mother was a happy woman and laughed a lot. She enjoyed talking with friends, but she felt nervous when called upon to speak in public. Although she practiced before she made her public presentations—this even included teaching—her blood pressure still increased when she took the stage.

Mother found her calling when she moved into the kindergarten classroom.[19] Her students always referred to Teacher Sheng as "Mommy." Her excellence as a teacher extended well beyond her four walls. Her well-known story, "Little Tadpole Looking for Its Mama," won first prize in a children's book competition. Later it was made into a film. This film won the first prize at the Yugoslavia film festival, the "Silver Sail" prize for a short movie in a Swiss competition, and similar prizes in France. Mother's research focused on ways to help students speak and develop language skills.[20] She composed more than thirty children's songs and published some of them. Her interest in music is reflected in her work as editor of *Music Games and Music Appreciation.*

Teacher Sheng frequently forgot her lunch and dinner as she helped the younger teachers prepare for class. And on those occasions when she received letters from small-town kindergarten instructors, she ran to the bookstore, bought some books, and immediately sent them to her correspondents. Even with all these teaching obligations, Lude made time to get acquainted with Ma Geshun.

Ma Geshun, my father and his parent's first child, was born in Nanjing on December 27, 1914. Ma Shaorui wanted his son to pursue an engineering degree at the university. When Geshun's high scores on his qualification exams demonstrated the boy's promise, the Central University of Nanjing readily accepted him into their engineering program. At this point it seemed certain that the boy who was to become my father would pursue a technological career, for Chinese children rarely challenged their parents' wisdom and authority. Still, Geshun spoke with his father about an alternative career path. "My heart," the boy said," is set on the study of music. This is a field in which I will be able to serve God and his Church." My grandfather's love of music may have helped him understand.[21] His son started school in 1933 and graduated four years later—with a degree in music. Pastor Ma had changed his mind after listening to his son's gentle and persuasive words.

My father's studies took him in two different directions. At home in Nanjing, he served as the accountant and the "letter-answerer" for his parents' orphanage. He also trained and conducted the orphanage school choir in Western music.[22] This choir gave Christmas and Easter concerts. But in the summers of 1935 and 1936, Geshun worked in Shanghai. There, in my maternal grandfather's church, he played the piano and helped out with the music. There, in that same church, the missionary Nettie, a tireless matchmaker, introduced Ma Geshun and Sheng Lude.

The man whom Lude met was slim and of average height. Geshun was calm in demeanor, except when conducting. But when he mounted his podium, he inspired and empowered his choirs. His friends rightly described him as talkative and blessed with a good sense of humor. Indeed, his stories could be quite entertaining. His gift with languages reflected his good ear and keen mind. In addition to Mandarin Chinese and the dialects peculiar to Nanjing, Xian, and Sichuan, he spoke English and a little German and Japanese. Early on, he determined that he would steer clear of politics, an arena that he saw as dirty, corrupt, and possibly even dangerous.

Dangerous indeed! Geshun escaped from Nanjing on December 12, 1937, just before the Japanese ruthlessly raped and occupied our capital. He fled inland, to Xian, where he took up teaching, a calling that, at least in comparison to politics, he saw as relatively pure. Here in Xian, he taught music at the Second High School, the First Girls' School, and the Zunde Girls' School. Later, when he became the Director for Xian's Battle Field Children Education Home for Orphans, he resigned from two of his three teaching positions.[23] For the most part, Geshun focused his energies on his professional responsibilities. But at least on one occasion he did become involved in politics. He conducted a children's choir in Xian as a protest against the Japanese invasion.[24]

After two years in Xian, Geshun started home to Shanghai. He took a southerly route through Vietnam so that he could avoid the Japanese. Although Miss Nettie had already passed away, her matchmaking paid off. My parents were married on January 18, 1940.

1

Exiles in the Interior

1942–1945

Within six months after the bombing of Pearl Harbor in late 1941, Japan carved out a territorial empire in Southeast Asia and the Western Pacific. They conquered the Philippines, Malaya, the Dutch East Indies, and more. The tide turned in 1942 with Japanese losses in the Coral Sea, at Midway Island, and off the Solomon Islands. Slowly, the Allied forces engaged in island hopping. Insistently, American planes attacked Japan itself. Finally, in August 1945, after atomic bombs devastated Hiroshima and Nagasaki, Japanese Emperor Hirohito called for an end to the war.

It may be that Japan's Pacific War eased the conflict in China, at least for a while. But it certainly did nothing to ease the conflict between Jiang Jieshi and General Joseph Stilwell, the American officer who tried to organize Jiang's forces and coordinate the war effort in China. Stilwell simply could not remedy the corruption, the timidity, and the poor leadership he witnessed firsthand. In fact, Jiang chose to save his weapons and his troops for the inevitable showdown with the Communists. He also met with

Winston Churchill and Franklin D. Roosevelt in Cario in the fall of 1943. There, the three leaders set war and post-war policies favorable to China.

Unfortunately, Jiang still had to face the Japanese. In April 1944 they launched Operation Ichigo, a successful offensive into the interior of China. China's forces abandoned Changsha and worried about the fate of Chongqing. None too soon, the Japanese called off this offensive. For those who lived in the interior of China, like Nettie's family, the enemy had come plenty close before they surrendered.

By 1942, Shanghai residents had endured more than four years of Japanese occupation. Elsewhere, in southern China, these "liberators" had shot my future husband's grandmother—eight times in the back—until she fell over, dead. On another occasion, a helpless young man had stood by and watched Japanese soldiers as they gang-raped his sister, hanged her from a tree, and, to end her life, disemboweled her. Similar occurrences, even in Shanghai, were too common. If only these foreigners would leave! Maybe then we could manage our own politics and live at peace with one another. But not yet.

Two years earlier, in January 1940, my well-educated parents had married and settled down. In Shanghai, they rented a small house and took up teaching posts, he at a music school and she at a kindergarten. Two years later, on February 2, my uncle's wife took my very pregnant mother to the doctor's office for a check-up; she still had three weeks before her due date. (Her husband hadn't come along for the visit because Chinese tradition excluded prospective fathers from obstetrical matters.) The doctor assured his patient that everything was in order, but this did little to relieve her anxiety. As a palliative, he invited her to spend the night in his clinic; in the morning, he suggested, when she realized that all was well, she could return home. It turned out that the patient had judged her condition better than her attending physician. Early the next morning, the patient cried out, "The baby is coming, and I can't wait!" An emergency. No time to warm a bed or to administer an anesthetic. Years later, my mother always referred to these events when she wanted to explain her chronic back pains.

It is here that I made my grand entrance into the world: at the wrong time, but in the right place. Such good care from my family. I needed a name that reflected my parents' hopes and commitments. "See how pretty she is; look into her intelligent eyes. Maybe we should call her Shu ('gentle beauty') Hui ('intelligent')." "But remember also the missionary who served as our matchmaker, the woman who left her country to show us God's love. Like our parents, we too have embraced that Way; and we pray that in God's time she will do the same. Let's call her 'Nettie.'"

I received such good care from my earliest days, as my parents' love embraced and nurtured me. Mother nursed me and tended to my other needs. One hundred days later, when Mother returned to work, she put me on the bottle. During my infancy I slept in a small crib beside my parents' bed. Each evening at midnight my father got up to prepare my milk and feed me. Eight months later, when I uttered my first sentence, I offered him my hungry and grateful response: "Papa, milk!" Later, and in a different setting, I spoke my second sentence: "Pick up a flower." These words reflected my simple recognition of the beauty of God's creation. Although speaking came early to me, walking came late: I only rose up off all fours and attempted this unnatural, bipedal method of locomotion when I reached my sixteenth month.

Grandma Sheng became my special baby-sitter when Mother was away at work. All my cousins were female, so we knew nothing of the preference that Chinese families normally gave to boys. Still, these cousins thought they should be higher than me in the pecking order because, unlike me, they bore Grandpa Sheng's name. Grandma would have none of this, for she knew that the two of us shared the same blood. Day after day, week after week, month after month, we spent so much time together! Grandma spoiled me as only grandmothers can do. When I was too young to learn, she, like my parents, taught me that love is patient and kind, that love bears all things, believes all things, hopes all things, endures all things; that love never ends. Wonderful households! The right place indeed!

Shanghai, however, was less than hospitable in February 1942. Admittedly, the violence had subsided, but the indignities continued. When the Japanese met us on the streets, we suffered a double humiliation: they searched us for weapons and they demanded that we bow to them. The first was tolerable; the second was not. Another year of this and my parents decided to move on. They abandoned Shanghai in summer

1943. Such a sad departure: we were leaving my maternal grandparents behind. This decision to flee, made well before my memories were formed, marked the first of those lengthy and painful separations that would characterize much of my future life.

My father chose to take us inland, to Xian, a city he knew well. Six years earlier, just before the Japanese had occupied his native Nanjing, Father had fled to Xian. Now, under even more difficult circumstances, he would try that journey again. We knew that my paternal grandparents, who still resided in Xian, would welcome us. But we still needed to survive the distance and the dangers of the trip. Seven hundred and fifty miles to go, with uncertain means of transport, a young daughter, food shortages, and enemy airplanes. No guarantees, even for a family that generations earlier had, through the ministry of Western missionaries, embraced the Christian faith; but sufficient hope for a family that, during these dangerous days, knew how to pray.

We spent forty-one days on our long march. My father rented a wooden "wheelbarrow-like vehicle," a commodious, single-wheeled contraption that accommodated me and our valuables. For a month and even more, Daddy pushed and he pushed, through the dry bed of the Yellow River and beyond. Then he rested and we traveled by bus. We hoped this would be an improvement, but the bus people lost much of our luggage, including all of my things.

The last week of our trek, we had to pass through Tongguan. This was the only way to get to Xian. My father had been reluctant to purchase train tickets, for he knew that the huge locomotives—and their long tails—served as easy targets for Japanese bombers. So he paid extra money to secure our seats in this train's only armored car; that car, a kind of caboose, held on for dear life as we readied ourselves to make the final run. But first, the conductor and the engineer laid out survival tactics. For the moment, we would stay hidden in the mountain passes, but only until the skies cleared. Meanwhile, the coal men stoked up our steam engines until those iron giants were near ready to burst. We were preparing for a sudden sprint across the vulnerable valley.

At last, we sprang forth, like Olympian runners. We knew the railroad tracks would refuse to give us any maneuvering room should a Japanese plane sight us; we also hoped these same tracks would lead us through the valley of the shadow of death and into our city of refuge. These tactics, undergirded by our prayers, worked. We felt grateful when we pulled into the railroad station in Xian, for we suspected that others had tried the same trick and had offered the same prayers but had died in tombs of torn iron, victims of aerial attack.

Even after our arrival, all was not well, for I stood by death's door. I had become severely dehydrated not long after we had left Shanghai; and during the last two days of our trek, I had had nothing to eat and little water to drink. My grandparents must have worried when they saw such a tiny and scrawny toddler. They prescribed goat's milk, a nutritious fluid they knew that I could digest more easily than cow's milk. "My" nanny goat, raised at the nearby orphan's home, served me well. I sucked my first bottle dry and waited for more and more. In time, I recovered from my dehydration; but I also remained sickly and frail. I must have frightened my parents on those too-frequent and unexpected occasions when, as my temperature shot up beyond 100 degrees, I passed out. Years later, after I reached my teen years, I recovered from this condition. But for now, my parents restored me to health as best they could. And for now, we waited out the war in central China. As we waited, we enjoyed tolerable political conditions, even as the winds from the Gobi Desert blew over our temporary home. While we put down these tentative roots, we remembered and wondered about our families.

My paternal grandparents opened their home and extended their hospitality to us in their native Xian. I suspect we could have stayed indefinitely, but that wasn't necessary. Soon enough, the same organization that offered us employment also provided us with housing. My mother took a teaching position in the YWCA kindergarten and the three of us moved into the "Y" dormitory. My father, hardly one to shirk his duties, taught music at both the Northwestern Conservatory and at Zunde's Girl's School.

Elsewhere, even as too many vulnerable people suffered the horrors of war, China and her allies became convinced that the Japanese were less than invincible. Far away, in Cairo, Egypt, in fall 1943, Jiang Jieshi, Winston Churchill, and Franklin Roosevelt met to formulate end-of-war policies. In the end, these bold men spoke unequivocally in their Cairo

Declaration. For Japan, it required unconditional surrender; for China, it called for the return of the territories lost to Japan.

Even further away, in the Pacific War, those who followed the conflict learned of successive and bloody Allied victories. Carrier-based bombers hit Tokyo itself. But not so far away, B-29s from Chongqing hit industrial targets in Kyushu and Manchukuo. Equally close to home, the Japanese retaliated with Operation Ichigo.

My parents, who saw the end of the war approaching, took their first cautious step, admittedly circuitous, in what would prove to be a long and slow trip home. We decided to head southwest. Our destination? We chose Sichuan, a province where many colleges and universities had temporarily relocated during the war years; more particularly, we chose Chengdu. More than 300 miles, straight as the crow flies. But we still had to get there.

Unfortunately, we weren't crows. The best we could do was strike a bargain with a man who had access to a large old truck: we offered him enough money, and he agreed to drive us to our new home. My mother and I sat up front beside the driver, while others, including my father, rode in the back. The first half of the trip proved uneventful. Then I spoke up and made my presence and discomfort known: I cried and cried. Mother, who was at her wit's end, threatened me with a spanking. Our driver, less frustrated and more suspicious than Mother, spoke out: "Why don't you wait just a bit for the paddling? Your little girl may be trying to tell us something. There may be a reason why she's wailing so." He pulled over to the side of the road, parked, and inspected his vehicle. He quickly discovered that one of the rear wheels was coming loose. He retightened the lug nuts and spoke once again: "If your little girl hadn't caught our attention, we would have continued on our merry way; and then, once the wheel had worked its way completely free, we would have crashed! Little Nettie has saved us from wrecking this fine truck. So she rides free—but the rest of you must still pay." Apart from this incident, we made it safely to Chengdu. As for our driver, he may have ended up with more than he bargained for: the story has it that in time he became a Christian.

We had no relatives to care for us in our new home city. But well before we hopped into that fine old truck, we had established helpful contacts there. The Chengdu YWCA had offered us the same arrangements that we had enjoyed in Xian. Once again my mother would teach in their kindergarten and our family would set up house in their dormitory. My father, not one to neglect his duties or to be outdone, found three part-time jobs. During the week, he taught music in a school—the English called it "Oberlin in Shanxi"—in Mingxian. On Friday evenings he peddled his bicycle for 40 miles and rejoined his family in Chengdu. Here, on Saturdays, he taught music at a normal high school and also at the Provincial Institute of the Arts. On Monday mornings he biked back to Mingxian, where he resumed his weekday teaching position. In time, the administrators at the Chengdu Fine Arts Institute recognized my father's gifts and offered him a full-time position. He accepted their offer, resigned his other two positions, and gave up distance biking.

Soon, we had a surprise visitor. Uncle Robert, Mother's oldest brother, had no thought of frightening his little niece when he drove up from Chongqing. After he arrived, the adults agreed that we would go on an excursion to visit one of the famous sites. He drove us to Dujiangyan, in Guangxian County, and parked by the Guang River. The four of us planned to walk together across the famous bridge that spanned the chasm below. Bamboo and rope, that's all I saw. Slowly, carefully—and fearfully—I started out. One step after another, one-quarter, and then one-third of the way across. Underneath us, that bridge swayed, back and forth. Way down below, that huge River threatened to swallow any who lost their footing. Enough! I refused to go any further. My parents understood my fright and walked me back to our starting point.

Emperor Hirohito spoke to his people in a radio broadcast on August 15, 1945. "This war has not developed to Japan's advantage. We must endure the unendurable and we must suffer the insufferable." Cryptic words, for the emperor had never mentioned "defeat" or "surrender." Stunning words, for Japan's army and navy had more than met their match. And true words, for during the past ten days, General Tojo Hideki, our Prime Minister, had led us into a war of frightening proportions. Hiroshima and Nagasaki were hit with atomic bombs. Enough. Formal surrender took place in Tokyo Bay aboard the battleship the U.S.S. Missouri. It was September 2, 1945.

It took time for much of this news to span the long distance—nearly 2,000 miles—between Tokyo and Chengdu. Still, my parents understood that the war had ended and that it was now safe for us to take a second step in our journey home. Our bus headed southeast on its 200-mile trip toward Chongqing, the city that offered us the best travel connections in Sichuan. We stopped for the night in Zigong, for we had completed almost half of our trip. The next morning we continued on until we reached our destination. Here we felt the heat; here we saw the haze. And here, Jiang Jieshi had maintained his wartime capital.

In Chongqing we could look down from our promontory and see the confluence of the Yangzi and the Jialing Rivers; and we could look up, into the hills and the mountains, and remember the words of the psalmist: "I will lift up my eyes to the hills. From whence does my help come? My help comes from the LORD, who made heaven and earth." Here, my mother's reputation as a famous kindergarten teacher, as a woman who loved and was loved by her students, had preceded her. Her reputation served her well, for once again she secured a teaching position with the local YWCA kindergarten. For this move we found housing elsewhere. Several years before our arrival, Sheng Zhenwei, a graduate of Northwestern Law School and president of the famous Dongwu Law School of Suzhou University, had moved to Chongqing, the temporary site where that university had set up shop for the war years. This president, the man we knew as Uncle Robert, had left his family in Shanghai during his self-imposed exile. It was he who invited us to live with him in the house the university had provided him.

My enduring memories from these days are what one might expect from a small child. One evening I woke up and watched a huge mouse—surely he was as big as any house cat—as he scurried across the floor of my room. I screamed and cried out in fear. My mother came quickly and spoke words of comfort: "That little mouse won't hurt you," she said. "He only looks so very big because you are so very tiny." Her soothing voice, her soft lap, and her strong arms calmed my fears.

My father had more to worry about than my huge mouse, however, for Chongqing was filled with refugees who, like us, wanted to return home. So many people, and so little space on the airplanes and the few passenger ships that headed east on the Yangzi River! We stayed an entire month in this city, and then Father secured the best transportation he could find. Our enterprising ship captain had devised an ingenious way to make extra space and sell more tickets. That man had pulled two wooden boats up alongside his center ship, secured these boats with heavy ropes, and invited his additional passengers to climb in. We followed his instructions. Afterward, we watched as we pulled slowly away from the docks—in this tugboat like-arrangement, jury-rigged, sitting dangerously low in the waters.

They say it's a tourist's delight to take a boat trip down the Yangzi River. But we traveled as refugees, not as tourists. Our journey took us past Fengdu, Pingdushan, and Fengjie, and into the Sanxia Gorges: eight kilometers for the Qutangxia, and more than five times that distance for the Wuxia. Calm, so far. But we had yet to reach the halfway point through these three gorges. Our captain, unafraid, steered onward, into the longest, the most dramatic, and the most hazardous waters. Finally, we entered the Xilingxia. On either side, the cliffs extended upward, sometimes as much as 1,000 feet, into the heavens. Ahead, the rugged rapids welcomed us: they wanted to test the sea-worthiness of our contraption. They suspected that they could best us. Unfortunately, they turned out to be right. We failed their test. Too soon, disaster struck: the ropes on our boat broke and we were cut adrift. Mama and I cried out for help. Another boat, one that had a motor, passed us by; but then, after its captain heard a child's voice, it turned around to help. Later, Mother would suggest that he had responded to my cry. Perhaps, but unlikely for one whose parents had trained her, however imperfectly, to remain quiet even during her tears. Our rescuers insured the safety of the men in our helpless "skiff"; new ropes made it near impossible for the twin "barges" to break loose. The women and children did even better than the men: our rescuers helped us board our central "flagship." Best of all, a generous woman shared her private room, deep down in our boat's belly, with Mother and me.

We were spared further near-disasters, but only until we reached Nanjing. There, the two outside boats, both of which had been riding lower and lower in the water, discharged their passengers and promptly sank to the bottom of the river. Fortunately, we stood safe, our feet firmly planted on dry land. "I will fear no evil, for Thou art with me." *Are we home yet?* As we strolled around the city, I clung to Mama's neck, for I preferred riding to walking. Mother wondered why I refused to walk, but then she noticed that I had lost a shoe. We spent one night in a hotel, and then we boarded the train to Shanghai. There, outside the station, we saw Sheng Zhendong (Uncle John), my mother's youngest brother, sitting in a horse-drawn carriage. After we climbed in, our royal coachman loosened the reins and guided his horses straight to my maternal grandparents' home. Strange and marvelous to this tiny princess. Afterward, relatives came to visit and listen to the little Chinese girl who spoke and sang in a quaint rural dialect. These strong and distinct memories remain to this day. We had found our way home!

2

Life During Our Civil War

1945–1949

After Japan's surrender in 1945, the Chinese Communist Party and the Guomindang resisted American mediation of their "quarrel" and got on with their long-expected civil war. Early on, in December 1936, Jiang Jieshi had agreed at Xian to cooperate with the Communists, but only after he had been kidnapped and pressured into this arrangement.

The Russians, foreigners but not brothers, remained in northern China. They had promised toward the end of World War II to withdraw soon from all of China. But before their protracted withdrawal, they extracted "war booty" from the Manchurian industrial plant. Brother "Joe" Stalin took what he could, even while he declared his support for our Communist revolution. More important than his rhetoric were his policies: these favored the CCP over the GMD. It thus came as no surprise that he did little to foster cooperation between the two.

The Americans, foreigners but not strangers, remained in China for well over another year. During this time they tried to mediate a lasting alliance between the GMD and the CCP. Ambassador Hurley initiated these conversations in August 1945 in Chongqing. When Hurley resigned in

November 1945 he had made no progress. Indeed, that same month, the GMD attacked the CCP in Manchuria.

General George C. Marshall, Truman's special envoy and Hurley's replacement, seemed to do much better than his predecessor. By January 1946 Marshall had secured a ceasefire and a promise from Jiang to convene a national assembly. But broken agreements and military clashes insured failure. In short, it seemed like cooperation was impossible. In January 1947 Marshall delivered his farewell address and abandoned his mission. So the foreigners—Japanese, Russians, Americans—had all gone; even so, the Chinese enjoyed anything but peace.

Shanghai witnessed in small measure the disorder and suffering that others elsewhere knew only too well after the Japanese occupation. Unemployment. Inflation. Strikes. Government emergency measures. Citizens of Shanghai experienced limited relief from times of troubles when their leaders tried to bring order to the poor city. But more was needed than they could do. By spring 1948 the shops were empty.

Jiang's northern military victories in the fall of 1946 had made him over-confident. "I will win this war against the Communists," he thought. Wrong. By 1949 the CCP had more than reversed the situation. Closer to the Ma family, Mao's forces occupied Nanjing and then Shanghai. Finally, the CCP founded the People's Republic of China in their "new" capital of Beijing: it was October 1, 1949. As for Jiang, he had taken up residence in Taiwan. And as for little Nettie, she had grown a lot and learned even more during these past four years.

In the fall of 1945, at last the war ended! Very soon, the Japanese would be returning home. Such good news! So exciting! A time for good people to work on reconstruction. "China will be saved, and we educators will certainly play a central role in that process." My parents spoke these unforgettable words before their young daughter.

Relatives helped us set up housekeeping in Shanghai. We lived with my maternal grandmother, but only for two weeks. Here I watched my Auntie Bessie gargle; so strange and so funny. She returned my attention and thought I was equally amusing. These two weeks gave us enough time to find permanent housing with Uncle Robert and his wife Rachel (Xianying). They rented us the third floor of their large home. Down below, on the second floor, they had their own bedrooms; and further down, on the first floor, they had a large dining room and a spacious living room.

Uncle Robert, still president of the Dongwu Law School and a man with political connections, suggested that my father take a government job. "Here, with the United Nations," he said, "you will be able to serve our country. And the money is good, certainly much better than anything you'll make in education."

My father's reply came as no surprise. "But politics is such a dirty business! Now teaching, that's a profession in which a man can keep his conscience clear and his life pure." Father spoke these words frequently, but only once to Uncle Robert—that was when Daddy turned down the political appointment.

Shanghai offered my parents more attractive ways to make a living. Soon, each of them found teaching positions that suited their gifts and goals. Mother signed on to teach kindergarten at the McTyeire Second Elementary School; before long she would move on to the Juemin Elementary School. Neither of these institutions paid well. Then Uncle Robert introduced Mother to a better-paying position at the kindergarten associated with the Shanghai City Gongbuju Elementary School.[1]

Daddy took on three jobs. He taught at the First Division of the Shanghai City Music Central College during 1945. (After this, it closed down.) He also served as principal of that school. At the same time he taught music at two girls' high schools. In 1946, my father accepted a part-time teaching position in the music department at the China Baptist Theological Seminary in Shanghai; Carl Culpepper, an American with Texas connections, served as that seminary's president. So while our country faced the beginnings of a civil war, we as a family did reasonably well.

Chinese children begin the first of two years at all-day kindergarten when they are four years old. This meant that in fall 1946, it was off to school for me, to the kindergarten of the McTyeire First Elementary School. My schooling complicated matters for my parents, for they both had their own professions to tend to. In the mornings, Mother prepared breakfast for me; while I dawdled over my food, she fidgeted impatiently. "Must you eat so slowly, child?" I simply couldn't make the food go down quickly.

Normally, my parents paid a rickshaw driver to take me to school. When they complained that he had too many passengers—six children—to transport us all in comfort, he agreed to make two trips. But his agreement meant little, for he crowded all six of us into his relatively small space; this left me sitting on the floor. Occasionally, however, my mother had to take her unhurried daughter to school.

When I returned home from school, again in our crowded rickshaw, I cared for myself. I had few choices as to how I would spend my time. Mother only permitted me to visit Uncle Robert's and Aunt Rachel's when they had invited me down to play. On those occasions, after first going to our apartment, I walked back down the stairs, past the second-floor bedrooms, and then, on the ground level, past the spacious living room, the big dining room, and into the familiar kitchen. My cousin Roberta was my special playmate. We became especially close, in part because she was only a year older than I. When we snacked together, I had a good appetite, but when I stayed upstairs by myself, I ate little. It was no fun eating alone. After the two of us ate, we climbed back up the stairs to the second floor where we played together in Roberta's bedroom; sometimes, her sisters Yvonne and Betty, who were eight to ten years older than me, joined in our fun.

Although I was a lonely little girl when I stayed alone, I found inventive ways to entertain myself. On one occasion, for example, I took the scissors to Mama's magazines, cut out the flowers, and glued them onto her bedsheet. Somehow, Mother failed to appreciate my decorative talents. On another occasion, I turned my attention to my hair. I had watched my father in the mornings as he greased his hair down. Since I didn't have his Vaseline, I turned once again to my trusty glue. When Mother came home, she found my beautiful hair sticking straight out into the air. She tugged and she scrubbed until she eventually cleaned up my mess. In time, my parents discovered an audible clue that would alert them as to what they should expect from their little daughter when they returned home from work. If they heard me singing, everything was fine; but when I quit my warbling, they rightly suspected that I was into mischief.

After a single year of this (school, not mischief), I was ready to be promoted. I skipped the second grade of kindergarten and advanced, at age five, a year younger than most, into the first grade. This put me in the

McTyeire First Elementary, the school where my Auntie Bessie served as principal. She would soon return to the United States—this would be her second trip to America—where she would work on her master's degree; like my father, my aunt believed that educated leaders would play an important role in her country's development. As for me, I followed the teacher's instructions well, except sometimes during our after-lunch naps. When I couldn't sleep, I peeked out from under my arms to see what my teacher was doing.

During those days, at the time when I was preparing to attend the first grade, my parents were preparing themselves for their first significant separation. Father, with the help and encouragement of Dr. Culpepper, had, in the summer of 1947, received a Lottie Moon Scholarship. He would study for his master's degree at the Southwestern Theological Seminary; and when he had finished his work there, he would move on to the Westminster Choir College. Mother chose to remain in China. Before Daddy left home, Mama sought three pledges from her husband: Father must never travel by airplane; he must always wear his wedding ring; and he must never dance. To outsiders these promises might seem odd, but not to us. Each in its special way would help promote fidelity and safety during a time in which my parents would be separated by thousands of miles of land and ocean. Daddy made good on his promises, beginning with his memorable and long trip to the West. His freighter stopped first in Japan and then in Manila; more than a month later, it docked in California. Then by train, by bus, and by car, Papa made his way to Texas. Meanwhile, Mother and I moved back into my maternal grandparents' home.

In China, as the Civil War escalated and as the balance in the struggle for power gradually tipped in favor of Mao's forces, troubles came to Shanghai itself. It was particularly hard on us when, in spring 1949, the Communists entered Shanghai and expelled "our" missionaries.[2] We watched in sadness as our friends Rev. Anderson and Rev. H. N. Hestekind and his wife[3] departed from their adopted country and left behind the good people to whom they had given their lives. (Still, my family kept in touch with the Hestekinds, who served in Japan until they retired in the United States.[4]) Meanwhile, Mother did what she could to make up for the difficulties in our church. Among other things, she filled in as the official pianist. Eight years later, when the Communists finally closed down our church, she was still sitting at that piano bench. If the missionary expulsion had not made things bad enough, our situation worsened when a number of instructors fled the country. This left a significant teacher shortage, and not only at the China Baptist Theological Seminary. The Shanghai City Music Central College, however, faced no such shortage, for it had already closed its doors. As for Father, he kept up with Chinese affairs, for student friends spoke to him about our troubles in a 1949 letter that they wrote to their professor.

That settled matters. It was time for our family to be reunited, even while Mao and Jiang readied themselves for the final stages of their struggle. My father decided that he must return immediately to China. He was coming home—it was April 1949—to help remedy the teacher shortage. In making the difficult choice to leave the States early, he hoped to participate in the reconstruction of his country. Surely there was nothing wrong, nothing political, in this! Surely no one could suspect him of partisanship or disloyalty! Surely the Communists, the forces most likely to win the Civil War, could have no complaints! True to his early commitments, Father had stayed out of politics. And true to the promise that he had made to his wife, he returned to China by ship. For him, returning at this time meant missing the June graduation at Southwestern Seminary, the occasion when he would have formally completed his work and received his diploma.[5] Soon after Daddy came home, he became the chairman of the music department at the China Baptist Theological Seminary in Shanghai; about that same time, the three of us moved into the recently vacated missionary home. We paid the church a monthly "love offering" as an alternative to rent.[6] Meanwhile, I had attended much more than just the first grade.

3

Education and Re-education

1949–1953

The dangers to Chinese citizens increased significantly when, on June 25, 1950, the North Koreans invaded South Korea. Two days later, the Americans sent their Seventh Fleet into the Taiwan Straits. By mid-fall, China had joined the fray. Between 1948 and 1952, the Communists initiated land reform, beginning from the north and moving south. With the advent of the Korean War, they sanctioned violence and initiated the "Suppress the Counter-Revolutionaries Movement." In order to identify these enemies, they categorized the Chinese people into five groups: landlords, capitalists, petite bourgeoisie (teachers, lawyers, doctors), farmers, and workers. At this same time they also introduced thought control into the educational system and required self-criticism and confessions from its members. Everywhere, the Chinese people saw widespread arrests, mass trials, and accusation meetings. Shanghai shared in these troubles.

In October 1950, Chinese forces crossed the Yalu River and attacked the imperialist forces. After three years of war, a ceasefire was declared in July 1953. The Communist world had demonstrated its strength and endurance against its enemies. In March 1953, China's Soviet ally lost its leader, Joseph Stalin. The government required its citizens to listen to his national memorial service on the radio.

Meanwhile, in China Communism had taken on a darker and more authoritarian cast. Mao Zedong forbade the free exchange of ideas and permitted only the Party line. At the same time, he looked to classical Marxism and its idea of class struggle. The Party and its chairman thus insisted that they must ferret out hidden enemies of the people. Mao's new stratagems changed Chinese politics and society in important ways, and this more than a decade before our awful and all-too-familiar Cultural Revolution. In making these changes, the chairman also enhanced his personal power and strengthened his dictatorship. Mao's self-serving policies brought death and destruction to many individuals and families. As for the survivors, many witnessed Mao's supposed apotheosis. The chairman, a god-like figure, now encouraged his people to worship him.

Mao's government sponsored two major campaigns that eliminated enemies—a foretaste of what would be faced in the future. Some cadres, thinking the revolution was over, had taken on bourgeois mentalities and become careerists. To correct this, the authorities attacked corruption, waste, and bureaucracy in their "Three Antis- Movement." By summer 1952, when they brought this campaign to an end, many Party members had been expelled.

Following this, as the regime noted the corrupting effects of business on the cadres, the government launched its "Five Antis- Movement." In this, they sought to eliminate the evils of bribery, tax evasion, theft of state property, shoddy work, and theft of economic information. In response to this, the authorities looked into cases of corruption, heard denunciations, and began to transform the private sector. It is here that the re-education of many of China's citizen continued, just as the first of many years of education began for Nettie.

From early on, politics, national and local, intruded upon my innocence. An older child might have understood these matters at once, but it took me several years to understand their import. During the spring of 1949, my parents heard much about our civil war. This was especially true after the Communists crossed the Yangzi River; thereafter, many small cities close to us feared the worst. Then, on the evening of May 26, 1949, the night before Shanghai was liberated and not too long before Mao's forces triumphed in China, my nervous mother looked to my financial future—just in case I might find myself in desperate straits. I watched her as she sewed silver money into the lining of my underwear; none but I knew this secret. On this same day, she explained that if I got lost and was unable to find my parents, I could use this special silver to buy food. Fortunately, I did not have to face that dilemma; peace prevailed in Shanghai, beginning on May 27, the day the Communists freed our city. Such festivities; we could see the PLA everywhere. Mother took me to an afternoon parade that celebrated our victory over Jiang. Such fun! Especially the drummers. Soon thereafter my parents bought me my own set of drums. Such noise at my practice sessions at home!

Victory! At last, the Communists had soundly defeated Jiang's forces. Now, there was so much for our leaders to do. How quickly shall we implement socialism? Can we use or adapt a Soviet model? What shall we do in agriculture and in industry? How shall we reform education? Who, at home and abroad, are our friends and who our enemies? Who will help us and who will oppose us? How shall we treat those who refuse to support us? So many questions! For the next decade, Mao and his colleagues cooperated and argued; for the next decade, they charted and re-charted our country's future.

As for my family and me, we focused on education. Mother and Father taught, while I played the student—all the way through high school. During this "decade," we still hoped to remain apolitical, to do much good for our country, to be left alone, and to practice our faith. We had few questions, until the regime challenged our loyalty, again, and again, and again. In time, we wondered whether we would be able to render unto Caesar that which was Caesar's and unto God that which was God's. Could we be good citizens in a Communist country? Perhaps, but in our case, only with difficulty. Our missionary friends could not help us, for they had been expelled. Fortunately, no backlash accompanied their expulsion: we faced no immediate troubles.

As a first grader, I had settled into a comfortable and enduring routine. Each morning, I walked next door, stepped into the garden, and called from outside my grandparents' house: "Good morning." A cheery voice from their little granddaughter. Grandpa responded first. Then came Auntie Bessie, who, having never married, lived with her parents. Grandma answered my greetings less frequently.[1] Now that I attended my auntie's school, she could walk me to school and back home. This meant that I gave up the crowded rickshaw.

After a morning of simple study, we took our lunch in shifts. The three younger grades began their half-hour noon break in the cafeteria, while the older students enjoyed a recess; afterward, we swapped places. Even before I entered the cafeteria, I knew what to expect. The cooks served us at least three separate dishes—they frequently included meat or fish, a vegetable, rice, and soup. On Wednesdays, we got noodles. On Fridays, they prepared a special meal; I couldn't wait to taste the crispy fried food from the bottom of the pan.

Our lunch routine was pleasantly predictable. As we stepped into the line, we picked up chopsticks, a spoon, paper napkins, and a tray. My Auntie Bessie, generous as always, had used her own money and bought those trays, 300 of them, when in the late forties she had returned to China from the United States. After we received our food, we gathered in groups of ten and stood at our tables. Before we sat down and ate, we children took turns offering thanks for our food: "For all we eat, for all we wear, we thank you Father, for all you share." Simple, yet meaningful. In time, the teachers assigned the slowest eaters to the same table; not surprisingly, I joined them. At the end of the meal, we took turns cleaning off the dirty dishes and returning them to the kitchen.

Most of my classmates hurried outside to play during our recess. I preferred to visit the library—I was the youngest one in my class. Here, I could read old books and learn new things. In my younger years, I began with folk tales and mysteries. In time, I turned to more classical literature; later, I learned to enjoy Russian writers such as Turgenev and Tolstoy and French writers such as Balzac and Rolland. One can read a lot of books in twelve years. But not during this one lunch break. It was time for me to return to class where, following the teacher's instructions, I tried to take a nap. Couldn't we get on to more important things?

At the end of the day, I entertained myself while my Auntie Bessie tended to her work. I headed first to the library; there, I read until they shut the doors. Then I returned to my classroom and finished my homework. Done. Time to go outdoors. I ran over to the McTyeire Girls School, which was connected to our school by a gate. When I reached the lake, I stopped and watched the fish swim and the water lilies as they floated on the invisible surface. I looked further out and saw the older students row their boats to a wooded island and then meander down its paths. Maybe when I got older, I could do this too. On other days, I visited the gymnasium and watched children exercise. Maybe, when I got older . . . . But for now, I returned to my school, where Auntie Bessie was waiting to walk home with me.

Hot days were my downfall. When my temperature soared above 100 degrees, it still did me in. I simply shut my eyes and fainted. Too much for this little girl to bear. Unfortunately, I had more than my share of sickness. On one such occasion—it was close to Christmas—my teacher sent this ailing little girl home to rest. I couldn't have been more than six or seven at the time. I fell asleep on my bed. Then I heard my mother's voice. She and a staff member from my school, a man whom my Auntie Bessie had asked to play Santa Claus, were talking quietly outside my room. Here he was, ready to deliver my gift. But how could he place it by my bed without disturbing me and waking me up? He tried, but he failed. I feigned sleep, but I understood well what was happening. Thus, I lost just a little of my childhood innocence; even so, I didn't let on.

On normal days, I had little to occupy my time. My parents prohibited me from playing with the neighbor children. I tried talking with them through the bamboo fence, but they had better things to do. So I read, and, inspired by my reading, I acted out my own personal "plays." I was an Eskimo who lived in the arctic. I built a wonderful "igloo" out of sheets that I spread out over the household furniture. Or I was a Norwegian who fished for a living. Or when my imagination ran dry, I went to Grandmother's bathroom and opened the window to watch the activity down below in the alley. There, I looked at hopeful peddlers who strolled around and hawked their wares in songs that they themselves created. I can still remember their ingenious lyrics and pleasant melodies: "Let me sharpen your knives. Let me fix your bed." And more. Simple fun.

Every day I waited at home, hoping my youngest uncle, John Sheng, a bachelor who still lived with his parents, would stop by. He brought me such wonderful surprises: an ice cream cone, a newspaper, or a comic book he had rented. In time, "we" would surprise Uncle John, but not in such a pleasant way. As a hobby, this uncle raised expensive flowers and birds; it was the birds that caused us problems. My father, hoping to provide companionship for his lonely daughter, had bought me a cat. That cat, a creature ruled by instinct and hunger, caught and ate one of my uncle's birds. That's it, my parents decided: the cat must go! We took her away from home, dropped her off, and left her to fend for herself. It took that cat three days to find her way back home. We tried it again, this time at a greater distance; harder to figure out, but she returned in a week. Maybe she enjoyed my company, or maybe she had developed a taste for uncle's birds. We tried it one last time, at an even further distance. That did the trick. Either she got lost or she understood the message: she should adopt other parents or she should eat other people's birds. About this same time, my parents got me another pet,[2] a cat who, if he knew what was best for him, would stay away from Uncle John's tasty birds.

We also owned a dog, a pet that provided companionship for me. "Spot" had a good deal going for him: He didn't eat birds, and he knew and loved my grandfather. And maybe he had a sixth sense. One day in 1950, even while that dog was sleeping, he cried out, as if something were wrong. Indeed. That day, Grandpa died. As Spot grew up, we children enjoyed playing with him. He and my cat walked with me each morning on my way to school. They stopped at the gate door, and in the afternoon they met me there. Lots of fun, but my father still worried: *Maybe that dog will bite and injure somebody. Maybe I should get rid of him.* The authorities settled the matter when, in 1953, they prohibited private citizens from owning dogs. So much for this pet. We cooperated, willingly but sadly, with the law. Spot thus found a new home, with the police, new masters whom he would learn to serve well.

In 1951, the regime began to remold the intellectuals and we faced politics at the local level. It looked like the Chinese Baptist Theological Seminary would have to close, for it was short on both teachers and money. At that point, my father and some friends devised a plan by which they could save the school. They organized a concert and charged for attendance. Meanwhile, Professor Ma practiced with the united church choir. The day before the concert, we felt optimistic, for all of the tickets had been sold.

Then, much to our dismay, the government forbade us to continue. "This is hardly an "innocent' concert," they insisted. They had secured an advance copy of the program, and in it they had discovered subterfuge and disloyalty. In one line of one of the scheduled works, Mendelssohn's "Hymn of Praise," the German composer had written the "Night is Departing, and Morning is Approaching." "So," the authorities said, "a cryptic attack on the Communist Party. We understand the symbol of 'night' in this work. But you are wrong. The CCP is not about to depart."

As a consequence of this accusation, the authorities claimed that my father, the man in charge, was an American cultural spy and a dangerous "rightist." They thus pulled Professor Ma's "political file" and placed this damning information inside. At the same time, they locked my father, the traitor, in an isolated room and forced him to confess that he had participated in sedition. With no concert, no money, and no support, the seminary closed.

Still, my father had plenty to do. The ideological remolding movement took in my own father, who was accused, placed in a single, small cell, and interrogated. Here, he ate his meals; here, he used a chamber pot; here, he remained isolated. In these difficult circumstances, Father savored his few small luxuries. Each morning the guards gave him water so he could wash himself and brush his teeth. *So hard to know how I should respond to persistent inquisitors when one has so little to confess*, Father thought. *Easier to know how to spend my time when they work me over. Focus on your music!* During his imprisonment, Father composed a Christian cantata and more.

Three long months, and finally they released my papa. They offered no compensation for his privations. Even so, he had made the best of it. He found some satisfaction in having enjoyed a productive period as a composer under such harsh conditions. Soon after his release, he published his compositions. Later, at Christmas and at Easter, he conducted the all-church Shanghai United Choir. Two hundred and fifty voices, blended together in magnificent harmony. Two hundred and fifty voices singing together classical Christian music, Mr. Ma's "prison musings." *Laudate Deum!* [4]

That same year in Shanghai, my mother's older brother, Sheng Zhenwei ("Uncle Robert"), was arrested. This good man had taken us in when, during the Japanese occupation, my family had sought refuge in Chongqing. Following the war, this distinguished man had continued to serve as the president of the famous Chinese law school at Suzhou University—but only until 1951, when he and three famous university presidents were jailed. The Campaign to Suppress Counter-Revolutionaries showed no respect of persons. My uncle received a twenty-year sentence. He began his imprisonment in Shanghai. Afterward, he was reassigned to Anhui, close by the Hua River. At this last location he joined other prisoners in heavy labor at a site noted for its regular and serious flooding. *Will he ever get out?* One night each week our pastor and the deacons from the church gathered at my grandmother's room to pray. She kept her door open during her frequent visits with friends, but only until it was time to seek God's face. Since the regime prohibited praying for an anti-revolutionary person, they conducted their meetings in private. I never witnessed these intercessory sessions, and I never asked about them; still, I understood that Grandma and her friends sought God's mercy for Uncle Robert. After eight long years, he joined other famous political prisoners, including China's last emperor, in being released from prison.

The authorities also made many charges against my paternal grandfather before they took him in. "You exploit those young people whom you pretend to care for in your orphanage." Untrue, as many of the residents in this "school" would have testified. In reality, Grandpa had showed no favoritism, even when it had come to his own sons. Indeed, because he had hoped to make his boys models of propriety to the orphans, much of the time he had treated them more severely than the others.

"A friend and supporter of Jiang Jieshi, the former president of our country." Untrue, as the government's own investigations revealed. In reality, the relationship had worked the other way around: Song Meiling, Jiang's wife, had donated ten silver dollars to Grandpa's orphanage.

"Friendship with an American spy, and then helping this traitor to recruit young Chinese spies." Untrue, as anyone knew who understood the real work of the accused Mr. Simpson, an American missionary. Of course Mr. Simpson visited the orphanage regularly, but only to tell the children about Jesus and to help the local Chinese people. He was no spy, and he certainly didn't train the orphans in espionage. Unfortunately, the Communist Party didn't see it that way. Indeed, they pressed Grandfather to sue Mr. Simpson as a spy.

"A spy for the United States, based on previous associations with American missionaries, and upon having a son, John Ma, who now lives in the United States." True with regard to Grandpa's friendships and his son. But surely neither of these simple associations substantiated the charge, which was patently false.

Unfortunately, the truth made no difference when, in September 1951, all of these accusations came to a head. The authorities expropriated the church Grandfather pastored and the land on which his orphanage was set. They put my grandmother on a train for Shanghai so that she could move in with her son Silas.[7] Worst of all, after Grandma's forced train ride, they arrested Grandpa and imprisoned him for life. In the end, he died in jail during the Cultural Revolution.

The authorities cast their net well beyond my relatives. In time, we learned about the fate of familial friends and other acquaintances. Reverend Chang, the manager of the Xian Orphanage, and Reverend Wong Keji, the manager of the Taidong Orphanage, were both imprisoned on charges that were identical to those the government had brought against Grandpa. In time, Rev. Wong, who shared a cell with my grandfather, was released and declared "innocent of all charges."

In 1952 the authorities sought to "reclaim" a number of petite bourgeois intellectuals. My father joined those they sent off to Anhui for "re-education." He attended the required land reformation meetings during which they brainwashed their "needy students." Several months later, they sent my father back home to Shanghai. We were glad to have him back, for the number of victims and executions in these movements must have been huge. But we refused to welcome the passengers he brought with him. Mother quickly discovered that her husband's luggage and clothes were infested with lice and fleas. "Burn it all. We will not offer these miserable creatures the hospitality of our home!"

During these same politically trying years, my father met each week with his pastor; together, the preacher and the minister of music planned the worship service. They talked in particular about the subject and the biblical text for the next sermon. Thereafter, my father composed a simple song based on the relevant Scripture passage. Early on Sunday morning, before the service actually began, he taught the congregation his new composition. He hoped that during worship the music and the message would reinforce one another. Toward the end of this endeavor, he published 100 of the short choruses he had composed.[6]

After the Communists had implemented their revolution, they organized children's groups at school. At first these groups were known as the "Young Pioneers" or the "Red Tie." Superficially, they resembled the Girl Scouts or Boy Scouts, for they, like their Western counterparts, played games, sang songs, and participated in other enjoyable activities. Ideologically, however, they differed considerably from the Scouts, for the Pioneers swore an oath of loyalty to Communism. This was reflected in the slogan-like song they sang: "We are the new generation of Communism; we carry the faith of Communism." In membership, the Pioneers were both more inclusive and more exclusive than the Scouts. Ninety-eight percent of all school students belonged, but not me. When I learned about this group, I asked my teacher whether I could join. I hoped that my attitude and my behavior—I was a good student—would get me in, and that I could keep quiet about my faith. With this in mind, I spoke with my teacher. "I am a Christian," I explained, "I wonder whether the Red Tie will accept people like me?" My teacher responded with a straightforward and emphatic "No."

The authorities had taken a similar approach to religion in the schools. They prohibited public prayers. The most we could do was pray silently, and in a posture that would not indicate to others what we were doing. Something similar happened with the Christian hymn we were used to singing. They replaced it with a Young Pioneer's song.

"Why don't you just keep quiet about your faith?" friends suggested. "You'll have less trouble that way."

What to do? To what group do I belong? Church? Although I attended regularly and shared in my family's commitment to Christian faith, I had not yet made my public profession of faith in baptism.

School? I sat with the "outsiders," the boys who were disciplinary problems and the children who had not yet joined the Communist Youth Group. But I also envied the "insiders," those who belonged: I saw for myself that they had the most fun.

Once again I spoke with my teacher about joining up.

"Listen carefully Ma Shuhui," she replied. "You will need to choose between Jesus and the Communists!"

"But wouldn't it be possible to choose both?" I queried.

"No!" She had no doubts.

Neither did I. Simple enough, even for a little child like me. Since choices had to be made, I chose Jesus.

Thirty years or more later I met Rebecca Zhang (Zhu Chongde), one of my former elementary school classmates. Her husband, a graduate from Southwestern Baptist Theological Seminary, served at that point as a Chinese pastor to a church in Texas. Back in our Shanghai classroom, so many years ago, Rebecca, who came from a Christian family, admired the brave ways in which I identified myself as a follower of Christ, especially when I spoke publicly to my classmates about my grandfather's faith. As for my alleged bravery, I'm not inclined toward self-congratulation. But I can easily testify about my weariness.

4

New Directions in School

1953–1961

China's leaders charted its first Five-Year Plan, Soviet-style, in 1953. The Soviets had provided China with aid and with experts in implementing such a plan. China's focus on heavy industry, paid for by the agricultural sector, demonstrated significant growth. China also modeled its educational system on that of the Soviets and soon witnessed impressive achievements in literacy. Still, Mao Zedong was not one to let his people rest on their laurels. In spring 1955 he purged dissidents. The following summer he demanded rapid industrialization.

Elsewhere, Communist leaders from around the world temporarily relaxed the severity of their regimes, or so it seemed. In February 1956 Nikita Khrushchev, First Secretary of the Communisty Party in the Soviet Union, made his "secret" de-Stalinization speech at the Twentieth Party Congress. Three months later, in a similar "secret" speech made before Chinese Party leaders, Mao called for China to "let a hundred flowers bloom." The following spring, Mao's call took concrete form in a campaign that invited intellectuals to offer gentle criticisms of the Party.

Freedom reigned, but not for long. When Hungarian students pressed on these matters, Khrushchev demonstrated his true colors: Soviet tanks rolled into Budapest on November 4, 1956. Similarly, when Chinese intellectuals took Mao's "gardening call" seriously, Mao turned on the intellectuals. Later, Mao maintained that he had initiated his Hundred Flowers movement only as a ruse. His strategy, he explained, had been to tempt the poisonous snakes to come out of their caves and to make their dangerous ideas public so that he could destroy them. In July 1957, the chairman initiated an anti-rightist movement, a campaign in which the authorities caught so many people who were close to Nettie.

Soon the government also extended its crackdown beyond human enemies when it attacked the "Four Pests." In 1958, Chairman Mao called for a campaign against lice, mosquitoes, and rats. Even sparrows, who ate the seeds the farmers planted. It was a happy day for school children, who were sent outside to scare the birds by making noise and jumping. This happened all over China, in its rural sectors and in its cities until they had succeeded in exterminating the sparrows. However, soon locusts had no enemies to prevent them from devouring the crops. Other insects went rampant and destroyed the forests. Without the forests, there were no roots to hold the soil when the rains came. In short, the successes against the sparrows had interrupted important environmental loops.

Mao initiated the Great Leap Forward, also in 1958, to hasten Chinese modernization. Everywhere, people worked to produce steel. They took down their iron windows and their doors, and they used their kitchen utensils to secure materials for their backyard, steel-producing ovens. This campaign intensified when, in summer and fall 1958, the authorities announced the "Three Red Banners"[1]—a people's crusade with exhortations, slogans, and dramatic economic victories.

China changed directions in several significant ways between 1958 and 1960. In economic policy, its leaders moderated the disasterous Great Leap Forward and then, in the summer of 1960, quietly abandoned it. In govenment, Liu Shaoqi replaced Mao Zedong as head of state. In foreign policy, China's friendship with the Soviet Union cooled significantly.

Middle School, which in China included three years of junior high and three years of senior high, brought significant changes and challenges my way. My small elementary school had limited its entire enrollment to 400 students and kept its average class size at thirty. But my new middle school enrolled 1,000 students and expanded the average class size to forty.

McTyeire Junior High ranked as a top-level school. Successful applicants scored high on written entrance examinations, which included both academic and political elements. Peiming Junior High, a private, second-tier girls' school, required equally high scores on their entrance exams, but they only emphasized academic excellence. Third-tier junior highs enrolled those who failed to secure admission to the more prestigious institutions. These schools differed not only in their selectivity, but also in the quality of their teachers and their facilities.

I set my sights high when, in spring 1953, I sat for the entrance exams: I hoped to attend McTyeire. The scores said everything! Quite promising academically, but most worrisome politically. The authorities had not forgotten my "capitalist" Auntie Bessie, the elementary school principal whom they had fired in 1951. Rejected! Now, for the first time, I faced a political situation that determined the direction of my own life. McTyeire was closed to me, so we turned instead to the Peiming girls' school, a place where a Christian family friend served as principal. Accepted. And only two blocks from our home. I could walk to school by myself.

At Peiming Junior High, the curriculum and the style of instruction followed a Soviet model. This was most apparent in language arts and music. I began, for example, to study Russian in my third year of junior high; tolerable, but hardly memorable. I had much more fun when the muse took over and introduced us to Russian folk songs; indeed, some of those wonderful melodies and lyrics remain with me to the present.

As young teens we pulled our share of harmless juvenile pranks. Who could resist? Unnecessary and unsupervised nap times invited trouble from junior high kids. Once, when the bell rang, we climbed out the open window—our kind of air conditioning—and hid. Just in time. The teacher returned to the class, only to find an empty room. Before she gathered her wits about her, we jumped back in and surprised her with a "Good afternoon, teacher." Her sense of humor hardly matched ours.

In 1954, the Communist government extended their investigations into the Chinese schools. We saw firsthand the fruit of these investigations: the authorities discovered and arrested two spies, my own teachers! Who would have believed this? My history instructor, a woman who knew everything. This polymath, a master teacher who engaged us with wonderful stories that included the lives and work of important writers. This sedentary Buddhist, a person who lived in the dormitory and, we thought, had never even left the school building. Hard to believe the accusation against her! The authorities claimed that she sneaked out of the window at night. They portrayed her as a famous woman who could ride horses and shoot two guns at the same time. True, although hard indeed to believe.

The political persecution I had witnessed during my elementary years continued into junior high. In Beijing, they arrested Rev. Wang Mingdao and his wife. A year of brainwashing in prison, and this beaten man gave up: he wrote a letter of confession and secured his release from prison. In the end, however, Rev. Wang's conscience got the better of him. He began to regret what he had written and to speak openly of himself as a "Judas." Two years after his release, he and his wife repudiated their written confession and turned themselves in to the police station. The result? Twenty years of prison.

One night in fall 1955, during the Campaign to Eliminate the Counter-Revolutionaries,[2] I awakened to a knock on our front door. Mother was still at work, caring for the students she loved, following the vocation to which she was called. In China, when parents worked the night shift, they left their children at school. That meant extra hours for the teachers. Mother never complained, but I did.

On one occasion, for example, when I suffered from the flu and a high fever, I wanted Mama to care for me twenty-four hours a day. She looked after me and nursed me during the suppertime. But then she returned to school to tend to the needs of Zha Guozheng, a small boy who also needed her attention. At four years old, Little Zha had never spoken a word. To make matters worse, his busy parents rarely had time to spend with their son. Earlier, when the doctors had examined Little Zha, they had found no physiological explanation for his muteness. Understandably, they had suggested his difficulty was psychological. Mother understood that her boy needed patience and love. In time, Zha learned to speak. In time, Zha told Mother's story about "Little Tadpole" to the folks at the Shanghai School. Scripture speaks approvingly of what my mother had done. "I was hungry and you gave me food; I was a stranger and you welcomed me; I was mute and you gave me words." Not me. I failed to appreciate the range of Mama's love. Indeed, I was mad that she would not spend all of her time with me.

A knock on the door. Mother? Gone. Father? He sat in an interrogation room on the campus of the Eastern China Teachers' Training University of Shanghai. That left me, a thirteen-year-old, alone to answer the knock. "The government has sent us to search your home and to question you." *No sanctuary anywhere!* "Have you heard any typewriters or radios at home?" I shook my head. "Okay. Now let's see what we can find." They checked out my long, woolen socks that had been made in America. They looked over everything else I had, including my dolls. "Ah, what do we have here? A diary." Nothing was private. Fortunately, my parents had warned me not to put anything controversial in this required school journal. So all these inspectors read was meaningless girl talk.

When my mother returned home at 10 P.M., I told her what had happened. In order to spare me further trouble, she took me to Grandmother's. Unfortunately, the authorities had also included this house in their search. At midnight, I was exhausted and still awake. Finally, Mother put me to bed in my auntie's room. So the child got some rest, but none of the adults slept that night. The next morning as I prepared for school, Mother issued a stern warning: "If you think someone is following you, you must not look back!" She also offered me words of comfort. "Don't worry. Your father has done nothing wrong. God is with us. All will be fine."

Indeed. During Daddy's most recent imprisonment he had developed four-part sight-sing exercises that he had noted down on small scraps of paper—he published these exercises later. After the authorities released my daddy, things returned to near normalcy. Although he had plenty to do at his school, he also made time to help me with an experiment. He knew about my love for the music-making cicada; he also discovered that I wanted to raise them in my room. Stern parents might have offered an explanation before they responded with a firm "No!" Not my daddy. He climbed the trees on the university campus and caught the members of my proposed in-house orchestra. One at a time, he handed the cicadas down to a colleague-in-crime, Dr. Ying, the chair of the music department; together, they collected my newest pets. Spoiled—me, not my instrumentalists! Ultimately, my experiment failed: my music-making insects never gave a single performance.

During the normal routine at Peiming, I plugged away at it; I studied, but not hard enough to earn superior grades. The energy and discipline I brought to mastering the piano equaled that which I brought to my academic work. At home, close to our piano, I kept a novel, an engaging alternative to the boredom of practicing. The day before each weekly lesson, the deadline when my teacher and I would both have to face the music, I started working on the assigned material. I suspect that my instructor understood only too well why I progressed so slowly. Those who knew me understood that I was a young girl who had more interesting things to do than hit the grindstone.

"A little money goes a long way." So I discovered when my mother started me on a fifty-cent monthly allowance. I kept ten cents back for the church offering and saved five cents. That still left me with thirty-five cents to spend at the school square, the place we students visited each day during the long break between our four morning classes. School authorities had scheduled this break with purposes other than shopping in mind—noble purposes, supported by a simple routine. We began with a flag-raising ceremony, no doubt to encourage civic-mindedness if not patriotism. And we ended with calisthenics, performed in rhythm to the music they played over a microphone. Finished, and still a little time to play or to buy snacks. Once a week, I hurried off to the confectionery window. There, I bought a delicious slice of fried toast for seven cents, or a tasty cake for ten cents. Afterward, my friends and I got together to chitchat while we ate our light snacks. Enough calories to tide me over until I walked home for lunch. There, I would join Huang Shunzhu, the woman who served as our housekeeper. Indeed, I cannot forget her sad story and how she came to live with us.

As a young woman, Shunzhu, a poor village girl, had found herself in an unpromising marriage. It was customary in those days for Chinese parents to arrange an older daughter's marriage for mercenary reasons. The bride, who was usually about ten years older than her mid-teenaged husband, would take care of the boy, and the girl's parents would get the marriage fee. In time, when Shunzhu's husband became sick, she lacked the means to pay for his medications. So her in-laws stepped in and sold her son to secure the necessary monies. When her husband died, Shunzhu's in-laws sold this poor widow to pay for their son's burial. Too much! Shunzhu ran away and ended up in the village where my maternal grandfather pastored a church. Unfortunately, he lacked the space to house another boarder, for Grandpa's assistant had already taken in and secured jobs for three or four needy women in similar circumstances. With nowhere else to turn, they sent Shunzhu, a woman by now in her mid-forties, to live with us. Thus, beginning around 1955, she served as our housekeeper, and we provided her with room, board, and a monthly salary that she rarely spent. Our family encouraged Shunzhu to attend evening church services, evangelistic rallies, and revivals. In time, she became a Christian. No longer content with being illiterate, she learned, with Mother as her tutor, how to read the Bible. For some reason, however, she could never read the same words in the newspaper.

I tried a wide range of sports before I found my niche. Although I lacked training and special shoes at the beginning of my athletic career, I did not let that stop me. I participated in the 100-meter dash as our best runner. This meant I competed in the district championship. At the end of the season, I lost in the final competition. In my second year in junior high I tried out for the girls' basketball team. In other arenas, I discovered that I could hurl the shot put but not the discus, that I could get a good vertical leap for the high jump but not much horizontal distance in the long jump. Aspiring decathletes with such deficiencies might have avoided such sports, but not me. When, however, my teacher told me I had promise at gymnastics, I focused my attention on this new sport.

I took up bicycling during my second year of junior high. My Auntie Bessie found her old bike, one she had not used in a long time, and she gave it to me. My father started me out in the churchyard, a safe enough place for beginners. "Steer straight ahead while you pedal!" "You've got to maintain enough speed to keep your balance." "Not so stiff and rigid with the handlebars." "Make wide rather than sharp turns; that way you won't fall over and hurt yourself." "Anticipate when you want to stop, and bear down gently on the brakes." At first, Daddy ran alongside me and held onto the bike. Then he let me go. "Not bad. Now, let's move out into the streets and see how you do." In time, after enough falls and more than enough skinned knees, I managed on my own. "Well done, Nettie, you've got it down. Are you ready to join me on a longer ride?" More than ready. The two of us pedaled down the street, past those slow pedestrians who chose to travel by foot and those who couldn't afford a bike. Father led the way, out of the city and into the fields and parks. Such fun, again and again and again.

Chinese adults practice corporal discipline to insure that their children turn out right. In support of this practice, they cite an old aphorism: "Only with the rod can you teach a child to respect his parents." Both my parents and my grandparents saw the wisdom of this saying, which, they knew, corresponded in many ways to the biblical proverb "Spare the rod and spoil the child."

In my early years when I misbehaved, my father spanked me. For this, he preferred the ruler, either on my hand or on my backside. Between spankings, I composed and sang my own song about that awful ruler. In later years when I needed correction, my father resorted to reason. What a fine tenth birthday present!

But not from my mother: she spanked me, although not too frequently, well beyond that fine birthday. When I dawdled at breakfast—too slow, she complained—she warmed my backside. When I broke a glass while cleaning the bathroom—too careless, she complained—she paddled me. On this particular occasion, my grandmother came to my defense. Mama, as a good Chinese daughter, remained silent, out of respect for her mother. Later, however, Mother insisted that I go to Grandmother's house and confess that I had been wrong in this matter. Not to be bested, Grandma consoled me with her kindnesses: she had seen through the charade and guessed who had made me do this.

Paradoxically, such corporal discipline, neither excessive nor brutal, made me a better person. It's odd, but I suspect that caring parents who spare the rod actually injure their children in profound and spiritual ways.

"What's all the excitement about down at your church?" I looked up from my homework in response to my friends' inquiry. A sensible question, for they had to walk past our church to get to our house.

"Simple," I explained. "They're having a revival."

"What's a 'revival'?" they asked.

By now they had me curious. "I don't know, but I'll find out and tell you about it."

The first time I attended one of these special meetings, I was visibly touched by what the pastor had to say. Several deacons from the church noticed that I was moved. So at the end of the service they talked and prayed with me. Since my interest in the revival moved well beyond the curiosity stage, I returned to the services, night after night.

On the last day, the preacher proclaimed the gospel in a particularly powerful way. "Some who are in attendance today still need God's forgiveness. Christ has died and risen again to make pardon and new life possible. As Living Lord, he invites you to repent and in faith to accept him as your personal Savior. Why wait any longer?"

He's right. This is for me! I accepted Christ as my Savior and publicly professed my faith in believer's baptism. Now this eleven-year-old understood what a revival was all about.

I could hardly wait for Sundays, for these were the happiest times in my young life. From 100 to 300 parishioners worshiped and attended Sunday school at my maternal grandfather's church. They filled the sanctuary for both the morning and the afternoon services. Here, first my mother and then my aunt played the piano. Fewer came for evening services. My father served elsewhere, at the Grace Baptist Church, as minister of music and as choir director. When church let out, we found time for fellowship. People sometimes brought their lunches with them and visited while they ate. And my grandmother frequently invited friends over for lunch.

Many children preferred to come over to Grandma's house rather than go to the afternoon worship service. We gathered together in her big living room; there, I orchestrated activities. My charges played together in simple games. They listened to my stories. They joined my amateur "drama troupe," each playing his or her part in a play that I designed and directed. Teaching and school: these were my elements!

Since I was a grade higher in Sunday school than most, I naturally became the children's leader at church. I worked with the younger children, those in kindergarten and elementary school, while the adults held their own services. The church had no prescribed curriculum, so I improvised. We sang songs and played games, and then I told the children Bible stories. I also gave them "picture cards" that had special Bible verses at the bottom. The missionaries had left these with us when they were forced out of our country. At last, time for a treat: I handed out the candy or cookies I had brought from home. Such affection for me, their special teacher! If we had extra time, I told them stories I had read. A simple ministry, just suited for me. We heard Christ's words—"Let the children come to me, and do not hinder them; for to such belongs the kingdom of heaven"—and they proved true. More than ten of my friends followed me in accepting Christ.

In summer 1956, soon after graduation from junior high school, two other students and I received a distinct honor. School administrators chose us to attend the Middle School, Summer Camp Campus in Hangzhou. A recreational camp. We climbed mountains; we watched farmers make tea; we rode in boats in a lake. It was only a week, but my first time away from home. Although I had a good time, I would have enjoyed it more had I not suffered from homesickness. We couldn't even write our families, for we found no place where we could post our letters. Not a political camp, or so they said. Still, they emphasized the superiority of group loyalty over family loyalty. In doing this, they instructed us in the five loves: motherland, people, labor, group, and public facility. By the end of the week, I was ready to return to my family in Shanghai.

When I entered Peiming Senior High School in fall 1956, I looked forward to a normal life. I had simple hopes: three years, with some study and plenty of fun, and much of this in the company of my friends. The first twelve months were promising indeed.

After school, friends joined me at home for study and for play. Once we got our homework out of the way, we looked for inviting ways to entertain ourselves. We talked; we played games; and we took on roles in the amateur dramas we invented. I made music at the piano, and my friends listened. Occasionally, my father came home early from work and visited with us or took our pictures. Away from home, we went to the movies, but only when we had money. By this time my mother had increased my allowance from fifty cents to a yuan a month. Better, but hardly enough to pay for the cinema and necessary refreshments. Fortunately, my father came to my rescue. He slipped me money on the sly—sometimes even enough to pay for ice cream—and told me to keep the change. Neither he nor I told Mother about his generosity. Then there was the new cat my father had gotten for me. Even that cat helped make these happy days: she walked with me, but only as far as the church door, on my way to school. I remembered when, in earlier days, my dog had joined me for the same walk.

When school finally let out and vacation began, I adopted new routines. I lived one month during the summer at my grandmother's house. Mother said this time away from home served me well, for it taught me to be independent. Right. But I still lived close enough that I could run home every day. Not that I could complain about life with Grandma. Such a modern home, with electricity and a ceiling fan! And such comfort: we shared a bedroom, and I got the soft bed.

During summer 1957, I set aside my studies and took up athletics and community projects. I started my swimming practice every morning at 6 A.M. Three hours later, at 9 A.M., I arrived at the Children's Palace. There, I took my Red Cross training. As a practicum in that training, I cared for children who had suffered minor injuries. Then I took a break. I ate lunch and spent the afternoon at Grandmother's home. There, I practiced the piano and did homework that had been assigned. At 6 P.M., I headed to the city sports center for gymnastic training. In this I excelled, so much so that some considered appointing me to the city early youth team. I tried to return home by 10 P.M., but sometimes I stayed late, took a shower, and returned at midnight. My father, uncertain when I would show up, worried and waited for me at the bus station close to our house.

My second year of high school gave us all more than enough to worry about. We faced dark, ominous clouds, and then storms that rarely let up. Our troubles began innocently enough, with a school requirement that students pair up and share a double-drawered desk. My "desk-mate" and I developed a friendship that extended beyond the classroom. "Do come home with me after school today," she said. "We'll have a good time visiting together." I readily accepted her regular invitations. Why not? Indeed! Her whole family suffered from tuberculosis.

I hardly expected the disease to be contagious. But then my father's friend, a man known to be an excellent doctor, saw the telltale signs in my face. "Nettie," he declared, "I'm afraid you've got tuberculosis." When he recommended I undergo a routine x-ray examination, I tried to avoid it. I explained to him that I had already had these tests at camp. It didn't work. He and my father insisted that I have them again. The results confirmed the doctor's preliminary diagnosis: positive!

No more school until I recovered. No more sports activities. I was not even allowed to walk downstairs. I cried and cried. Isolated! But not entirely. Many of my classmates stopped by for a visit. I feared that I was contagious, so I wore a mask. They kept coming. Some joined me for lunch and brought me a heated box meal. One gave me a little kitty. In response, I called my friend the kitty's "grandma." *So hard for me to express my appreciation to busy friends who extended their care and affection to me.*

My mother's visit to her doctor brought an equally threatening situation. When the physicians talked with Mother about her condition, they did so in private. Not even my father was allowed to be present for these conversations. In fact, when Daddy left the doctor's office, they locked the door behind him—excluded, frustrated, and saddened. In the end, the doctor reported that they had found sixteen tumors on my mother's uterus. This meant only one thing. A hysterectomy. My illness and my mother's impending surgery only added to the political tests that had been a regular part of our lives since I had started school.

Ma Geshun, Rightist." I opened the newspaper and read the article on the new Anti-Rightist Movement. There, I discovered my father's name. This can't be! Then it appeared again, in a magazine. Alarming! My parents had told me nothing about this. I asked my father about what I had read and he told me the truth. The regime had singled him out and given him a Rightist's cap. Soon, the authorities took him back to the interrogation room.

Others got caught in the same campaign. Uncle David, my father's youngest brother and a senior engineering major at Nanjing Industry University—"Rightist." The authorities interrupted his schooling and sent him away, first to a factory and then to the country, where he worked for a year. When he eventually returned to the university, they prohibited him from continuing his science major. He chose ceramics as an alternative course of study. But that choice reversed his progress in school, for he had to begin his major once again as a first-year student. Uncle Silas, the general senior engineer in the China Ministry of the Railroad (called the "Signature Bureau"), another of my father's brothers—"Rightist." My literature and my physics teachers—"Rightists." Our pastor, the good man who had replaced my maternal grandfather when he had died—"Rightist." The authorities allowed only one church in each school district to remain open; ours had to close its doors. And Mother? They moved her back to her school from the hospital; and they refused to allow her to return home, even after her surgery. The prescribed cure for all petite bourgeoisie, these misguided citizens, was re-education, brainwashing.

As for me, I stayed home by myself. Aunt Barbara, my father's sister-in-law, would not allow my paternal grandmother to come see me. Still, my maternal grandmother visited me daily. Apart from her, I had no one. *Alone. What would I do when the authorities came for me?*

They came to our house, but not for me. The security department policeman explained that the vice-governor of the district had decided that he liked our home. Since he would move in soon, I would have to move out. At the same time, he told my grandmother that another governor wanted her house: she would have to leave. "Where then," I asked, "can I go?" The authorities showed me a home in which two to three families already lived; they said I could make my bed in the hall. *Who will help me move? I'm so alone! Helpless.* In desperation, I turned to God in prayer. "God," I pled, "I don't want to live in a hall." This was the first time my difficult circumstances had driven me to prayer.

My classmates tried to help me, but they found nothing. Then a family close to our neighborhood offered to let us rent three downstairs rooms. They had sensible reasons to make us this offer, for they feared that the government would turn this part of their home into a cafeteria for the nearby commune. Maybe, if this space were already occupied by good people, the cafeteria would be set up elsewhere. Yes. God had answered my prayers.

But I still faced the logistical problem of getting our belongings from one place to another. I turned to the government and asked them to let my parents out of detention so they could move with me. They released Mother permanently, but they only let Father out for one day. Moving everything proved to be an impossible task. Still, we did our best. We rented a rickshaw and we used our two bikes to carry our belongings. Even Grandma got settled in another house where she rented two rooms. Once we completed the move, the government reduced my father's salary by two entire levels and sent him to the country to work.[9]

Three rooms offered us little space or privacy, especially since we shared the dining room and the toilet with our upstairs landlords. Partitions helped. Part of the living room became the master bedroom. We used two curtains in our third room to give Shunzhu and me separate bedrooms and to create a small office for my father. Finally, to complete our "apartment," Daddy built us our own kitchen from a portion of the walled courtyard.

We still had our piano, which served as the centerpiece of our living room. I might have continued my lessons had I not suffered from tuberculosis. As it was, I lacked the interest and the energy to continue. Each month, Daddy had two days off from his work in the country; on those occasions he returned home.

I found Father's office more inviting. He and I had desks that faced one another. After I recuperated from my illness and Daddy returned from the country, we became regular "suite" mates. Each night, there in that office, the two of us sat down to do our work: I did my homework and he prepared his lessons. We continued in silence for an hour and then, simultaneously, we raised our heads. Time for a short break. Tea for Daddy, sugar water for me. We chatted for a short while, and then we returned to our studies. In this simple routine we became particularly close. As for Mother, her work consumed much of her energy and kept her away from home much of the time.

During this time, everywhere the Chinese people endured hardships in order to raise production. Such a shortage of daily necessities! Not enough gas for commercial and household use. Innovative bus "engineers" developed a new technology that was visible to the naked eye. On top of their vehicles they placed a large, refillable bag they stocked with simple and cheap gaseous materials. Desperate cooks resorted to stoking their home stoves with a combination of coal and mud. Neither the buses nor the stoves worked well. A scarcity of clothes. The regime tried to help us cope with this by introducing ration coupons. Basketball players may have had more difficulty than most when it came to clothes, for their coupon allotment was grossly inadequate to cover their large bodies. Fortunately, generous and smaller folk shared their rations with these tall, needy athletes. As for food, we, like many, lacked enough groceries to get by on. Mother responded by raising a chicken to supply us with eggs. Had she raised more than one such creature, she would have violated the specific limitations the regime put on urban folks. Still, many simply did not have enough food. This in turn contributed to widespread sickness. Everywhere, hungry people suffered from swollen bellies. Although Mother suffered from malnutrition, as was evidenced by her swollen legs and feet, she still shared what she had with others.

So much for a young girl to deal with. Then our own situation improved significantly. The authorities had sent most Rightists to northern China, near the Soviet border, for work and re-education. We had done better than that. The leaders of the Shanghai Conservatory, the school where my father had taught since 1956, wanted to keep their unusually talented professor close to home. So the authorities assigned him, in 1958, to a farm in the nearby countryside. A year later, and Daddy lost his Rightist's cap. Even better, the authorities apologized and said he could return home—but only if he agreed to one condition. He must promise that he would not go to church again. This might have been a particularly difficult decision, had it not been the case that most pastors had been removed from their churches and sent to work in factories. Father gave them his word—"I promise"—and he returned home. Henceforth, he would attend church only in his heart. As for Mother, she had recovered from her surgery and stayed busy at school. Thus, within a year my entire family had been reunited.

Meanwhile, I continued to recuperate from tuberculosis. The doctor treated me with Rifadin[3] and streptomycin. I regained my energy levels and took up the Chinese martial art of Qigong. Such exercise helped restore my strength and health. After a year at home, I felt ready to return to school and studies. Unfortunately, my parents would have none of it. Even my tears failed to persuade them. "You'll go back to school, all right, but only after you have completely recovered. That's the way it's going to be!" I spent a second year at home before the doctor and my parents relented.

At last, I returned to high school to begin my junior year; it was fall 1960. Not quite what one would call "normalcy." Most of my friends had graduated, so I found new confidants. My teachers understood my circumstances, but they gave me little slack. "You will have one month to catch up in all your classes; during that period of time you will have no exams. Thereafter, we'll treat you just like all the other students." A serious challenge for one who had been less than diligent at her studies in her earlier days. Now I must really hit the books if I want to succeed. I even quit sports. It worked. I earned all "A's" in my course work, and I was selected as the distinguished physics representative from our class.

Soon, I began helping my teachers by tutoring less capable students. I located additional physics and math materials that would help them, and I quizzed them over this subject matter. I set up two tables at home so that as many as ten of my friends and I could join together in study. Pretty soon, everyone in the class could pass the physics exam. My classmates loved it even though no one in the class equaled my performance in these subjects.

One of the leaders from school invited a few of the students to take college-level math and physics classes. With this encouragement, I enrolled in two separate night courses that met two or three times a week. I was pleased to be selected and honored in this way.

The honors continued. Because of my high test scores, I was selected to participate in the Shanghai Physics Corps. Then the Communist Youth asked me to join them. A version of a dream from years gone by.

"Is it possible for me to join and still be a Christian?" I had asked this question before.

"No!" I had heard this answer before.

Some suggested that I sign up and keep quiet about my faith. "You can," they said, "still honor God silently."

I must not do it that way. I turned down my opportunity for political advancement. But not academic advancement: I graduated from high school in June 1961.

Nineteen years old with a good education but too much politics. Hardly a normal late adolescence. Even when it came to romance, I had neither the time nor the opportunity to pursue those very real interests that Westerners find so compelling. Of course I noticed the other sex.

I knew this boy from church . . . but nothing ever developed between us. Our families lost contact with one another because of the political situation. Thirty years later, I ran into his parents and siblings, but not him, for he lived elsewhere. There was also my grandmother's neighbor's son, who asked me out during my bout with TB. The two of us took in several movies together, and then my parents told me to break it off. That was that. Chinese children, unlike their Western counterparts, obeyed their parents. Finally, my best friend's brother wrote me a few letters and asked me for a date. I responded gently but directly: "No." He wrote me again in 1968, after he had graduated from college, and tried once again. This time I told his sister that I already had a boyfriend—I spoke of the man who would eventually become my husband.

Three years earlier, our government had announced that no student could date. We should choose school or love. Well before this announcement, I had chosen school. Hardly a normal adolescence.

5

A Communist College Education

1961–1965

Mao Zedong and other key Communist leaders had plenty to tend to during Nettie's college years. Early on, they encountered serious problems with declining agricultural production, millions of unexpected deaths, and a shortage of experts. Each problem seemed to have its origins in foolish policies and programs from the late 1950s. In mid-1962, at the Tenth Plenum, Chairman Mao and his comrades tried to chart a new course in such critical areas as agriculture and education. Should politics and pragmatism prevail? Should they temper or renew the class struggle? They argued over these matters for three years before their conflict took on new, dramatic proportions.

These particular national problems and high-level arguments rarely intruded into the life of "third-tier" universities, even in such prominent cities as Shanghai. These students lived "normal" Communist lives: they studied; they attended regular political meetings where they confessed their failures; they witnessed the occasional suicide; they participated in rural re-education; they occasionally relaxed with their friends. Nettie Ma, at the Shanghai Conservatory, was one of these "normal" students.

Following graduation from high school in summer 1961, I prepared to take national qualifying examinations. My scores would be crucial in determining the post-secondary institution I could attend. In China, the top tier of universities focused on science and the second tier emphasized medicine. Teachers' colleges and "arts" schools sat firmly at the bottom of our hierarchical educational system. Those students who scored highest on the exams would be free to choose their school, or so we were led to believe. My teacher predicted that my results on the exams would complement my excellent grades and thus qualify me for admission to my top school. In the applications for the exam, the instructions asked us to list three schools in order of preference. My teacher helped me choose the best school for physics.

Both the contents of the exam and the circumstances under which we sat for it tested us to our limits. We faced a long day and a wide range of difficult material. So many questions, on politics, literature, history, geography, mathematics, physics, chemistry, and even a foreign language.[1] In the early morning, as we stood outside the building in which we were to spend the day, the administrators required us to produce an identification picture and written certification that we had applied to take the exam. All they allowed us to bring into the building was a number two pencil. Their vigilance made cheating impossible. I sat down at my assigned desk and spent the next four hours writing and solving problems. At noon, they gave us an hour's break for lunch. I felt more than ready, for they had prohibited us from bringing food or drink into the building. Daddy waited outside and joined me for a light meal: he had brought a bottle of water and some bread. At 1 P.M. we picked up where we had left off. Another four hours of testing. They made only one concession to human frailty: we could use the toilet facilities when we felt pressed. It was such a hot day, especially in a building that lacked air conditioning. So exhausting that some even fainted. They carried the weak to a recovery room where fans made the conditions marginally tolerable. At last, done! I stepped outside and my father and I returned home.

I, like other students, had been nervous when I began the exam. But nine hours later, when I had completed the last test, I felt good about my work. Now came the wait, first for my scores and then for my school assignment. In time, my teacher inquired about my grades and brought us the results: "You scored 96 percent on the physics section of the exam. Excellent!" My family and I breathed a sigh of relief. I waited several more weeks for the public notice that would match students with their "preferred" schools. At last, the notices appeared, with our names and university assignments, on our school walls. I checked several times and discovered that my name appeared nowhere. *What could this mean? So distressed!* I went home and cried.

In time, the principal of the Peiming girls' school visited my family and offered her explanation of what had happened. "Your family has enjoyed extensive contact with foreign missionaries. Your grandpa is serving a jail sentence. Your father is a Rightist. Two of your uncles live in the United States." I remembered Uncle John, my father's brother, and C. H. Sheng, my mother's brother. "The authorities," she continued, "will not permit you to study science. Politics prevails! You could sit out of school for a year, study intensely, and retake the exams. However, although you might raise your high scores, it will do you no good. The political objections to your appointment will remain." My parents were grateful that the principal had told us the truth.

Not me. *Political matters? This makes no sense! If my family is the obstacle that sits in the way of my getting the best education, then I must leave them. I will travel to northwest China, study for another year, and retake the exam.* A fine idea, until my parents interfered. I never even made it out the front door. Mother locked me in my room and she and Father called a prayer meeting. We all needed divine help and guidance. What to do?

At last, Father spoke to me about my future education. "You will surely be prohibited from medical studies if you apply. Politics won't change. So, you must study music. Third tier arts schools will still be open to you. And within the field of music you should choose the harp as your major instrument." What a strange idea. The only harps I had ever seen were in pictures and in movies. My father must have looked to the Old Testament, to the harpist David, for inspiration. Thus, he encouraged me to play a "Christian" instrument. As Daddy spoke, he reminded me that we Chinese read the Bible characters from the top to the bottom of the page; in doing so, we silently nod in agreement with what is said. Our counterparts in the West read their Bibles from left to right, and silently nod in disagreement with what is said. A simple illustration, and sage advice. I didn't like the idea of studying music and playing the harp, but it seemed to be the only possibility open to me. Like other Chinese children during these days, I again obeyed my parents.

Obedience also meant practice, practice, and more practice. My father decided that my first piano teacher had been too lenient with me and had spoiled me. So he hired another woman to supervise my keyboard work. He himself took on the task of teaching me ear training, harmony, sight-reading, and even a little music history. For an entire year, for eight hours a day, I studied and I practiced. We knew that the competition in the entrance exam for summer 1962 would be stiff. I hoped to be among the few students selected to attend the Shanghai Conservatory of Music. Such an exam! Besides politics and history, it included separate sections on sight-reading, music history, and performance. I played a Mozart sonata (Klaviersonate KV545), a Schubert piece (Scherzo in B flat major), and a song by a Chinese composer.

Only four spaces available, and forty students with whom I must compete for those special slots. How will I fare? Success! Xie, Zhang, Huang, and Ma—that's me—made the cut. Relief, but only until we learned that the conservatory had to winnow us down yet again, for they had a shortage of harp teachers. So they gave us a month to practice, after which they would make another "selection." As the four of us prepared, we discovered that each of the other girls was a Christian. Stiff competition? Yes. Ugly envy? No. We determined not be jealous of the girl who was chosen! As the end of the month approached, we found out that they would be able to take two of us, for a second harp teacher had recently returned from her studies in Russia. Xie made it and Zhang was out. Huang and I had similar scores, so they decided to measure our arms and our fingers. I had slightly longer arms and more flexible fingers. They thought that this would probably make me more successful at the harp. I was in.

Shanghai Conservatory of Music normally required its students to attend five years of school. Most of these people were more than ready for advanced work, for they had spent their last ten years with a singular focus. The government had selected this elite group for specialization when they were third-graders. Thereafter, these children had taken up music at three-year elementary schools and at seven-year secondary schools. Equally important, they hadn't suffered from distractions in their homes, for they had lived in boarding schools. The government had paid for room and board, books, and instruments; it had even provided the particularly poor with pocket change. Shanghai students had returned home monthly, or at best weekly. Those from out of town had visited home only for the winter and summer vacations. So these children really had "lived" at their schools. There, they had learned the importance of collective education as opposed to familial education. There, they had also received extraordinary professional music training, for these schools had had more faculty than students. These budding musicians had thus found it nearly impossible to shirk their work, even in their practice sessions—which the teachers supervised. Diligence prevailed. In reflecting on this situation, we used to say, "Every window has a cannon"; by this, we meant that the teachers peeked in the windows to insure that their charges took their music seriously. In short, the government recruited the best students in China and prepared them in the best possible ways. In doing so, they demonstrated that Communism was superior to capitalism.

Of the seventeen students in my first-year class at the conservatory, only six of us came out of traditional secondary schools. We could not compete with the eight new specialists in our class or with the three "older" specialists who, although they had entered school a year before us, had also joined our class. So in order to bring us six newcomers up to speed, the faculty gave us special instruction. "You are too far behind your other eleven classmates. Before you enroll in the first year of classes, you will spend an entire year in this 'catch-up,' or preparatory program. Maybe then you will be able to compete." Indeed. From this first year on we six faced intense academic pressure; it seemed even worse when we discovered that our better-prepared peers enjoyed perfect pitch. Even though our teachers gave us remedial instruction, we fared poorly. The conservatory dismissed one of us after his first year, and another two dropped out between their third and fourth years. The three of us who remained had to complete a total of six years of college.

Academic requirements pressed me plenty hard. And if that were not sufficient, I brought more than enough political baggage to an educational world that was infused with Communist ideology. The leaders at the conservatory knew me as Ma Shuhui, the daughter of Ma Geshun, the famous professor at Shanghai University, the notorious Rightist.

"We sincerely hope that each of you students is studying to be a Red professor, not a White professor. The former are serious in their music and in their commitments to Communism; the latter are interested only in musical proficiency." A serious warning. The regime feared that the White students, unless cured of their errors, would eventually try to escape from China. They thus provided us with regular indoctrination and brainwashing. In this training we learned that humans must be divided into two groups, the exploiters and the exploited. The Marxists dreamed of a society in which only the exploited, now freed from their oppression, would remain in the country. They hoped that their political instruction, even here at the conservatory, might inoculate the weak and might cure the exploiters from the ideological errors that contributed to their mistreatment of others.

Since I lived at home during my first year at the conservatory, I enjoyed the regular company of my family. When, however, the school officials recognized the noxious influence my parents had on me, they required me to move into the dorm. Thereafter, I returned home only on weekends. I never told Father or Mother about my political difficulties, for I feared it would only add to their problems.

My instructors explained to me that loyalty to the Party, the central virtue of life, requires that I hate its enemies. I looked around and noticed that the good students at the conservatory belonged to the Communist Youth. Because of this organization's strength, they helped out with indoctrination. I tried to join, but they rejected me, the daughter of a Rightist father. Rejected again! This was hardly the end of the political pressures.

The intensity of academic demands contributed to my unhappiness. If I wanted to catch up with the stellar students in my class, I had to practice six to eight hours a day. I attended classes from 8 A.M. to 11:30 A.M., and then relaxed during lunchtime and the scheduled siesta. I skipped the nap and ate and studied with the other harp students; rules prohibited us from playing our "noisy" instruments and disturbing others. During the winters, we retreated to the hall in the first floor of our five-story building to stay warm. I stepped outside after lunch, bought bread, and returned to the floor hallway. There, sitting in the middle of this corridor, was a stove that warmed this large building; there, we prepared toast for several friends. We enjoyed light talk, but only until the school authorities found out about our jokes. They required me to confess this failure. In this way, they insured that their students embraced the proper ideology.

My neighbor in the dormitory and a senior at the conservatory, "K," faced trouble when a Youth Leader asked her for a date. She turned down her Communist suitor because she had decided to go out with another schoolmate. The rejected suitor retaliated with a vengeance. He and other Youth Leaders held repeated indoctrination and brainwashing meetings during which they forced K to confess that her family's influence on her was stronger than that of the Party. "So, you like to wear nice clothes!" "So, you read the wrong kinds of books!" Among those books was Charlotte Bronte's *Jane Eyre*. The students in my future husband's class were among those who attended these meetings and witnessed K's humiliation.

Too much of this pushed K over the brink. During the lunch period that followed the last indoctrination meeting she ever attended, she ran up to the fifth floor of the south building and jumped to her death. No slow, torturous death for her. That same day, after having eaten, another harp student and I stepped outside and headed toward the practice building. We never reached our destination, for security had closed the access road. Unknown to us, they were cleaning up the mess K had made when she had landed on the street. A friend called us back into the dorm, explained what had happened, and warned us against making any inquiries. "Just keep your mouths shut and take a nap." It didn't take long for the word to spread about K's suicide. Other friends urged us to remain quiet about the entire affair. "If you show any sympathies for her, you yourselves will be in trouble. Just go to class, practice, take your naps, and pretend that nothing has happened."

So much for dating. Indeed, the authorities still cautioned us against dating and advised us to focus on our studies and on proper political thinking. *Good advice. School is more important to me than romance.* But not all Chinese young people listened. Those who married frequently received work assignments that placed them in different parts of the country. The government gave them a fourteen-day vacation each year; during this time they could visit with their spouse or with their parents. If they combined their vacation with the Chinese New Year, or with "off days" that they had accumulated because they had worked on Sundays, they might get a little more time together with their loved ones. A common custom and a simple explanation of why, during these years, so many Chinese children were raised by their grandparents.

Each year during the winter vacation, and sometimes during the summers, the authorities sent us to the country for "re-education." Nighttime. Intense, psychological pressure during the evening indoctrination meetings. They uncovered my erroneous thinking and they forced me to confess again and again and again. "Since I see all people as equal I must confess my wrong-headed sympathies for the landlords." "I know that it's wrong, but I love one of the little lambs that I came upon out here in the country." "My family's failures about which I have repeatedly spoken have made it difficult for me to see the truth." So hard. Will they ever let up?

Daytime. Intense physical labor during the supposed respite of daytime work. Once, when we lived in a village, we had to cross a makeshift bridge that was made of plumbing pipe. *Scary!* Fortunately, one of the boys helped me across. The next morning I woke up early to practice crossing on my own. Often, they set us to work in the field. *So hard!* The farmers were accustomed to working barefoot, but not me. I always wore my shoes. Until now. I took them off and stepped out into the dirty, muddy rice field. *Scary. Will leeches attach themselves to my feet and suck my blood? Will a snake get angry at me and latch onto my leg?* Then they instructed us to collect and distribute excrement, some of it human, as fertilizer for the plants. *Surely I can cope, just as the others do. But such an awful smell! So nauseating, working my hands in pig dung! So hard! Will they ever let up?*

Nighttime. More indoctrination. "Once again I've failed. I'm bothered by this awful task of working in the manure." "My mother always told me to clean my hands. But now I see that on this too she has been a bad influence on me." I confessed publicly, and I wrote my confessions down on paper. *Such a change from high school, when I took comfort in helping people. Now I'm the enemy.* I cried and trembled when they singled me out to speak in these public meetings. But my re-education required even more than this. A youth leader instructed me to read the many books he handed me. These books demonstrated that the Bible was filled with errors. *Will they ever leave me alone? Isolated, with no one here who will listen to my troubles. So hard! So unfair! Will they ever leave me alone?*

Gradually, I drifted away from God. When I returned home after my time in the country, Grandmother noticed my spiritual declension. "Remember, Nettie, you are God's child. Never give up! I will pray regularly for you. Most important, you must return to the Lord!"

While I lost my spiritual moorings, and while Grandma prayed, friends in college provided me with the encouragement and emotional strength I needed. Odd that the diversions of simple play did me so much good. We repeatedly took to our bikes. The one of us who organized the outing sent each of the others separate letters with instructions on where she should bike. When we arrived at the appointed place, we found further directions, in a small loaf of baked bread that we were to purchase on the streets, or under a stone, or elsewhere. Start and stop; stop and start. Toward the end of the day, and at the end of our enjoyable adventure, we all met at a park. Someone had already paid for the food we shared in our picnic. So refreshing, small talk and time together! Our play also took us into the boats and out onto the lake. We splashed one another until we were thoroughly soaked. Then we lay on the grass, staring up at the heavens as we dried out. On national holidays we headed to the City Square to watch the fireworks. Then someone suggested that we cross the Huangpu River and watch the brilliant nighttime explosions from a different angle. Surprising that diversions of simple play molded us into a surrogate family and created lifetime friendships.[2]

Some relationships among the students in my college class never jelled. This suited the Communist leaders just fine, for they tried to prevent us from having close friendships. Of the six girls in our class at the conservatory, two came from workers' families. "T," one of these girls, repeatedly tried to borrow money from me. Not easy to get blood out of a turnip! My mother gave me only twenty yuan each month—this barely covered my expenses. I used fifteen of those yuan for food coupons and the other five for necessities. When I "pinched my pennies," I had a tiny bit left over, just enough to help T out. Unfortunately, the school authorities found out about my generosity and charged me with violating class lines and having a bad influence on T. One more crime for me to confess. So the next time T asked me for money, I refused her request. T, not easily satisfied, complained to me about my stinginess. *What should I do? There's no way I can satisfy both.* In the end, I told T she should check with the school authorities and see what they recommended. I would be more than glad to follow their suggestions. In this case it looked like it was class differences, precisely those matters that the government accentuated, that kept the worker, T, and me, hardly a peasant, from warming up to each other. "W," my best friend, found these distinctions especially distressing.

The next time such supposed class differences caused tensions between T and me, W saw only too clearly the true reasons behind our differences. During the summers, we set our suitcases outside so they could get some air. On one occasion I had knitted a vest and left it sitting inside my suitcase. Everyone knew the vest belonged to me. Then it disappeared. We all felt certain that someone had stolen my vest; it was W who discovered its whereabouts. She told me it was hidden in the bottom of T's suitcase. I didn't know what I should do. I felt sure that if I said anything about this to those in charge, I would likely get into trouble. So I kept my mouth shut. My friends in the dorm knew exactly what had happened, but they too lacked the courage to speak up. No one wanted to invite the school authorities to settle such matters. We knew that while they stressed indoctrination and confession, they had little interest in real justice.

After my third year at the conservatory, and just before the Great Cultural Revolution, the authorities sent me to the country for 100 days to take part in the socialist educational movement. No school studies for me during this "school holiday"! Because they knew my story, they watched me closely. Indoctrination continued to be a troubling part of my life. Normally, the authorities paired two students together and required them to work and live as a part of a rural production team. For some unknown reason, they treated me differently. They sent me by myself to join one of these production teams. Now I faced the dangers of walking home alone at night. This lasted only until I met Xu, the man who would later become my husband. Xu held a relatively important position, secretary to the leader of our region, no doubt because he wrote so well. He was also a member of the youth cadres. Part of his job required him to interview students who worked in his area during the winters. During this special early spring, Xu walked with me and offered me his protection and his company. These were good walks. Still, he must have wondered about this strange, Christian woman, for he, like most of my countrymen, had been taught by our government to reject any belief in God.

6

A Budding Romance Amidst the Great Proletarian Cultural Revolution

1965–1966

The high-level, restricted, unresolved political debates of the previous five years turned out to be the calm before the storm. In 1966, China witnessed the beginnings of Mao Zedong's decade-long attempt to reinvigorate his revolution. China and too many of its leaders, he said, had abandoned their early Communist fervor and ideology. He insisted that old thought, old culture, old customs, and old habits be eradicated. At the highest levels, Mao demoted Liu Shaoqi and others who had opposed Mao. He also mobilized the Red Guard, discontented youth and Party members, as the vanguard of his new Cultural Revolution. These zealots visited homes, destroyed Buddhist temples, confiscated Christian bibles, burned Western books, and, at least on occasion, pocketed capitalist money. Many, including Nettie and her family, learned first hand about forced confessions, brainwashing, torture, and prison. Some victims chose suicide to escape the brutality.

I listened attentively to my father's prediction: "We better get ready, for a powerful political movement will soon wreak havoc on China." In summer 1965, Mao Zedong and his wife Jiang Qing had moved temporarily to Shanghai. From here, he attacked his enemies. Newspaper editorials spoke about these matters and more. Although journalists wrote obliquely, Father read between the lines.

I listened again, this time with optimism and anxiety, to my father's declaration: "I don't think I have done anything wrong. But as an old 'athlete,' I expect they will force me back into the 'games.'" Such prescience! The authorities would once again accuse Daddy of capitalist thinking. Brainwashing and forced confessions would follow.

A second athlete took charge of these "games." On July 16, 1966, our seventy-two-year-old chairman swam in the Yangzi River. Amazing! Nine miles in sixty-five minutes. That's what everyone heard. No decrepitude or lack of vigor in our leader. Thereafter, Mao returned to Beijing and took charge. We heard radio reports about these and related public events. Red Guards, the vanguard of the Cultural Revolution, were sent out to eliminate the "four olds." Their mission required them to search our homes, our temples, our schools. And when they discovered unacceptable property, they would confiscate or destroy it. That would put an end to capitalism and feudalism. So much for old culture, old customs, old habits, and old ways of thinking. Many students joined our Great Proletarian Cultural Revolution.

That revolution threatened everything we did at the Shanghai Conservatory of Music. The Red Guard, young people who understood little about music and cared even less about our muse, prohibited us from practicing. *Surely they will identify the tools of our trade as capitalist musical instruments. And if we don't act quickly, they will destroy these priceless possessions. Risky, but necessary.* We hid our capitalist harps, instruments the Red Guard called the "queen of the orchestra," in the spacious garbage room. We sealed and put away our pianos and the special music and the books from the library. *Just maybe we will be able to use these irreplaceable goods once more, but only when the Cultural Revolution comes to an end.* The school staff burned our less valuable capitalist goods to show that they knew how to dispose of reactionary materials. That still left our instructors—we couldn't seal and hide them. Time for our professors to sweep out the monsters and the demons through self-criticism. A dangerous task indeed.

Mother, who had retired from work, expected the Red Guards to search our home. With this in mind, she prepared as best she could for our unwelcome visitors. She found my necklace, a cheap piece of costume jewelry I had bought and kept secret. She flushed it down the toilet, for she knew it would cause problems when the "home inspectors" discovered such a prized possession. She also tried to send my music to the recycling company. Too late. She heard the knock at the door. The Red Guard had arrived. They found and confiscated Bibles and music. It could have been worse.

We witnessed "more" at the conservatory, for here the revolutionaries criticized each of our monstrous and inhuman professors. Such humiliation! Such debasement! The Red Guard corralled two friends, the chair of the piano department and the chair of the secondary department, and forced them to criticize one another. Their re-education began with the two women kneeling face to face. "Now, you must explain how you have poisoned your students' minds with your teaching." *Impossible.* In time, the poor professors confessed. "Not enough. You must slap the other's face." *Impossible. We can't.* In time, these friends struck one another. "Not enough. You have spoken such evil words. Your mouths must be cleansed." Their tormenters fetched a toilet bowl brush and issued their instructions. "You must brush each other's teeth." *Impossible. We'll become sick and vomit.* In time, the poor women obeyed. "Enough, but only for this day. We'll pick up tomorrow where we left off." The second day began with more interrogation and ended in death. The two professors, these good friends, committed suicide.

These suicides served as a portent of things to come. The principal of the secondary department and her husband, the chair of the conducting department,[1] ended their lives by inhaling gas from the kitchen stove. Their son, a cello major from our department and my friend, saw to the funeral arrangements. He had the bodies cremated and then attended their simple memorial service. Such a tragedy, and so sad! But no tears. The school authorities would not allow the poor boy to cry.

Not yet enough. The criticism and the violence continued. I remember well the day the members of the instrumental division gathered together to continue the "cleansing" process. This time they singled out an instructor from the wind instrument department. The authorities picked away at him as they tried to find something wrong with what he had taught his students. They failed, but only until "T," a student who had been taking a nap, arrived. Since she came late, she had no idea what we had been talking about. That didn't stop her. "I'm from a worker's family," she explained, "and this professor tried to teach us capitalist ideas." Then, she took off her belt and began to beat this enemy of the people with its buckle. Awful!

In time, a courageous person spoke up. "Why don't you leave the miserable man alone? He's not worth your anger."

Another brave girl tried to stop the violence. "That's enough. When we criticize, we must restrict ourselves to verbal attacks. We must not injure physically those who are addicted to the old ways."

In this case I watched; and when most of the other professors were beaten; and on those occasions when the inquisitors slapped my father.

It requires no census-taker to provide a final tally of the suicides at the Shanghai Conservatory. They were so common. The chair of the conducting department, the chair of the instrumental department, the vice-chair of the instrumental department, the chair of the piano department, the chair of the secondary department, and the chair of the traditional instruments department. Each of these professors was my father's close friend. Still not enough. Ten more, administrators and faculty from our small school, took their own lives.

I might have sought refuge at home, but I worried that the Red Guard would use any visits I made as a pretext for further accusations. I imagined what they might say. "We understand what you have done. You went home and collaborated with your parents. Then, when we interrogated the three of you separately, you all told the same story in the same words. Unbelievable!" So, I stayed away for as long as I could. In time, on at least a few occasions, I secretly left the conservatory to be with Mother. By this time, she had been forced to find accommodations elsewhere in the same building. Now, she and five other families lived in a single house. They all shared a kitchen and a bath and one-half; Mother got a whole room and a half to herself. Unfortunately, they simply had no space for Huang Shunzhu, our maid and friend for many years; she had to move on. But before she disappeared, the Red Guard tried to persuade her to criticize my parents. It didn't work. Shunzhu insisted that her benefactors had treated her well. She would not accuse my parents of wrongdoing.

In these difficult days, I thought often and hard about the suffering I witnessed. The Communists taught us that we could create an earthly utopia, a communal kingdom. No need for heaven, the opiate for the masses; they could create heaven on earth. Indeed, we all could participate in the inevitable victory of the Communist vision, if we would only abandon our traditions and join in the class struggle. Mao and his cohorts promised us peace, equality, and the good life. A distant dream, not a present reality! After a decade and a half of class struggle, re-education, and too many visits from the Grim Reaper, what had we won? A social system in which new class differences had emerged and become entrenched, a social system in which each new political movement created fast-growing and destructive enemy groups. So many broken families; so many tragedies. It simply didn't work. The only way to solve the class problem, I believed, was through Jesus Christ. A crucified Savior, a resurrected Lord, the forgiveness of sins, a new community in which "there is neither Jew nor Greek, . . . neither slave nor free, . . . neither male nor female." Although I rejected the Communist vision of class struggle and embraced the Christian vision of the Kingdom of God, I had much to learn. Helpless, powerless, I started praying to God. "Please, Father, show me the truth."

During the first year of these persecutions, my father went to work early and came home late. Each evening after supper my mother walked to the bus station to wait for her husband. When will he come home tonight? 9 P.M.? 11 P.M.? 1 A.M.? Will bad weather make it impossible for me to meet Geshun tomorrow night? Even the heavens cooperated. Father understood and appreciated Mother's encouragement and love. Still, he wondered; still, they talked.

"How much can a man endure? So bad! So hard! Maybe it would be better if I ended it all and took my own life?"

"Please Geshun, don't take the easy way out. Remember that I love you. And God loves you too. We both know that suicide is not the Lord's way. Please, don't give up!"

She's right. And she cares. Each night she shows me her love by meeting me here at the bus station. I also know that Christ calls us to take up our cross each day. I must not abandon my wife. I must not deny my Lord. "Sufficient unto the day is the evil thereof." "No temptation is given us that we cannot endure." I'll stick it out, come what may.

These late night meetings came to an end when, in the Fall of 1966, the authorities made it impossible for Father to return home. They incarcerated him in a concentration camp that was attached to our school. For seven long years, he lived in what could best be described as a "cowshed."

Long before Father's incarceration, the regime had encouraged children to criticize their parents. In the early 1950s, my cousins, both of whom were in high school, were drawn into this net and criticized their father, my Uncle Robert. Afterward, the older of the two children spoke to my mother about what she had done. "I only read out loud what other people had written for me to say. Loyalty to the Communist Party seemed like the most important thing in life to me. I'm so sorry for what I have done." My cousin cried and asked my mother to forgive her.

"I'm not the one to whom you need to confess," Mother replied. "You must ask your parents and God, not your aunt, for forgiveness."

My cousin carried this burden of familial disloyalty with her for many years. How could she have betrayed her own parents, those who had given her life and love for so many years?

And now, during our Cultural Revolution, many faced this same test. In our homes and at our workplaces, criticism prevailed. In this highly charged, politicized atmosphere, the Communists turned husband against wife and wife against husband. Chinese families reaped the whirlwind. Divorce was common, and children turned against their elders. The Red Guard, led by students, took center stage. In their own homes, these praiseworthy revolutionaries denounced their own parents while they and their comrades ferreted out capitalist goods.

I could not escape my turn. The Youth Leader at the conservatory told me that I needed to participate in the criticism against my father. I knew

Daddy was far from perfect, that he had made many mistakes. But he had never acted against his own government. *I must not falsely accuse my own father. But they will never permit me to remain silent. What can I say?* I secured a large poster and wrote out my accusation in big characters. "My father, Ma Geshun, has erred in his judgments about the novel *Tough Road*. The author of that book claimed that true proletarians must be baptized three times in water and three times in blood. My father has enjoyed too much this comparison between proletarian 'education' and Christian baptism." I put my pen down. *I've been too hard on my cousins. Now I understand what they faced. Hopefully, this poster will satisfy the Youth Leader; hopefully it won't cause Father too much trouble; and hopefully they'll leave me alone.*

Father would have been glad to respond to my trivial complaints rather than deal with the more serious charges his interrogators brought against him. "You might as well confess, Mr. Ma. It's clear to us. Not only are you an American spy. You are also a cardinal in the Roman Catholic Church." How could they have reached such an absurd conclusion? My father had a red choir robe, the one he had bought when he was a student at Westminster Choir College in the United States. When the Red Guard had discovered this robe among his belongings, they had put it on public display—along with a sign, just to make certain his crime was clear: "American Spy and Catholic Cardinal!"

If only I had listened to Daddy earlier, before all this had happened. "Nettie," he had said, "you take this robe and make yourself a skirt out of the material." *It's pretty, all right. But if I wear something new, I'm liable to get myself into trouble.* I did nothing, and they found the incriminating evidence. Much later, Daddy joked about this matter. "The next time I plan to make you a dress, Nettie, I will remember your reservations about new clothes."

For now, Father answered his accusers as best he could. "It would be an honor, indeed, sirs, to have been appointed to the highly regarded position of cardinal. Unfortunately, as a Baptist, I lack the proper qualifications to serve as a leader in the Roman Catholic Church."

Public accusations against my father continued. The authorities pressed me to continue with my criticisms. An impossible situation. I cried, morning to evening. After one of these public meetings that they called "Help Ma Shuhui, to cut off the string that has tied her to her family," two boys came separately to my practice room. One reminisced with me about the good times we had enjoyed when we were young. "My parents," he said, "held my hand when they took me to play in the park." Another boy came to me and lamented that we all had become people who had no homes. I remembered my own story. Back in the late fifties and early sixties, when food had been in such short supply, Daddy had set out for the Black Market to buy us eggs. He had tried to board the crowded bus but people pushed him off. He was deterred, but not defeated. In time, he caught another bus, secured the eggs, and returned home to feed his family. I remembered, and I cried.

I could not live in the past, and I could not endure the present. *Maybe I should commit suicide. Then others will realize that I have done no wrong.* Most people in those days just walked away from me. They feared that if they did anything more, the Red Guard would interpret this in the worst possible way—namely, they would be seen as Nettie's sympathizers, people who themselves deserved criticism. Not "S," though, who, from the six girls and seven boys in our class, was one of the two students with worker family origins. This good friend looked out for me and, in doing so, made me realize that I was not alone. After one of our indoctrination meetings she sought me out. She knocked on the door of my practice room and spoke briefly. "Why don't the two of us get together for lunch?" Few words, but enough to show people that she understood me and that she objected to the way I was being treated. Not much, but plenty brave. With these words S saved my life. During these troublesome days, S and then Xu Dingzhong, the man who would later become my husband, joined me regularly for lunch and supper. *Such good company. I'm not isolated. These sympathetic friends have strong shoulders. They'll help me persevere.*

I needed such strong shoulders, for the destruction and divisiveness of the Cultural Revolution persisted. We witnessed so much madness as our leaders tried to destroy the old world and create a new one. Their foolishness extended even to city streets; there, they politicized traffic regulation.

One morning the Red Guard discovered an ideological flaw of major proportions with our stoplight system. "Why," they asked, "should 'red' mean 'stop?' Red is the color that represents the Revolution, the progressive movement that will bring in the new order. And why should 'green' stand for 'go'? It represents at best reactionary revisionism." With such profound insights they reversed the meaning of our stoplights. Now when a vehicle approached a red light, it needed to proceed through the intersection; and when that same vehicle approached a green light, it needed to stop at the intersection. Confusing indeed. Chaos resulted. Hundreds of accidents. People simply failed to understand the change. The next morning the government discussed these matters with the Red Guard and decided that we must, at least for the present, return to our reactionary system: red once again meant stop, and green meant go.

The government also prohibited or eliminated many of the remnants of the old order. Western practices and goods represented capitalism; old Chinese customs and artifacts represented feudalism; and traces of Russian influence represented revisionism. The attacks against these subversive influences continued. Mao proscribed flowers and flower gardens capitalist creations at their root. This affected in particular our parks and our campus. Here at home, at our conservatory, we refused to abandon our aesthetic tastes: we landscaped our gardens with vegetables. Visitors and residents noted our delicate designs and our rich colors. With another mandate, the authorities banned virtually all of the fine arts: no public performances! Of course we could still sing our "Chairman Mao songs." The Red Guard, not to be outdone, went after the ancient statues located in our parks and our temples. These feudal icons, mostly from the Tang and the Song Dynasties, suffered accordingly. Hands, noses, feet, and more: the zealots mutilated their defenseless enemies. Years later, more sensible folk tried to repair at least some of these statues. Nearly hopeless. It doesn't take a sculptor to distinguish between ancient art and modern plaster. So much for our cultural heritage.

Red Guards, much like those young people who had visited Mother's house, continued purging our residences. Destroy the old; expropriate the useful. Where these goods ended up, no one knows. None was exempt from these surprise calls. Our friend, the wife of the former president of what had been Shanghai University, looked on helplessly as such hoodlums ransacked her home. They tore her bedsheets, ripped up her clothes, and broke her China dishes. When they had finished, her cupboard was bare. No bowl from which to eat her food; even no undergarments. Fortunately, friends looked after her needs. They collected simple clothes, set them in a basket, and pretended that they were going to the market. Then, at the right moment, they gave their basket to the poor woman whom the Red Guard had victimized. A good start, but only until the weather turned cold. What would this former university president's wife do for winter clothes? So hard. How could we make sense of this search-and-destroy movement? The guilty committed no crimes; and the innocent confessed their errors.

In summer 1966, the students and the teachers divided into two groups, the rebels and the royalists. We royalists remembered only too well what had happened to the innocent during the Hundred Flowers Movement. Initially, the authorities had invited the "birds" to "sing." In time, many intellectuals had joined the chorus and had foolishly criticized the government. Trapped! Our leaders offered their familiar explanation: they had used this ruse to tempt the snakes to come out of their holes; and then they had beheaded the evil and poisonous creatures. And what now? Although we understood little, we suspected another trap. How could we protect our teachers? Mao made such protection difficult when he initiated the "Establish Revolutionary Ties" Movement.[2] In response to this, the city authorities, people who wanted us to serve the royalist cause on their behalf, organized our school and sent our royalist students to Beijing. "You must," they insisted, "go to the capital and visit the universities there. They are at the vanguard of the Cultural Revolution. You should 'establish revolutionary ties' and learn from them." In saying this, the authorities clearly spoke of the rebel students in Beijing, young people who had already begun their Revolutionary Ties movement. Thus, our sponsors got us train tickets and, in August 1966, sent us on our way. So much to worry about. *What will happen to the faculty children, we who are known as "Black Sheep," we whom some called Lau Bao? I'm frightened. I hope others will protect and care for us.*

The crowded Beijing "Express" offered little room—for sitting or for sleeping—in the passenger sections of the train. So several of us, including

Xu, moved outside, to the small space between the railroad cars. Open air, more space, and even a chance to talk, but only if we shouted. In Beijing, "S" and I spent most of our time together. The two of us visited the different universities where we established revolutionary ties. We looked forward especially to the grand celebration in Tiananmen Square. Finally, the big day arrived: on September 13, we joined the masses in the city center. We had heard that Chairman Mao himself would appear. *Maybe we can get close and see our leader.* No luck. We tried but failed to get near the platform. Too many people. So we waited, at a distance, for the special moment. At last, he stepped up onto the stage. "Is that him? Yes, I'm sure. Can you see him? Yes. I do! I do!" So exciting. Later in the day, when we had more time for reflection, we felt less certain that we had really seen Mao.

Soon after we returned to Shanghai, the authorities called the students together for a public meeting. This time they singled out and accused four couples. "So, you have betrayed the Revolution. The evidence is clear. You have failed to suppress your capitalist affections: you have fallen in love. We expect you to confess your errors."

Two of the couples immediately acknowledged their guilt. "You are correct. Western capitalist ideas, especially those about love that we have read in Western novels, have led us down the wrong path. An evil influence. We hope hereafter to support the Revolution wholeheartedly."

Xu and I, and the other couple, chose to remain silent. Why should we criticize ourselves and thus add to the difficulties that hounded us because of our families' supposed failures?

Everyone knew that Xu had been sympathetic with me. That could do him no good, given my father's situation. Even apart from me, he carried enough baggage of his own. Xu's familial story, the source of that "heavy baggage," extended back two generations. Sun Zhongshan (Sun Yat-sen), the GMD leader, had sent Xu's "grandfather" to Japan to study printing. When he had competed his studies, the new graduate returned to his home in Guangzhou to set up a photography shop. A sensible career path, but not after the 1949 October Revolution. Thereafter, his failures became clear: a member of the bourgeoisie; an officer in the GMD. Too successful for his own good. A historic counter-revolutionary.

Xu's grandfather, like many men of his generation, was a polygamist. His first wife bore him two boys, the older of whom was Xu's father. The second wife also bore him several children. Xu's father only tolerated his unhappy home situation of having to put up with two mothers in the same house. None too soon, he left home to study at the Guangzhou Art Institute. He lived a relatively quiet life, but only until the Japanese annexed Manchuria in 1931. This in turn provoked a broad-based protest movement. Students from the north to the south cried out against the Japanese: "They rob us of our land and they rape our women. Something must be done!" These students took to the streets and sang their songs. "We must boycott the purchase of all Japanese goods. Our military must force the enemy out of our land." Xu's father and his future wife, then a senior in high school, joined the protesters. In this way they earned—the hard way—their credentials as Chinese patriots.

This protest movement offered a most unlikely setting for romance. Still, it happened. Xu's father and mother met and fell in love. Upon her graduation, they married and set up their own household. Soon they had a full house. They started a family, and Xu's father invited his mother and brother to live with him and his new wife. In the late 1950s, a decade after the Revolution, Xu's father played an important role in designing a new historical museum and military exhibit in Beijing. Once again he earned his credentials as a patriotic Chinese. Not enough. His father, Grandpa, was a counter-revolutionary. Because of this, the family faced repeated troubles. Eventually, Grandpa was forced to quit his job. During the Cultural Revolution, the Red Guard criticized Xu's father and searched his home.

In short, Xu's familial problems may have been nearly as bad as mine. That meant that if the two of us started dating, we would only complicate our problems. His friends urged him to end his friendship with me. "If you maintain or even deepen your relationship with Nettie," they warned, "you will not be fair to her." Xu listened but didn't reveal his mind, not even to me.

In time, I wrote Xu a letter. I spoke about our need to talk and told him a bit about my own thoughts. "Perhaps," I said, "I will need to confess publicly that I have read *Jane Eyre*." I concluded by asking him what he thought. Unfortunately, he never received my letter, for the authorities intercepted it. Even worse, they read it before one of our many criticism meetings. I cried, both then and on similar occasions. Finally, Xu and I took a long walk together far from the conservatory. Finally, we found a quiet place where we could talk. Soon thereafter—it was October 1966—we started dating. Ironic that the Communist opposition to our supposed love had encouraged what it had hoped to discourage: it had brought the two of us closer together.

Our situation worsened as our relationship deepened. Where would all of this lead? I knew that He Xiaoqiu, the daughter of the conservatory president, had committed suicide because of intense pressures. And I was not as strong as she, at least in the eyes of the other students. Even so, Xu and I continued to see one another. So much had changed over the past four years. We had started as acquaintances and then become friends. Now we were dating. Soon we would become even closer.

Certainly close enough to enjoy the 1966 Chinese National Days together. On that occasion, Xu invited me to join him for a walk around the park. When we came to the small lake, he suggested that we rent a rowboat. "Sure, that sounds like lots of fun. Except that it's quite crowded and we'll have to wait in line." Afterward, while we meandered around the park, we ran into some of our schoolmates. Surprising. Such a small world. Toward evening, Xu took me to meet his aunt and his cousin. They welcomed us and asked us to join them for supper. During the meal, I understood little of what the others said, for they talked in the Guandong dialect. It sounded almost like a foreign language to me. Later, when we were alone, I asked Xu what they had said. He summarized their judgments: "You've introduced us to a nice girl and a good catch; you must not let this one get away." *Nice.* That evening Xu and I walked to a new place, the People's Park, and took a boat across the Huangpu River to Pudong. There, together, we watched the brilliant fireworks as they lit up the heavens. *So strange. Normally on these National Days my friends and I have gone together to watch these fireworks. And now, I'm going with my boyfriend. So nice. Maybe things will settle down.*

7

On the Road for the Revolution

1967–1968

Chairman Mao "invited" China's youth to hit the road during the Cultural Revolution, to "join the revolutionary storm" and travel around the country. Some might retrace the challenging and lengthy escape route that Mao and his fellow Communists had taken when they fled Jiang Jieshi during the Long March of 1934-35. Others might visit Beijing or chart their own courses. On such trips China's youth, including Nettie, could toughen their soles and reinvigorate their souls. Both could serve the Communist cause well. Too soon, Mao called the youth back home, but not for long.

While the youth hiked, Mao continued his struggles with Liu, the Red Guard continued their persecution under directive from Mao, and Mao's wife turned her attention to the Beijing Opera.

The Red Guard, responding to official "directives" in the summer of 1966, attacked the "four olds" and more. Not surprisingly, our schools ceased to function that fall. At the same time, Chairman Mao encouraged us students to join the revolutionary storm; in this way, he explained, we would secure an alternative and valuable education. Many Shanghai students sought revolutionary enlightenment outside our fine city. Some headed north to Beijing. The more adventurous headed south to Jiangxi, where they would follow in the steps of Mao's 6,000-mile Long March—west southwest to Yunnan, and then north to Yanan in northern Shanxi. A great adventure that might incidentally include sightseeing. Xu and his two friends chose to see Sichuan and the Emei Mountain, a place that had the reputation of being the "most beautiful mountain under heaven."

That takes care of Xu. But where should I go in order to participate in Mao's revolutionary storm? And what will happen to Mother if I leave Shanghai? Maybe I should stay put. By this point, most students in my department at school had already hit the road. Many of our elders wondered about the few of us who remained. Nothing was wrong with me, except that I couldn't make up my mind. Undecided. So I visited with Mother and sought her counsel. "Don't you worry about me, Nettie. I have God and Grandma to take care of me. If it would be good for you to make this trip, then you better go." Sensible advice. Friends and I organized our own travel team: three harp players (one from my class, one a year ahead of me in school, and me); a cellist; and, before our cohort was complete, a flautist.

Well before we took off, I understood that my family would not be able to give me much money to help me out on my trip. Earlier, when the Red Guard had searched our home, they had also taken my parents' entire bank account. That cupboard was bare. At the same time, the authorities had reduced all professors' salaries to fifteen yuan per month. My father had tried to negotiate with the paymasters. He rightly claimed that he could not support his family on such a small income. It worked. He secured a minor victory and an additional five yuan to allow Mama to pay her rent. But nothing for Daddy on that score. "You," the authorities explained, "live at school and pay nothing for your room and board." Father had also requested twenty yuan in order to provide for my grandmother's living expenses; they cut that request in half. "Your brothers," they claimed, "must also contribute to her upkeep." Finally, Father had asked for a fifteen-yuan stipend for me. No luck. "Your wife," they reminded him, "is a retired school teacher. She can support your daughter from her pension." So, I would get nothing from the government.

Mother understood these hard times. On her recent birthday a friend had brought her a cupcake. This generous but poor woman hadn't even had enough money to buy frosting. Embarrassed, she had hidden her present in a newspaper as she walked over to our house. No one would see her insignificant gift. Mother responded predictably and graciously. She thanked God and her friend for the cupcake. And then she invited acquaintances over and shared the sweet—cutting it in tiny pieces—with them. Hard times indeed!

I too understood and expected nothing. Wrong. Mama came through. She dug deep, gathered together the small savings that she had squirreled away, and gave it all to me. Forty yuan. So much, and I didn't really need it. For with my own fifteen to twenty yuan, I could buy rice and bread with vegetables every day; and two to three times a week I could even afford a slice of meat. Poor Xu was much worse off then I was. So I gave him Mother's forty yuan.

Still one more thing to take care of. Before Xu and I left, he invited me to meet him in Guangzhou—after we each had completed our trips. A good idea. He gave me his mother's address and directions on how to find her home. That was that. Each of us went our separate ways to join Mao's revolutionary storm.

As 1966 came to an end, I slipped on my small backpack, and my friends and I walked to the pier. We planned to travel by boat up the Yangzi River on the first leg of our journey. When, however, we came to book our passage, we saw a long line. Many others had similar plans. Eventually, we secured a small room and boarded our boat. While we were standing around, two male schoolmates, a piano and a composition major, recognized us and asked whether they might link up with our troupe. "The school authorities have already criticized us more than enough," they explained. "And now, if we don't have witnesses, they may accuse us of not taking the revolution and the trip seriously. We're not going to play, but they might not believe us. You could testify on our behalf." We empathized, and we welcomed our new traveling companions to join us.

When our boat docked in Wuhan, we still needed to plan our itinerary. Although we had not yet decided where we would go, we knew we needed accommodations. I visited a bookstore and bought a helpful map. We located the route to the university and hopped on a bus—at no cost to students. The school officials pointed us to our free "suite": a large room that held between twenty and forty students. Simple and tolerable. Now where? We started our second day by reading all the political posters that decorated the classroom walls in our "hotel." Thereafter, we visited the other colleges in the city.

After we had seen enough of Wuhan, we moved on to Changsha, the city where the young Mao had lived and studied. Equally inviting, Changsha was located close to Shaoshan, the chairman's birthplace. Unfortunately, too many others had the same idea. Students filled the train station to overflowing. It was an interminable wait for anyone intent on entering properly, through the front door. The "back door," however, was another matter. We walked several hundred meters, circumvented the fence erected to prevent irregular access to the trains, and found our way to the passenger cars. They too were packed like sardines, especially at the doorways. We knocked on a train window and asked whether they had space for a few more people who needed a ride. Someone crawled out the window, and I climbed in. A good start. And then, one by one, I pulled my traveling companions, both the boys and the girls, in through "my" window. Hard work! Now, where should we sit? Others had already beaten us to the luggage racks. Standing room only? Right. But only until I found a spot on the back of one of the seats. There I perched, for nine hours straight. Impossible for anyone to win access to the toilet facilities. Simply too crowded.

At last the train braked to a stop and we arrived in Changsha. Egress was no easier than ingress. I told the boys to jump out the window and then let me hand them our luggage. Done. We girls exited the same way as our compatriots. Soon thereafter we all hopped on the bus to Changsha Normal School, the college where Mao had studied. Booked. No room at this "inn." In time we checked in at Hunan University—they offered us room and board. Our second day in Changsha we visited various schools and then wandered westward, toward the nearby "mountains." We found the Xiang River—it separates the eastern and western sides of the city—and walked along its shallow shore. Green water. Safe enough to drink? No need to take unnecessary risks. Soon, we crossed over the river, passed through the urban setting, and hiked up the 300-meter-high Yuelu Mountain. So much to see on this outing. Later, we read the local paper and listened to the radio. The announcer suggested that students walk rather than travel by bus or train. Why not?

Eighty miles southwest to Shaoshan, Mao's birthplace. A long walk, but not too far, even with luggage, if we gave ourselves three days to get there. Our trip required only minimal preparations. We secured a map and selected the villages where we hoped to spend the night. I suggested that we start early and stop before dark. We stuffed covers and clothes into our backpacks and stored the rest of our belongings at the university, the Changsha school that had given us lodging. We were ready to begin our "Short March." Many hours later, we arrived at our first day's destination. The hospitable villagers gave us bread and water. We might have bought meat and other fancy foods, but we were short on funds. Since we all came from "black" families, our parents had lacked significant resources to help us out. Even so, we could not complain. We had enjoyed our day together—walking and singing—on the road. Still, not quite a perfect day. When we took off our shoes, we discovered blisters. No doctors around. Home remedies would have to suffice. We soaked our feet in hot water and then punctured the blisters. Better. We still had time and energy to learn about rural China. So we found our way to a farmer's house and asked those present to sing for us. They obliged us with local songs and local opera. Fascinating, especially for music majors. We transcribed the melodies as we listened.

The next morning we once again started out early. Not so much fun this time. Our feet hurt! Still, we ambled along—at a pace that would have put snails to shame. One of the boys suggested we take a side trip to Huaminlou in Ningxia County. There, we could visit the birthplace of Liu Shaoqi, the young man who, along with Mao, had attended Changsha Normal School, the mature politician who now served as Head of State of the People's Republic of China. A harmless suggestion to people who knew nothing of recent events. What did we know? We looked forward to spending the night in Tanzicong, a place famous because of its association with Liu Shaoqi, one of our Communist heroes.

On the third day one of the girls threw in the towel. "I'm too tired to walk even an inch further. I can't and I won't go on." To make her intentions clear, she sat down, right there on the road.

I was as worn out as the next person, but I felt that we couldn't stop here in the middle of nowhere. I responded indirectly to "Q's" complaints and tried to encourage our troupe. "We can't just quit. Not now. I'll carry Q's luggage and you boys pull her along as best you can."

We all agreed to forge ahead, but without much enthusiasm and hardly congenial. Fortunately, fatigue reduced the level of our anger. So we trudged along, step after step until, amazingly, we arrived in Shaoshan. We secured lodging at a local elementary school and "crashed." The next day we visited Mao's ancestral home in this beautiful mountain village. Impressive but not refreshing. The revolutionary storm had for the moment subsided.

Eighty miles back to Changsha, as far one way as the other. Easy enough for the radio announcer to recommend hoofing it. Impossible for us to carry through. On the second day we caught the bus, all the way back to Hunan University. Our secret. We never told people that we had taken the easy way. Such a trip. We had collected treasures—special rocks, Mao buttons, and more—on our overly-ambitious "Short March." But we kept little of it. Memories would suffice. On what turned out to be our final full day in Changsha, we recuperated and finished up retracing Mao's steps around the city. At this point, one of our companions, one of the flute majors, decided to leave us and to go see her family in Wuhai.

Where to go from here? I thought back to Shanghai, to my last conversation with Xu before he and I began our revolutionary storm. At that time Xu had suggested that the two of us should meet together, toward the end of our travels, in Guangzhou. A good idea. Unfortunately, at just this point in our adventure, the radio announcer declared the new government policy: "It's time for students to stop these revolutionary trips." *Right, but not quite yet. Maybe, if we hurry . . . . But we can't find the two boys who have accompanied us on our adventures. Well, they'll just have to manage on their own.* That settled it. On this, our second day back in Changsha, we returned to the train station. We hoped to make our little "side trip" before returning to Shanghai. Simply no room on the direct trains to Guangzhou. But if we took the train into Guangxi and then booked passage on a boat, we could reach our destination. That's what we'll do. Except for the other female flute major. She left us and went back to Wuhan where her family lived. But for the rest of us, our passenger car had plenty of space, and was even quiet enough for us to take a nap.

We woke up when our train pulled into the Tianxin station—on the first set of tracks. We looked around, got our bearings, and speculated about the destination of the train that sat parallel to us on the third set of tracks. We called out our window, exchanged information, and determined that if we traded places with some of these strangers, we could each reach our destinations more quickly. Agreed! We jumped down from our window and stood on the tracks while we waited for helpful strangers to hand us our luggage. Suddenly, we found ourselves flat on the ground, lying under the stationary train we had hoped to board. None too soon. Another train pulled up on the middle set of tracks. Preoccupied, accustomed to the noise, we simply hadn't noticed. We'd have been pancakes, had not a more observant and kindly man pushed us out of the way. He had saved our lives. Once we recovered from the shock and the fall, we quickly looked around for our luggage. Success, for everyone except one harpist; her luggage was nowhere to be found. We lacked the time for an extended search, for our new train was already pulling out of the station. So, we hopped on board, found a seat, and settled in for the ride.

At last we arrived in Guangzhou. We found our way to the university campus; there, we booked a room and ran into several acquaintances. Within several days, the boys whom we had abandoned in Changsha showed up and rejoined our group. What next? "We ought to look up our many friends who play in the city's symphony orchestra." "Why don't we listen to a vocal ensemble and watch a dance ensemble?" So many things we might do. I said nothing about my private plans.

And then one afternoon I excused myself from my companions. "You go ahead with your plans. I want to visit a relative of mine." I felt reluctant to offer a longer explanation, which included my plans to visit Xu. I followed his directions, found his home, and knocked on the door. His sister and brother greeted me. *Oh dear. I wonder where Xu is?* We chatted until their mother arrived. She told me that Xu would be on the road for another week before he came back to Guangzhou. It was awkward, even after introductions. The family invited me to join them for dinner, but this didn't seem quite right. I declined their generous invitation and said I would come back another day. *So much for that.* When I showed up again, Xu had still not returned home from his revolutionary storm and his western wanderings. Nothing else to do but to get on with it. His family and I said our good-byes and we parted.

A month or so had passed since we had begun our adventure. Much had changed. We finally learned about the political storms Beijing had weathered for the past five or six months. A power struggle at the highest levels. Mao seemed to be gaining the upper hand in his efforts to oust Liu. So confusing. Apparently we had mistakenly taken Liu to be a Communist hero when we had visited his birthplace on our way from Changsha to Shaoshan. Or maybe this was just politics as usual.

We returned to Tianxin in hope of finding the harpist's lost luggage. When the train pulled into the station, we exited the usual way, out the windows. This time we looked carefully, both ways, for oncoming trains. Then we searched for the missing baggage. In vain. One last time we boarded a train—to Shanghai. When we got home we helped our friend replace her lost goods. My contributions? Clothes and food rations, and sheets I got from my mother. Good friends. And a good way to end our 2,000-mile junket around China.

After I completed my travels, I settled in at the conservatory in Shanghai. I had much to catch up on and much to sort through. Xu returned from his trip and filled me in on the details. Once again he thanked me for the forty yuan I had given him. "It made life easier in so many ways." He also told me that he had developed stomach problems that included internal bleeding. Worrisome. By now the continuing conflict in Beijing was public knowledge—it eventually ended with Liu's being placed under house arrest in summer 1967. This struggle adversely affected the political climate at the conservatory and in Shanghai.

During this phase of the Cultural Revolution, many people suffered religious persecution. Stories abounded. Pastor "T" told me about how the Red Guard found a Christian man in a village close to Ningbo and put him to the test. "Take a sheet of paper," they commanded him. "Cut it with only one single, straight line. And in the end, you must produce a cross. You have twenty-four hours to figure out how to do this. If you succeed in this impossible task, we will believe. If you fail, we will kill you."

The good man took up the challenge. He experimented, hour after hour, but he failed repeatedly. Late that evening, after he had given up, he sought God's face. He didn't fear death, for he knew that "to be absent from the body is to be present with the Lord." But for the present, while he was still "in the body," he needed his rest. "Dear Lord," he prayed, "please, if you could just give me a good night's sleep, I would be most grateful." He got even more than he asked for. A strange dream. In this, he understood exactly what he must do to survive his test. It would take various folds and intricate cuts to get it exactly right.

The next day, the Red Guard instructed their intended victim to get on with it. When the well-rested man finished his work, he produced what they required, and more. First, he showed them the cross. Next, he took the leftover pieces from the paper, placed them together with the cross, and created the Chinese word for "eternal life." Finally, he removed the cross from the cuttings and his persecutors saw yet one more word. "Death!"[1]

The Red Guard, surprised and amazed, spared the Christian's life. And the entire village in which the man lived declared their faith in God.

Here at the conservatory, we developed a tiny supportive community as a way of coping with the unending political pressures that a few of us faced. In time, "W," "S," "X," and I became close girlfriends. W's familial tragedy may have served as the initial catalyst to help bring us together. When her father had retired from work in Hong Kong, he had saved enough money to start a business. Thereafter, he chose to settle in Ningbo. He knew this city well, for he had served here before the revolution as a people's representative in the political arena. And as a Christian and an active church member, he hoped to return here, to his hometown, where he could tell his people about Jesus. At the outset of the Cultural Revolution, the authorities arrested and imprisoned W's father.

Sometime later, they called the daughter into their office to tell her the news. "Your father has died in prison. You must start a clean life, one unsoiled by association with your family. Finally, you must not cry." At this point, "T," one of our classmates, filled us in on the details of the story. She also suggested that we watch W to see whether she cried. Tears would be a sure sign that she had not broken the relationship with her family. Impossible for me to spy on this poor girl. I had my own problems. In fact, W and I developed a good friendship, especially after the administration allowed four of us to share a room in the dormitory. There, we sympathized with one another; there, we felt free to talk together openly. I spoke freely about my father's difficulties. And W told me about her worries: "the government has accused my entire family of being spies." I warned her that people outside were watching for signs of weakness and cautioned her against crying in public. But here, in my presence, I invited her to shed tears whenever she needed to do so. I wouldn't report her.

Closer to home, the Red Guard arrested "J," the pastor of our church. *We will destroy him and what he stands for. And we'll begin by ruining his reputation among his friends.* Thus, these cruel young zealots criticized Pastor J publicly in his neighborhood district. Not enough.

Relentless. *We'll take this a step further. We'll "persuade" this foolish Christian to renounce his faith and to embrace atheism.* "You might as well confess, old man, you have tricked the people into accepting the existence of God." Our pastor stood firm. He would not accede to their demands.

Vicious. *He's tough, but he'll crack if we make it hard on his boy.* The Red Guard tried criticizing the son. Not enough. Then they brought the boy outside to a public place, not far from where they had been pressing the good pastor to abandon the cause. Father and son watched as their tormenters created a simple apparatus that would serve their purposes. They set a chair on top of a table and a washboard up on top of that chair. Ready. They forced the son to climb up to the top and then to kneel down on that washboard. *The old man may not value his life. But with his own son, that'll be another matter. He'll crack. Wait and see.* For hours and hours, the son knelt and the father watched. "Renounce your faith, boy, and we'll let you down off your perch."

What will they do next? The helpless father softened, and then he spoke. "I'll understand, son, if you give in to their demands."

"No, Papa, I can't and I won't."

A standoff, until the boy fainted and fell down from his "tower." The Red Guard revived their victim and discovered that he had injured his knee. "We'd be glad to take you to the hospital, boy, a place where you can receive proper medical attention. Just say one simple phrase: 'There is no God.'"

"I can't and I won't."

Father and son survived this "interrogation," but not without a tangible reminder—the son's permanent difficulty with his knees—of their encounter with the Red Guard.

Back at home, my family wouldn't escape these vigilant visitors. Grandmother heard the knock on her door. The Red Guard came calling during these days, a time in which the leaders of the Cultural Revolution had confiscated people's Bibles. In small ways, Grandma had thwarted the Communist purposes of suppressing the Word of God. She had, in more tolerant times, memorized much of the Bible. "Thy word have I hid in my heart, that I might not sin against thee." Now, when Christian friends stopped by, she recited while they transcribed. She gave them back their Bibles. Perhaps word of her activities got out, for the Red Guard criticized her publicly. Then they knocked. Grandma came to the door, smiled, and held her peace.

"Speak to us, old woman. Do you pray? And what do you pray for?"

"I do. I ask God to help you grow up faster. And I pray for Mao, that God will give him more intelligence so that he will be able to rule better."

"So, do you think Mao is stupid?" A dangerous challenge!

"I just pray."

That was it for now. The Red Guard sought easier prey.

These strangers might easily forget Grandmother. After all, she lived such a simple life. This was especially the case during the Cultural Revolution. At this time she and my aunt lived in a single room in a house they shared with four other families. Somehow everyone managed, even though they had only one kitchen and one bath. Easily forgotten? Maybe for strangers. But impossible, at least for those of us who were close to her.

Before I began my whirlwind tour of China, I had visited with Grandma and told her I had a boyfriend.

"Really?" she had replied. "I would really like to meet him! Tell me, is he a Christian?"

"No." What else could I say?

"Well then, you can be sure I will pray for him. If he is God's choice for you, sooner or later he will become a Christian."

Some might have taken offense. Not me. I knew Grandma loved me. After I returned from my trip, I stopped by her room for periodic visits. During these times together she teased and told me she wanted to meet my Xu Dingzhong.

Although Grandmother was an old woman, she still had a thing or two to teach us. Her final lesson began about the time she turned eighty-five. At that point she still seemed to enjoy good health. She read the paper without glasses. She heard tolerably well—if we spoke loudly. And she still had her wits about her, as was evident when she did arithmetic in her head; no paper or pencils for her.

But maybe we had it wrong, at least about the question of "wits," for one ordinary morning Grandma spoke in an extraordinary way to my aunt. "I will see Jesus this very day. And now, if you will give me a hand, I need to bathe. I don't want to be dirty when I appear in God's presence." My aunt did what she could to help.

Once she cleaned up, Grandmother wanted to visit with the entire family. We humored her, even though we doubted her "prophecy." Mother found me at the conservatory and asked me to come pay my respects. When I showed up at the room, Grandma smiled and took my hand.

"Listen carefully to me, Nettie. You must not give up. You can lose everything, but not Jesus. It will do you no good to think about what is unfair in life. Instead, you must remember you're the other Nettie; recall your namesake, the missionary from America. She gave up so much to come to China and bring us the gospel. She will receive a magnificent heavenly reward for her work. And what about you, my own Nettie? You must seek a higher prize than honor and material goods. You must only consider eternal life and the cost of heaven." I had heard these encouraging words from Grandma more than once during these difficult days. Repeated instruction, however, still helped me. I benefited from Grandma's counsel and I understood how much she loved me.

When my cousin arrived, the familial choir reached its full complement. Now, Grandma asked us to sing the church song "Glorify." *A worrisome request. Surely she knows that if the neighbors hear us, they will report us to the authorities. Maybe we had better keep silent.* "If we sing for you, Grandma, the Red Guard will likely come back and search your home again."

Grandma refused to accept our excuses. What else was there to do but join the chorus? Pianissimo, of course. After this hymn of praise, I tried to persuade Grandma to eat at least a few bites and to drink something.

"Absolutely not! I want to be clean when I leave."

I pleaded with her, but it did no good.

That didn't stop the rest of us from eating. By the time we finished our meal it was 8 P.M. I needed to return to school. I told Grandma I would see her tomorrow and encouraged her to get a good night's rest. The younger members of the family left at about the same time I did. Mama, who stayed longer, walked her mother to bed and suggested that she lie down and relax. Done. Thereafter, my aunt and my mother talked. At 10 P.M. Mother decided that it was time for her to return home. One last time she checked in on her mother. Surprise. Somehow, Grandma had known this was her day. She passed away, peacefully, in silence. She was gone. It was close to Easter, April 14, 1967. She was standing in the presence of Jesus. Clean.

We all took Grandma's last lesson to heart. The Christian community, a group of people who had neither Bibles nor buildings, found encouragement from this dear old woman, this speaker who had joined the "cloud of witnesses." Her life also touched me in profound ways, even though she could no longer offer blessing or benediction. Except *in abstentia.* In fact, her words continued to touch me. The invisible God had made his mysterious and permanent presence known. My cousins and I knew what we must do. We must follow God and his ways. So we renewed our vows.

The day after Grandma's homecoming, when I was still at school, I found the message Mother had left for me. "Your grandmother has died." So many people attended the simple funeral. Apparently, the word had gotten out; it had spread quietly and quickly among Christian folk. Grandma's final, silent "good-bye" stirred our souls. At last, Grandmother enjoyed a special peace that worldly authorities could not take away. At last, Grandmother enjoyed a special happiness that money could not buy. At that moment I understood just how rich she was. Equally important, I realized that God is fair.

While my family and I profited from this unexpected and comforting death in Grandma's home, the constant public turmoil tested our resolve. Chairman Mao and Chairman Liu continued their struggle. An unequal contest. Finally, Liu was isolated, criticized, persecuted, and jailed. Thereafter, we saw the entire country turned topsy-turvy. Up to this point the authorities had focused their persecutions on the professionals. But they needed to go deeper. Now, the Communists discovered new enemies in the most unlikely places. "We must overthrow those within the Party who are taking the capitalist road. They will not be protected just because they occupy positions of power." Thus, the Communists had to build numerous "cowsheds," tiny buildings attached to concentration camps; here, they accommodated and re-educated the newly arrested criminals. Awful. Except for the remaining professors at the conservatory. They benefited from all of this, for they became less interesting to those who ensured the purity of the State.

Not so for Professor Ma. My father continued his life in his cowshed, which in this case was one of the small buildings in the camp attached to our school. Resistance was futile, so he made the best of it. He asked the Red Guard to give him copies of *The Sayings of Chairman Mao* in both English and in Chinese. In his limited leisure time, Daddy studied, not politics, but the English language. He compared the English to the Chinese, just to make sure he got it right. For seven years this linguist-in-the-making remained attached to that cowshed. The authorities refused to allow him to return home, even for a single day.

Daddy had only limited leisure, for most of the time he worked hard. He and his associate, the vice-president of the conservatory, served as a team. In time, they became close friends. As electricians and plumbers, they tended to the routine problems in our school buildings. Years later, my father told me plumbing stories. "Once, when I tried to fix a pipe, the leak turned into a flood that poured down on me. Still, when compared to enduring criticism meetings, this was nothing." As diminutive muscle men, my father and three other "prisoner professors" moved pianos by hand, from the fourth floor of the north building to the fourth floor of the south building. Exhausting. On one occasion Mao insisted that all Chinese citizens build air raid shelters. These orders included the conservatory. So Mao's imprisoned professors, those whom he called "monsters" and "demons," shoveled and shoveled that dirt. Daddy did more than his share of the digging because he was such a good worker.

Unfortunately, the authorities didn't leave the rest of us at the conservatory alone. We continued our meetings—Xu organized them for our department—but now they took a new direction. Not quite what we expected. The new leaders asked us to describe how their predecessors had treated the students improperly. In time, the matter of "K's" suicide came up. Her father told the story of how this had been handled. The authorities had taken her body to the hospital to see whether she was pregnant, but the physicians had found nothing. Thereafter, K's parents had suffered for a number of years because of their daughter's alleged misdeeds. In particular, the father was forced to declare that he and his wife had offered K bad instruction at home. Even worse, the authorities had coerced him to confess that they, their own daughter's parents, had been the cause of the poor girl's suicide. Awful. As others continued the story, they described how those students who had sympathized with K had faced four consecutive years of difficulties from the Party. This was especially true of the young man who had tried to date K. He suffered from guilt by association for so long; and periodically he was forced to confess his culpability in the whole matter. Somehow these stories gripped me in a new way. For the first time, I began to see the extent of others' sufferings. While we discussed this particular tale, the leader actually heard what we said. For when we finished with our testimonies, he admitted to the abuses and apologized. So surprising to hear his sincere words: "I'm sorry."

Outside the conservatory, the Party demanded pure rather than corrupt culture. In vocal music, this meant we could only sing Mao's songs. No more lyrics or tunes from the West or from old China or from the Soviet Union. For instrumental music, Mao's wife reformed the Beijing Opera in November 1967; about this same time she promoted "eight pieces of model revolutionary music." In this, Jiang Qing restricted orchestras to performing only eight pieces that she herself approved.

Strangely enough, this "reform" and subsequent related events gave me unexpected professional opportunities. My "advancement" began when some desperate musicians "borrowed" me from the conservatory; they needed me to play in their symphonic band. All well and good, except that when we performed on stage, we musicians had to dress like soldiers.

Since the proletariat didn't wear glasses, we who depended upon spectacles had to set them aside. No need for me to use music I couldn't see. So I memorized each of the pieces in our repertoire. There I sat, no glasses, playing alongside the percussion instruments. But not loudly enough. The conductor gesticulated and complained. "Louder," he exclaimed. "We are a part of the music revolution; we must play with extraordinary energy!" Indeed. The next evening I played so loudly that I broke eight strings. In this strange way I began my professional work with a symphonic band. Later, when the harp professor was prohibited from teaching, the Revolutionary Committee selected me as a replacement and ordered me to give interested students harp instruction. After each lesson I had to report to the committee on what had happened. Thus, while the Communists were politicizing culture, these unexpected developments ushered me into a teaching career.

During this same general period, spring 1967, I began an alternate career as a factory worker. Students rarely attended class during our Cultural Revolution. The Party pointed us to better activities in which we could spend our energies and show our revolutionary commitments. Our department at school, duly patriotic, sent us to the factories. In time, three girls and I joined Xu and his friends for work at the same place. We began each week by walking together across the bridge and then on to the plant. On weekends, we returned to the conservatory. A good hike, had it not been for unwanted dangers. Somehow, urban political factions formed—even here in Shanghai—and fought one another. Then the factories organized their own factions and, setting their priorities, closed down operations. Finally, to bring this brew to a nasty head, the army got involved. By this point, the situation had deteriorated to the degree that it resembled a civil war. People fought one another with military weapons. Hardly a safe walk for innocent bystanders. Fortunately, once Mao recognized what was going on, he worked hard to restore order in the cities. In time, peace prevailed.

Xu was supposed to graduate from the conservatory in summer 1966. Normally, the government assigned the graduates to particular jobs, and it took several months for graduates to get their assignments. So if they graduated in July, they might well wait until September before they started work. None of us needed reminders that these days in the Cultural Revolution were far from "normal" or "usual." Jobs were hard to come by. So Xu remained in school while his family struggled to support him. Early 1967, and still no assignment. This was not surprising, given the problems China faced.

China's educational situation resembled something between paralysis and chaos. Students in junior middle school and senior middle school could not advance to the next level of study because these schools simply weren't functioning. As for the elementary schools, they served as day-care centers more than educational institutions. Kindergartners were supposed to move up to first grade, but there was no space for them. Then there was the question of what to do with those youngsters who were ready for kindergarten. The poor teachers. If space had been their only problem, they might have managed. But they also had to deal with political realities that included the regular demands for confession. From top to bottom, Chinese society was stuck.

At last, in December 1967, some college graduates began to get jobs. Since most of the former educational bureaucrats had moved to the cowsheds for criticism and punishment, the Revolutionary Committee and select students worked on job arrangements. When Xu filled out his job application papers, he listed me as his fiancée. A promising step in our relationship. In time, he was offered a position with the Shanghai City Symphonic Band. Most people would have jumped at such an assignment, or at a similar one in Beijing, for these cities produced the best music. Not Xu. He recognized that if he stayed in Shanghai and we followed through on our commitments, my father's position would affect him adversely. For a time, Xu considered distancing himself from Shanghai and returning to his home province. At last, he was offered a position in Hangzhou, a city reasonably close to Shanghai. In these days, a one-way train trip from Shanghai took three to four hours. (Now, one can span the distance in less than an hour.) Hangzhou was a good place, almost like heaven with its beautiful West Lake. Mao had lived here for a number of years. Now, foreign dignitaries visited. Beijing was for politics, Shanghai for business, and Hangzhou for rest and relaxation. Here, artists entertained visitors with song and dance ensembles. Orchestras usually performed light rather than serious music. Relaxing for the visitor. In future years, it came as no surprise that Pompidou, Thatcher, and Nixon all visited this fun city.

So Xu began his Hangzhou job in December 1967. And I continued in school. At the conservatory, I faced more of the same: revolution, daily meetings, criticism of school authorities and professors. By this point it had become as boring as it was frightening. Just maybe, I hoped, the class of 1967 would graduate close to their scheduled time. They were ready. But only until Mao announced that students graduating from the older universities needed re-education. He planned to send them, and maybe those in subsequent classes, to farms that were under army control. There, Chinese young people might learn the proper revolutionary ways.

Before things got moving too fast, however, I had familial matters I needed to tend to. Sometime after Grandmother's death in spring 1967, I introduced Xu to my family. We "all" met in a restaurant for a meal and conversation. Auntie Bessie enjoyed this time together. She spoke well of my fiancé. "He's nice, polite, has clean fingernails, and carries a hankie." Mother loved Xu immediately. That left Daddy, who couldn't leave the cowshed to join us for this meal. He had no idea what was going on between Xu and me.

The summer of 1968, the scheduled date of my graduation, came and went. I still kept my student status, for the officials postponed my graduation until December. I couldn't complain, for conservatory problems were small when compared with those in the rural economy. There, the patriotic farmers joined the revolution. In doing so, they turned their attention away from sowing, tilling, and harvesting, the uninteresting and routine tasks of the farmer. Production declined accordingly. The government decided that if they greatly expanded and made mandatory the "youth to the countryside" program that they had begun in the early 1960s, if they now sent millions upon millions of young people from the city into the country to help out, this would reverse the production problems. As they put this new public policy together, most high-level officials failed to consider the enormous differences between rural and urban life. "No major problem. The kids will adjust quickly enough. We must listen to our hearts and follow Mao." Were these foolish old men blind? Could they not see how laborious it would be for citified young people, those with soft hands and underdeveloped muscles, to work the soil? I watched and I waited. My time might come. Eventually the government would graduate us, move us out, and thus prepare university slots for the many high school students who now had nowhere to go.

Beginning in the 1950s, Mao had encouraged Chinese parents to follow the Soviet example and raise large families. A sensible suggestion for a country that suffered from under-population. China, however, was not Russia. Still, we followed our chairman's counsel. Thus, when in 1968 Mao initiated his new "youth to the countryside" program, we had more than enough people to take up the hoe. "One child may stay home; the rest must go." Such were the orders of our chairman. So many from our cities, high schoolers, middle schoolers, and even elementary schoolers, headed off to the farms. Parents hoped to find nearby places where their children might stay together and live with relatives. Those who could not find such "refuges" were sent to the distant northeast. In all of this, parents cooperated, sometimes reluctantly. But so many naive young people, ignorant of what awaited them, participated with considerable enthusiasm. That enthusiasm waned soon after they reached their appointed places. How to survive? They earned food points according to the amount of work they did; sadly, they lacked the strength and the know-how to get enough to eat. They faced comparable problems in finding housing. Few of them found consolation in writing "misery letters" home to their parents, for poor education had made most of them minimally literate. So hard!

In short, we all witnessed much human suffering. One such story I read about after the Cultural Revolution remains firmly embedded in my memory. A Beijing couple, criticized for being out of "sync" with the Communist Revolution, was forced to send their two daughters to the country. The girls ended up in the far northeastern province of Heilongjiang. In time, the two grew lonely: they missed their mother. Hopeful, they tried to purchase train tickets back to Beijing. Impossible. Persistent, they hopped on the train, illegally, outside the last car. Desperate, they tried to get inside. The conductor refused to open the door. They stood there helpless, stuck, shivering. When the train arrived in Beijing, the officials discovered the "unticketed" passengers. Clinging together. Frozen. Holding the flower and the letter that they had wanted to give their mother. In subsequent years this story, and innumerable similar accounts, filled our collective memory with sadness. We knew too much about the tragedies the commoners experienced during the Cultural Revolution. In time, the Party acknowledged at least the awful part the Red Guard had played in these tragedies. For the present, however, Mao used these little people in his successful struggles against Liu. Then, when he no longer needed the little people, he threw them away.

8

Re-education on a Military Farm in Rural Jiangsu

1968–1970

In 1968 Mao Zedong announced his new "Youth to the Countryside" program. Many city folk would learn the value of dirty, back-breaking work on farms. Nettie was no exception. As Chairman Mao sent millions to the countryside in the following years, he said that they should be happy to take up the plow, for menial farm work would serve them well. Thereafter, he left these workers alone and tended to more important matters. During these days, then, weary farmers with dirty hands put up with indoctrination meetings and self-criticism. Happy farmers with callused hands appreciated their distance from the Red Guards.

We at the conservatory faced dramatic and worrisome changes in the fall of 1968. Following a directive from Mao, army leaders, factory workers, and the School Revolutionary Committee gave directions to our school. This made it possible for those of us in Shanghai to benefit from their wisdom. Our new "administrators" must have quickly noted the crowded conditions at the conservatory: the class of 1967 had not yet left us to find jobs in the real world. The new "outsiders" might have done us all some good, had we been allowed to enjoy their tutelage for an extended period of time. But then, still in 1968, we heard that Mao issued another directive: "Every student who graduates from an older university must be re-educated." When the government implemented this directive, they decided that student re-education should take place in army-controlled state farms. So the class of 1967 no longer had to worry about employment. They headed off to agricultural sites in nearby Hangzhou. When my class graduated, in December 1968, we received similar good news: "to the farms!"

I had to tell someone the news, so I hurried home and spoke with Mother. "I will soon be leaving Shanghai and heading to a military farm. My destination? Not yet disclosed. Nothing to do now but get ready and make the best of it." Mother put a package together—clothes and other things I would need while I was away from home.

I also wrote Xu, my fiancé, and told him about my new assignment. He responded by suggesting that we get married before my departure date. "I think," he explained, "that you will be much safer at the farm if you are a married woman."

"I might be safe," I replied, "but I also might be stuck at that farm, forever. Surely, that's not what you want in a marriage."

"That could happen," he countered, "but I wouldn't mind. Many couples in China live separate lives. Moreover, I just might be able to help you get away from that farm. Our orchestra still lacks a harpist. We could write the authorities and 'borrow' you, at least for a little while." Persistent indeed.

I felt very uncertain. I needed to think. I couldn't answer Xu right away.

Soon thereafter, "W" stopped by and told me that her fiancé had asked her to marry him before she left for the farm. "In order to do this legally," she explained, "I will need to apply for and get a marriage certificate from the Revolutionary Committee."

"I understand your situation only too well," I answered, "for Xu has offered me the same proposal, and for similar reasons. I just haven't made up my mind whether I want to get married now."

W resolved to follow my lead. This gave the two of us much to deliberate about. Age, however, was not one of these matters. In these days, the government required people to delay marriage as a way of limiting the size of the Chinese population. Couples weren't supposed to marry until their cumulative age added up to fifty-five. Xu, and I, at ages twenty-eight and twenty-seven respectively, qualified. W, a bit younger than me, and her fiancé, a bit older than Xu, also qualified. At last, W and I decided to apply for a license at the Revolutionary Committee. No problem there: permission granted.

Xu and I still had one more matter to deal with: we each needed time off from work. My superiors gave me a week's vacation, and Xu got about the same. The rest was simple: the exchanging of vows and a honeymoon weekend in Shanghai. Mother invited the guests, her brother John and two of my cousins, to serve as witnesses. We spent the night at "Mother's Motel." In short, she loaned us her room, and she moved into a small, windowless storage space.[1] Auntie Bessie couldn't attend our wedding because of her current status with the government—"under criticism." Saturday night, December 15, 1968, Xu and I tied the knot. Married! Mother prepared the wedding "banquet," a fine supper, as the first step in our celebrations. An auspicious beginning, except for a minor technicality. The government marriage office was closed on Saturdays; thus, they didn't record the official "married" entry in their books until two days later, on Monday, December 17. Thereafter, Xu and I spent five days together; then Xu returned to Hangzhou. Three weeks later I departed for the country.

A good number of students gathered together in the Shanghai People's Square on an early January morning. This included 1968 graduates from the Shanghai Conservatory and 1968 graduates from other national universities. The second group of graduates, engineering students, had accepted the government's assignment to the local Meter Bureau; this bureau planned to assign these students to other factories. Each of us carried a package; none of us had a clue as to our final destination. Some enjoyed the company of friends and relatives who had come to say goodbye and see them off. A word of encouragement, a hug, and then Mother and I parted. Time to board the buses the government had reserved for us. Time to get rolling. Several hours later we pulled into Wuxi, the city that housed an office for the 27th Field Army, the military group to which we were assigned. Here in Wuxi, we boarded a second set of buses. Later that evening, we stopped for a layover. Before our instructor allowed us to go to bed, he required us to attend an instructional meeting. The leader spoke frankly.

"You may write a simple letter to your families, but you may not tell them where you are. You must put our identification number on the envelope as a return address. With such a coded number, the government will make sure that correspondence from home reaches you. But none too quickly. Letters travel slowly these days. But enough of this simple stuff. I need to move on to more important matters. Let me describe your final destination. You will see mountains on three sides of the place where you will work. In time you will understand why many of the local folk go naked in the summers. The extraordinarily hot temperatures burn up the ordinary human inclination toward modesty. The story has it that when one military leader ordered the locals to don clothes, they ignored him. Not one to brook disobedience, he had them whipped. Still no success. Eventually, if my story has it right, the leader himself was punished. Let me be frank. You will tolerate nudity and you can survive the heat. Unfortunately, however, you can expect much worse than this. I must warn you especially about the dangers of quicksand in the undeveloped area where you will be starting a farm. If someone falls into that quicksand, they're sunk. And if others attempt a rescue, they too will drown and perish in the bottomless muck. Mark my words carefully." *Scary stories, if they're true.*

On the second morning of our trip we traveled partway by boat. Too soon, our "ferries" docked and set us back on dry land. As we ate a nutritious bread meal, we noticed the snow on the ground. Not enough to impede traveling by Shank's Mare. Curious instructions: "You must follow the leader." A tiring trek; we hiked most of the day. As evening set in, we found ourselves in a small town. We crossed the river, surveyed the wide expanse where we would build our farm, and settled in for the evening. That night we would sleep in an elementary school.

Before we settled in, we noticed the fancy facilities. Here, we enjoyed the luxury of outside bathrooms. The men and the women lined up at their own designated shacks. Here, we could take a "shower" with a portion of our water rations. Five pounds a day, for drinking—after we boiled it for safety's sake—and for washing. The next morning, when the women crowded into the bathroom to clean up, we noticed that some of the local men had climbed up and were peeking down through the large "cracks" between the roof and the walls. Voyeurs. They might have been harmless, but they still frightened us. One of the women threw a pail of water up, out the open space, and soaked those "dirty old peasant men" who were watching us. We celebrated our success, but not for long. Soon, "T" spoke to the military leader who, sometime earlier, had warned us about the serious class struggles China faced. Perhaps T also told him about the water episode. However it happened, the authorities learned that "W" had encouraged others to throw water at the men who had scared us as we were cleaning up. Thereafter, those in charge suspected W of being a class enemy; thereafter, her troubles never ended. And this very first day, ours began, in a criticism meeting.

Soon after we arrived at our farm, our military superiors organized us, perhaps as many as 400 "workers," into separate hierarchical units. To the 7th Company they assigned foreign language students from the class of 1967 plus a number of others who had lived at the site for half a year before we arrived. To the 8th Company they assigned those from the class of 1968 who had registered at the Shanghai Meter Bureau and those of us from the conservatory who had specialized in piano, instruments, conducting, composition, and more than a few traditional voice students. They further subdivided the two companies into platoons, and then into classes of seven to eight people. The female graduates from the Shanghai Conservatory were assigned to two classes. The 13th Class, to which I was assigned, belonged to the 3rd Platoon; the 14th Class belonged to the 4th Platoon. From this lowest level, thirteen people cultivated the vegetable gardens that provided food for everyone on the site; and six to eight of us staffed the kitchen.

None of us workers fit into the Marxist proletariat class. So the new Mandarins labeled us "intelligentsia," one of the nine bad elements in their classification system. Menial and laborious work assignments were central to our re-education. Among the six "intellectuals" whom they initially selected for the kitchen crew was a pianist schoolmate of mine. She and some friends collaborated privately and decided that I lacked the strength to work in the fields. After their colloquy, she volunteered to switch assignments with me; fortunately for me, the military agreed to this switch.

So on this first day of work we menials took up K.P. while most everyone else learned too much about extraordinary physical labor. When my comrades returned "home" that evening, some shed tears as they told us their harrowing story. "The river, that's where they unwittingly tried to kill us. The officers in charge ordered us to break the ice and then to jump into the freezing water. Thereafter, they commanded us to stoop down and clean out the riverbed with our hands and fingers. So cold! Like a knife, cutting us to the quick. To their credit, some student leaders stayed with us and helped out. Just take a look at our palms and our digits and you'll begin to understand our pain."[2]

I readily appreciated how easy we on K.P. had it. High costs and menial labor, but still easy. Once we graduated from school, we each received a monthly salary of thirty-seven yuan. The military deducted our personal food expenses, fifteen yuan, before they issued us our salaries. That left us with more than enough to buy a wok in which we could cook, and nearly enough to pay for the rice and the inexpensive radishes we ate. Not very impressive! Gourmets and gourmands had equal grounds for complaint. But not yet. For we were hardly ready to serve up our first delicacies. We still needed to clean the radishes—in the icy river—and build a stove, and cut our wood, and light the fire. At last we finished cooking. Now we pulled our load across the snow and on beyond the river to the site where we found and fed our hungry comrades. After these ravenous "intellectuals" devoured such fine fare, they had the gall to complain about their meager meal. "Sliced radishes? Yuck! Give us more! We're starved!" We fared better than they. Indeed, there were benefits—plenty of food—for those who worked in the kitchen. My comrades encouraged me to eat before we parceled out the leftovers to our friends. Good advice, had I not been such a slow eater. I chose instead to eat with my friends. Sometimes, W helped me fill my dishes; always, I was the last to finish my meal. As we, the kitchen patrol, returned home along the river, my mind frequently turned to the Volga Boat Song. "Yo-ho heave ho! Yo-ho heave ho! / Once more, once more, Yo-ho heave ho!" In time, particularly after the weather warmed up, we bought seeds, piglets, and chicks. Thereafter, we raised our own food. Fresh eggs, way out here in the wilderness. Not too shabby. If we didn't kill the golden goose—in our case the hens—that fed us.

For our first month on site we lived in town. Open-bay and open-roof barracks that were air-conditioned and even refrigerated during this frigid January. It didn't require much detective work to determine why—faulty carpenter work, or perhaps just dilapidated buildings. We saw huge, extended gaps between the walls and the ceiling. This allowed snow to accumulate on the floor where we slept. Too cold for it to melt. That first night the company commander cautioned us about cleaning up. "Just put a dab of water on your towels to wash your faces. If you use too much the towel will freeze and you will injure yourselves." I followed his good advice. At last, when we hit the sack, we wrapped our heads in dry cloth; we needed to protect ourselves from chilblain or frostbite. On those occasions when we were assigned to the night watch, we could at least keep the juices flowing by walking around, with real guns on our shoulders. As members of a military organization, our instructors taught us the proper way to use a rifle. Wary guards. No intruders allowed. Too early, at sunrise, the horn sounded. Reveille!

Off to work. For thirty days, most everyone helped build dikes around our farm. It might have been a scenic walk out to those dikes for those with good vision. But not for me. My glasses never completely compensated for my myopia. And also not for another student who lost her spectacles on one of these hikes. (Fortunately, on another occasion she got lucky and found them, hanging on a tree.) We hiked up into the mountains, where we got most of the rocks out of which we built our dikes. Innumerable backbreaking trips. Until, at last, our dikes stood, ten feet high, on all four sides of our farm. Safe from any floods, or so we hoped. At this point, because I was on K.P., I still got off easy. I only carried food, up to 66 pounds of it, to my dike-building comrades.

As a part of our army training, our military officers introduced us to "midnight scenic walks." They never forewarned us. Indeed, they sprang these upon us when we least expected them. Our walks always took place late at night, after we had spent a hard day in the fields and after we had all fallen into a deep sleep. Suddenly, the whistle alarm blasted us out of dreamland. Five minutes to get ready. We slipped on our clothes and prepared a makeshift rucksack—folded into a square, tied, and hoisted up onto our backs. Then we rushed outside and lined up. Ready for our midnight hike. Follow the leader. Through the fields, across the dikes, and up into the mountains. My first try at this military training went poorly indeed. My rucksack, which I had tied too loosely, started falling apart. And if this were not enough, I sprained by ankle. I simply could not see well enough to watch my footing. By this time I had fallen so far behind the others that I could not catch up. A "sympathetic" army officer recognized my plight and sent me home. When I explained that I had no idea what direction to take, he said I would have to find my way as best I could. Dark. Alone. Crippled. Toting a rucksack that refused to stay together. Frightened. When I finally made it back to the dorm, I discovered that my friends had returned home from another direction and had already fallen asleep. I did not look forward to future scenic walks.

Right after we finished constructing the dikes, we built new dorms, closer than our temporary accommodations to the area where we worked. To secure raw materials, some people returned to the mountains; there, they cut down bamboo trees, the only lumber available in the vicinity. Others collected weeds out of which they made thatched roofs; we hoped these roofs would protect us from the weather. It worked, at least from on top: snow no longer accumulated on our floors. A month on this job and we moved into our new and improved accommodations. Seventy people for each dorm. Oil lamps, a necessary improvisation for poor farmers who lacked electricity. Bunk beds, made of bamboo, just like those one sees in military movies. Every day, we prepared for inspections. Beds: flat and well made up. Every day, we filled our heavy containers with water from the river. Every day, as best we could, we purified that water with alum. We watched the dirt as it settled to the bottom of the container until the water became clear. Quite fancy! But not perfect. Our new dorms would have been tolerable, had not the wind found its way through those bamboo walls.

Normally, we cooks rose at 5 A.M. so we could serve breakfast at 7 A.M.; others got up later. On most days, we used "washbasins" in the dorm to clean up. But our schedule also allowed for one "full" bath each month, and, on less busy occasions, one full bath every ten to twenty days. Each platoon had one hour—travel time included—for bath time. On these special days, the women cooks got started at 4 A.M. We hiked for fifteen minutes, crossed a bridge, and arrived at the indoor "Roman bath," close to the site where the military company lived in their barracks. (Modern Westerners might have mistaken our "bath" for a swimming pool.) We women jumped in, took thirty minutes to clean up, and then made space for the male cooks, who had left the dorm half an hour after us, to clean up. The other platoons got their turn, one after the other, throughout the day. Not too bad, unless you were last in line. Since the authorities did not change the water throughout the day, it got quite nasty as evening approached.

By the time spring set in, our regimen was firmly set. We cooks lived in the dorm with the other students. Two military leaders, a mess officer and a staff sergeant, lived in a room connected to the kitchen, a building located toward the back of our tiny "hamlet." These two men supervised us to make sure we got it right. We served lunch, cleaned up afterward, and then had an hour's free time. When our comrades finished supper and left us to attend the political study groups, we still had to wash the dishes. Later in the evening, we joined these re-education groups. That first night as we walked together in the dark on our way to a political meeting, I heard an animal cry out. The mess officer comforted me with his reassuring words: "You needn't worry. It's probably only a hungry wolf. In our setting I must encourage you to stick together at night. Also, you probably ought to use flashlights so you don't lose your way." Understandably, we constructed a tiny commissary close by the dorms. There, we bought our basic necessities. Some folk, amateur seamstresses and tailors, even took up light sewing and repair work on the side. A set regimen, but only for three months. Then they transferred me to the fields and others took over my kitchen duties.

Musicians are nothing without their entertaining and harmless music. And accordions are perfectly suited for performances in primitive places. We unreformed capitalists knew that we, not the entire community, owned our accordion. Thus, when others wanted to borrow our instrument, we hid it. Bad ideology and bad judgment! When the military discovered our errors, they opposed us and forced us to confess our political mistakes. T, ever vigilant, blamed W. It was W's idea. A fundamental error. Class conflict. A bad family. The officers pressed the rest of us to criticize W but we remained silent. We all knew that she was a good and generous woman, and that these events were unrelated to her family.

At about the same time I moved out of the kitchen, W, two friends, and I enjoyed our first holiday together. Only a single day. A community-wide reward for good work. Military protocol required us to sign out before we left; thereafter, we traveled in teams. Simple enough. Like many of our other comrades, we hiked to a nearby village. Because we had been frugal with our salaries, we had a little extra money to buy something we really wanted. While we thought about our treat, we went to the post office. There, we bought and mailed special gifts for our parents. Afterward, we still had a little change left over. Why not pamper ourselves? Chinese women enjoy eggs that they have boiled in tea and soy sauce. Why not, just this once? Each of us bought two eggs. Our secret. Nobody else must see what we have. I hid under a bridge and wolfed down my special treat. Unfortunately, my delicacy got stuck in my craw where it caused me considerable pain. For weeks thereafter I found it impossible to eat eggs.

W's potential trouble with eggs surfaced when she developed a painful tooth infection. Fortunately, she had no need to worry about her well-being. Our medical clinic specialized in primitive dental care. Such an operation! Several people pinned W down so the dentists could extract the tooth without injuring their squirming patient. Secure. They then took a hammer and a screwdriver to the poor woman's mouth. At last, they had dug deeply enough around the abscessed tooth to allow them to extract it. Done. When W returned to the dorm, her jaw was badly swollen and she herself felt quite weak. Those in charge gave her three days to recuperate from her surgery. Equally important, the company commander allowed me to prepare her the special food, eggs, that we prescribed for the sick. When I asked my friend how she wanted me to cook her treat, she waved me off: "Unfortunately, I am unable to eat. I can barely manage to drink a little water." *Maybe, and maybe not.* I steamed and boiled her eggs—four of them. Afterward, I added a pinch of salt to my soft "medicine." It worked. She could swallow after all.

Some time later, T complained to the company commander. "I remind you that W comes from a counter-revolutionary family. We shouldn't have given her four eggs." This time T failed in her attempt to get W in trouble. The commander rejected T's complaint as he explained that out here in the wilderness we are all equal.

Perhaps the commander spoke in hyperbole. Too soon, I found out otherwise. I thought we had already taken more than "just a few small steps" toward taming and developing the rough country in which we were building our military farm. When, however, I moved outside into that rough country in early spring, I understood the extent of others' efforts and the frailty of my own body. Each day we still added stone and dirt to the top of the "finished" dikes. Normally, two people carried their loads on a board that they suspended between their shoulders. Our supervisors decided that they would pair up a weak student and a strong student for these tasks. Fortunately, W, a woman of considerable strength, invited me to team up with her. Initially, I declined her generous offer. "No, that wouldn't be fair to you," I explained. "You shouldn't have to do my work." W persisted in her offer: she didn't mind a little unfairness. An unequal team indeed. I carried the front and lighter part of the load; and she extended the board well beyond her shoulders so that she bore most of the weight. Helpful, but not enough. I simply wore out too easily. So W pushed as we walked up the hill. Some might have wondered about W's foolishness in choosing a puny "stringbean" like Nettie as a partner. Not me. I understood the heart of this good, Christian woman.

If we failed to break our backs while we worked on the dikes, we got a second and even a third chance to do so while we farmed the fields. We apprentice farmers started tilling in early spring. Since we had no draft animals, we hitched up a "human" ox out front of each of our plows. Each "ox" pulled; at the same time, two others on his team insured that he inched along in a reasonably straight line. We quickly discovered that our virgin land, baked and re-baked by the sun, resisted our best efforts to dig deep furrows. Although we were apprentice farmers, we weren't stupid. We soaked our prospective fields in water and the resistant soil gave way. Success. We sowed the seed and then waited, until our seedlings poked their heads up from beneath the dirt and sought the warm sun. When our plants measured three to four inches high, we transplanted them to their permanent residence.

Thereafter, we journeymen had to cultivate our crop so that it would grow better. Our military supervisors insisted that as a part of re-educating us, a notorious "bad element," we were to use no tools. Moreover, they required us to kneel down in the water-soaked fields. This might have been tolerable, had we not used "night soil," human manure, to fertilize our rice. So dirty! So nasty! We conservatory students tried an alternative approach, bending over, as we did this work. When, however, the military saw our attempt to subvert our re-education, they aimed their rifles our way and once again ordered us to kneel and work. We complied, unenthusiastically. The deeper the water got, the more it stunk. Understandably, the boys worked as fast as possible. I tried to speed up, but all I managed was my proverbial snail's pace. Degrading! A friend asked me whether I had seen the movie *Slave*, a Tibetan story that identified freedom as the distinguishing feature between servants and slaves. A rhetorical question. Too true! I cried while I worked.

As we moved further into the summer, the sun blazed above and sapped our strength. Even though the temperatures rarely exceeded 102 degrees Fahrenheit, some of us still passed out. When one of my friends fainted, we carried her to a walking path and splashed water on her face. After she regained her senses, she returned to the putrid muck.

We never complained when nature called, for that meant a long walk to the toilets—and at least a short break from work. Our military commanders, efficiency experts, experimented with methods to curb our laziness. At first, they weighed the advantages and the disadvantages of eliminating our daytime water rations.

"If they don't drink anything, they won't have to urinate."

"Right. But with no fluids they will become dehydrated. And then they will slow down."

With such tactics, they might win this battle; but they would lose the war. Finally, they hit upon an ingenious solution. We planted cucumbers, two to three inches apart, on one end of the field in which we grew our rice. Our supervisors permitted us to eat these water-bearing gourds while we worked. Such efficiency! It worked reasonably well, except for the day when another friend contracted a bad case of diarrhea. Too far to make it to the outhouse. She soiled herself. Humiliating!

On those rare occasions when our body temperatures exceeded 102 degrees Fahrenheit, the bosses let us rest. More commonly, we musicians invented our own form of relief. We chanted while we worked. We sang about our "home" on the Huangpu River. And we composed playful lyrics and a melody about a toilet that flushed with the wind. A strange term, "wind," but a simple explanation. Each of our two outhouses was equipped with primitive "toilets" that bore no resemblance to the comfortable commodes that most civilized people enjoy. Our "toilets" consisted of two narrowly separated pieces of wood and a hole. Users squatted over that wood and did their business down into the cesspool. So no real flushing, but plenty of wind.

In late spring, our generous "instructors" turned our single holiday into a weekly affair. This gave us the chance to wash our clothes down at the dike. While we musicians scrubbed away, we sang Russian songs. More important than washing was our weekly trip to the post office. There, we continued to send regular small gifts to our families. Occasionally, they responded in kind, even though the only thing they knew about our address was a postal box number. And then it happened. A package for me! How exciting! We dug among the clothes and found hidden foodstuffs. *Crackers and powdered milk. We must not let the others know about our goodies. We'll just have to wait until later at night in the dorm. Only one dim light there. We can hide and eat beneath the mosquito net without being spotted.* When the bedtime bell sounded, we hit the sack; we also took our goodies to bed with us. *Nobody will catch us now. Military regulations prohibit anyone from getting up out of bed except for an extreme emergency.* We finished the crackers and started on the powdered milk. It tasted good, but in time it left a sour residue in our mouths. *Unfortunately, they won't allow me to get up out of bed and brush my teeth. Still, it's been a good day.*

They canceled our holidays for the month of June because our crops demanded our attention. We tended to our first harvest and our second planting. We could be optimistic as long as the weather cooperated. The men reaped and the women sowed. Complementary but unequal partners.

When we fell behind in the harvest, the military commanders required all of us to help out with reaping. One person carried two bundles of rice. Each bundle weighed 84 pounds. Impossible, particularly for the women who, like me, were slight of frame and short on muscle. Unfortunately, the Communist rule stood firm. "Men and women are equal. Each bears half of the heavens." The origins of this curious phrase may be traced to a morning radio show during which Mao announced the equality of the sexes. They are able to do the same work, or, in his exact phrase, "women can hold half of the heavens." The power of Mao's rhetoric settled that matter. If pity had been in vogue, I would have evoked plenty from any sympathetic bystanders. As it was, I managed two or three steps, and then I stopped to catch my breath. At other times I pulled my load along the ground. Our bigger and more muscular male comrades finished their work on schedule and then offered to help the weaker women. The authorities would have none of this, not among equals. So the men returned home and ate their supper while we women worked late into the night. Complementary but decidedly unequal partners!

This heavy and exhausting work affected the joints of our fingers. So stiff! We could barely open our hands as we combed our hair or buttoned our clothes. We got no sympathy from those in charge. During the evening hours they ordered us to prepare festive music appropriate for such celebratory occasions. We from the conservatory took note and composed away. At times, our performances were laughable. Such was the case when we performed the officially sanctioned Beijing Opera Music. Toward the end of that piece the hero sings a high note. As he does so, he is supposed to extend his opening hand upward. Unfortunately, our stiff-fingered operatic star discovered that his fingers could not obey the instructions from his brain. So he improvised. In three separate steps, while we played the appropriate accompaniment, he gradually produced an open hand in concert with his open voice. Afterward, we teased one another about our difficulties with our digits.

Somehow, our military instructors found enough daylight hours to provide us with target practice. We cordoned off the area and put up warning signs for outsiders: Stay out! Danger! Firing range! After such basic precautions, we shot our rounds off in groups of ten. Once a person hit her target she could leave. I can only imagine the musings of those who watched me. "Poor Nettie. Sharpshooter she's not. She couldn't hit the broad side of a barn." Indeed. I hit everything but my target. When I gently pulled the trigger, my rifle jerked upward from the cradle in which

I held it. After the others had left, I stayed late and kept trying. I tried lying down, belly in the dirt, my elbow stable on the ground; once again I fired away. I managed to wear a thin spot on my coat sleeve, but that's all the success I can claim. So much for the aphorism "practice makes perfect."

Some of us might have fired well into the evening hours had not a local resident gotten into trouble. At about the time when the sun set, this illiterate poor boy took no note of our written warnings. As luck would have it, he wandered too close to our targets and took a bullet in the buttocks. Another "sharpshooter," not me, shot the boy. The officer in charge halted our practice and took the wounded noncombatant to our clinic. The military might have blamed the victim for class error. Unfortunately, they wouldn't have been able to make this claim stick, for our victim was a peasant through and through. In fact, everyone knew the military had been careless and bore the guilt for this needless accident.

On and on. We master farmers survived well into the summer, and our first rice crops did better than we. Not so, one poor pig. He was to be a part of our grand feast after our first harvest. We would have more than enough food on this occasion. As we got started, all 400 students met together to decide which group of re-educated intellectuals would win the honor of butchering the creature. The engineers and then the musicians pled ignorance: "We have no idea what we should do!" That left the biology students. When the female biologists squirmed out of their predicament, we drafted their male counterparts. They accepted the assignment, tied our supper to the stake, skewered it, and served up fresh pork. A festive celebration and a grand banquet, shared by comrades who had learned to work with their hands.

The threat of a flood, a yearly occurrence in this area, returned us to our senses and to the dikes. Once again we abandoned our weekly holidays. Once again we hauled stone and dirt to the dikes. When the rains began their periodic assaults on us poor "land-lubbers," the race began in earnest. Dripping wet, we returned to the dorms, changed into dry clothes, and took up our task with renewed vigor. Within hours we were soaked to the bone. We understood then that it would be impossible to keep dry. So we worked in wet clothes. It would only get worse, for soon we would endure a week's monsoon. The heavens had determined to fill the river basin full to overflowing. And as if that were not enough, the snows from the nearby mountains joined in the effort to destroy our dikes and to create a monstrous lake. "We will bury you!"

"Not yet!" We accepted the challenge and worked through the clock: night shifts on top of day shifts. Then the snakes came out of hiding and sought safety inside the barriers. Handwriting on the wall? The words seemed to say that we might not win this battle. The timorous military company understood the sign and abandoned us in the easiest possible way out, by boat. But not the site commander. He chose to stay with us, his two student companies.

That next morning, when we saw the severity of the situation, the student leaders deliberated about how we should proceed. In the end, we decided that the men should stay behind and work on the dikes, and that the women should flee to higher ground. We would take our most basic goods with us to the mountains. Some girls grabbed the chickens, while others packed up all the vegetables they could carry. That left one very big and very lively pig. We couldn't very well let that poor creature stay behind and drown! Witnesses watched an uneven tag-team match, four human females against one stubby-legged "oinker." Each of us took hold of one of that pig's legs and held on for dear life. Piggy refused to give up without a fight. Indeed, he squirmed so much that we all fell to the ground and rolled over. Although we got wet and dirty, we would not let go. That pig would come with us!

Earlier, when most of the military had abandoned us by boat, they had also instructed us clearly as to our options in the case of a flood. "If the dikes break, it will be because of faulty construction; in this case, you will bear the blame and you must stay behind. If, however, the water spills over the top of the dikes, you will be faultless; in this case, you may leave." The re-educated engineers studied the situation, identified weak points at the bottom of the dikes, and predicted that those dikes could not survive much longer. In order to reinforce weak points, men lay down—in rows—against the rock and dirt. Just maybe the extra weight would hold the dike together and force the water up, over the top of our manmade barriers. As we waited, we heard the explosive sounds for which we all had hoped. "Boom! Boom! Boom!" The site commander shot his rifle, three clear blasts, up into the sky. Our agreed-upon signal. This meant that the water was beginning to spill over the top of the dikes; more importantly, it meant the men could seek safety on higher ground. But only if they could extricate themselves from their precarious position in such a way that the weakened dikes wouldn't give way and bury them. We women watched from our mountain. Frightening. Just as the men pulled themselves out, the waters flooded in earnest over the top. But our male comrades made it out safely! Meanwhile, the expanding "lake," the place where we had built our military farm, picked up refuse from the bathrooms and covered the fields. Eventually it peaked at the top of our dorm roofs.

If we re-educated intellectuals could survive the demands and the dangers of the lowlands, surely we could adapt to higher ground. Our competent cooks had brought plenty of rice with them; they would feed us well. But where would we sleep? We raised this question with the local mountain people, who offered to let us sleep with their animals. Our generous hosts laid wooden doors down on the ground as makeshift beds. Dry, but also crowded—more than ten women to each bed. Shoulder room, but not much more. Tired beggars couldn't be finicky choosers. So we packed ourselves tightly together. Then the mosquitoes came to take a blood offering. We discouraged them from drinking too deeply by covering our faces. Alongside of us on the ground sat the ducks, also crowded together; perhaps they imitated our strange formation. When one moved, they all moved—ducks and people. We rotated guard duty that first night. On my turn, I watched both our broad-billed companions and my worn-out friends as they visited dreamland and renewed their strength. Strikingly similar creatures.

The next morning we set about creating a more commodious "dormitory," a temporary "home" that would offer space to each "class," the military subdivision of the platoons. We partitioned off "rooms" by hanging "sheet walls" on the trees. Simple and acceptable. What next? The military commander appeared on the scene and organized us into working units. He pointed out that we still had much to take care of; he emphasized in particular that we needed to store the fertilizer and the chemicals. We cooperated, but only half-heartedly. We were inclined to work in a leisurely way. Little by little, our boss lost control. And little by little, the friendships among us students deepened. Seemingly insignificant events brought us together. I remember a classmate from the conservatory, a man who, because he served on the vegetable teams, had plenty of time on his hands. He purchased two duck eggs, salted them, and shared his good gift with the rest of us. We each got a tiny piece. In such ways our affection for one another deepened.

After a month in the mountains, the lake disappeared and the waters returned to their pre-flood path within the riverbed. Before we returned to the mess down below, a student traded the local peasants a package of cigarettes for a dog. We named our dog "Pegasus," after the legendary Greek winged horse. Such a fine pet! He followed us almost everywhere. This included our trip back down into the valley to see what was left of our farm and our tiny village. The flood had damaged our dorms beyond repair. That left the military auditorium, a spacious and fancy brick place that could house nearly 200 women. A complete roof and walls and electricity. So bright! Even better, it came equipped with clear well water, an attractive alternative to hauling and then purifying water from the river. The Communists understood well the virtues of a classless society! Farmers could also enjoy the fine life.

Others might have been afflicted with sloth, but not us. We had so much to do to our farm. The flood had destroyed our rice before it had matured. This meant that we would have no second harvest without starting once again from scratch. Four o'clock in the morning. The military commander ordered us out into the fields for replanting. At sunrise, we shifted our efforts to rebuilding the dikes. We couldn't risk a second flood. At sunset we returned to the fields and continued what we had begun there so many hours ago. At midnight we collapsed in our bunks, exhausted from our twenty-hour days. Could we succeed, or were we doomed to failure? Some students from the class of 1967 yielded to despair and took their own lives.

When I surveyed the situation below the horizon, I understood their hopelessness. But when I turned my head up toward the heavens, what I saw with my weak eyes brought me encouragement and renewal. As a Shanghai city girl, I had paid no attention to the sunrise or the sunset, and I had never watched the moon go through its phases. But now, out here in the bleak wilderness, this re-educated farm girl understood in a new way the wonder of the psalmist's vision: "The heavens declare the glory of

God, and the firmament shows forth his handiwork." *Such a great Creator! So puny, we, his creatures. Strange that he should care so deeply for his children. For me, his daughter.* I kept my musings to myself while my friends and I cultivated the fields. There, we sang together until our voices gave out. There, we talked together until we grew too tired to utter a word. There, I spoke silently in prayer to God. "Please, dear God, help me to know you better." A strange prayer for a Christian woman who, in recent years, had found too few occasions to serve her heavenly Father or to meditate on his Word. I waited twelve years for God to answer that prayer.

After a month of such backbreaking work we made two changes. Our commander reinstated our earlier practice of giving us one day a week off from work. He also moved us from the auditorium into the dorms the military had vacated when the impending floods had threatened to drown us. On one of our "holidays," at a time when all of the women from the 7th Company were relaxing in their dorm, students from the class of 1967 received unexpected visitors. Local male residents. They walked right in the front door. Naked! They understood better than the women how to manage the unbearable summer heat. More hospitable and less modest women might have stayed. Not them. They fled. These imperturbable visitors made the best of the situation. They searched the dorm and took what they wanted. Fortunately, no one from the 7th Company suffered personally during any of this. Later, during the winter, we noticed that the locals did don clothes, at least when the weather called for it. When we looked more closely, however, we wondered about the strange fabric the local "tailors" had used. It was marked with return addresses. Earlier in the summer, when these men, nudists at the time, had paid the women a visit, they had taken the cloth wrappings from the gifts the women had received in the mail. Simple folk. They may not have even realized that they were wearing stolen goods.

What I wanted and needed was a real visit from my husband. Although Xu and I had been married for about eight months, we had not seen each other since our honeymoon. Fortunately, China had a law that provided for situations like this: "In cases where husband and wife are geographically separated from one another, they are allotted fourteen days during the year to be together." Our military leaders sympathized with our plight, for they too suffered from similar privations. Thus, after appropriate conversations on both ends of the line, we made arrangements for Xu to come calling. We gave him directions as far as Wuxi, where someone would meet him and tell him how to get to our secret location. After Xu got off the train at the rendezvous point and received his instructions, the riverboats brought him to his final destination. Such strange sights for a city boy to see along the way. Naked women taking a bath in the river; and in one small town through which they passed, a second group of naked men and women. When Xu arrived at our military farm, he and I got to use the "guest room" that the military provided for such occasions. We enjoyed an entire week together. Every day while we intellectuals worked, Xu hiked to town; there, he bought special goodies for the rest of us to eat. When evening came around, the conservatory students joined the two of us as we visited and tasted the treats. In the end, they spoke of Xu's generosity in terms of a "tooth sacrifice." We smiled, and we agreed. A good visit; a good law. Other women, including "W," benefited from arrangements similar to ours.

Sometime after Xu returned to Hangzhou, I wondered whether I might be pregnant. I always felt tired, and physical labor did me in too easily. Had I been in Shanghai, I could have gotten a pregnancy test. But not here, out in the boondocks. Nothing for me to do but limp along. Then the day came when I collapsed under the strain. That day started when I hoisted a heavy load up onto my shoulders and tried to carry it. Too much! I inched along, walking and resting, resting and walking. Until I fell down. *I can't quit. I must go on.* I returned to my feet and dragged the load along as best I could. That evening I suffered so much from severe stomach cramps that I could not sleep. Finally, in the middle of the night, a friend awoke to my whimpering. I responded to her inquiry and told her about my stomachache. She awakened our student leader, who sought help at the military medical center. No doctors there. Only medics, people who knew too little about medicine. They tried acupuncture on my poor abdomen. Ten minutes later and I hemorrhaged. I suspect that I had miscarried, but at the time I couldn't be sure. I should have returned to work the next day, but I was unequal to the task. Fortunately, my friends collaborated and figured out a legitimate way for me to take it easy. Once a week, each person was assigned to light rather than heavy work. My friends pooled their "light days" and gave them to me. Once I recuperated and returned to the fields, I gave them back these "loaned" days.

Recuperated. Also the proud owner of a useful pet who tended to an annoying problem associated with our post-flood living situation. Although in former days we had "picnicked" out in the field, now we always ate in the dorm. This might have worked fine, had not some uninvited guests moved in. Mice! I spoke with one of the male students and asked him whether he would help us in making a trade with the locals: a package of cigarettes for a cat. Few from my dorm relished the thought of owning a furry feline with whom they would have to share their food. Just me. So I secured the cat, housebroke him, and fed him. Within a week the mice left us, the third platoon, en masse. Perhaps the fourth platoon would be more hospitable. Wrong. They complained about the terrible infestation and borrowed my cat. When my ferocious mouse hunter changed dorms, the sensible mice returned to us. *This isn't working!* I retrieved my cat and refused thereafter to loan him out. In time, those in the fourth platoon bit the bullet and got their own cat. Better to share their food with him than to suffer those pesky rodents. As expected, they succeeded in their extermination efforts: the mice sought safety elsewhere. Unfortunately, the new "Tom" never learned his manners. He relieved himself inside and outside, whenever the urge came upon him. I tried to help out, but I failed to housebreak this one. Maybe, like the proverbial "dog," he was too old to learn new tricks when they adopted him.

At fall harvest time, most of the remaining military personnel from our site moved up north, close to the Russian border, where they relieved another Chinese garrison. They had neglected to tell us anything about the impending changes. Thus, we simply woke up one morning and discovered that our supervisors had left us. We also discovered a heartbroken dog: the mess officer had abandoned his pet. In former days, that faithful canine had guarded his master's money. But now, after his master had disappeared, he felt quite useless. So each morning at reveille, when the loud horns announced the advent of another day, that dog sat down under those horns and wailed away. Pitiful!

We students fared better than that poor dog. Our masters, the military commander and the military guardian, had stayed behind. It might be too much to suggest that a good relationship had developed between us. Still, something had changed after their ten months of re-educating us city slickers. They seem to have softened up. As they lost their mean streak, they treated us as more than hopeless and evil slaves. Or maybe they just found it too difficult for two men to supervise so many students. However one explains the changes, we benefited. After the relatively poor harvest, our superiors gave us more free time than usual. Thereafter, we spent eight hours each day rebuilding the dikes; during evening hours we were on our own.

The male students, bored with too much free time on their hands, took up hunting wild dogs. Fun and useful, for our comrades ate their prey. In time, they caught and cooked the mess officer's dog. A terrible irony. And no more morning wailing. Pegasus must have recognized the dangers, for he sprouted wings and fled. During the winter, months after Pegasus had taken to the hills, I received quite a surprise. It happened one day when we students were returning to the dikes from our lunch break. As usual, I brought up the rear—I still washed my hands before eating and I still dallied over my food. There by the dike stood a dog. Pegasus had come back! I called out to him and commanded him to stay while I fetched him some food. But when I offered him rice with gravy, he just stared. As I looked more closely, I'm sure I saw tears in my dog's eyes. My comrades refused to believe me: "Dogs don't become misty-eyed." They could believe what they wanted; I knew what I had seen in my pet's eyes. At that point I decided that I would share my table food with Pegasus. He would get one-third, my cat would get one-third, and Shuhui Ma would get the rest.

During the daylight hours, my two pets entertained themselves. But at night, from 7 P.M. to 6 A.M., when I shared guard duty with a friend, they helped out. Such a strange sight. A bespectacled woman carrying a gun she couldn't shoot straight. A cat that took the lead; and Pegasus, who brought up the rear. When we stopped to change directions, my cat watched closely and stayed in front. He never missed a step. No wonder people enjoyed pulling guard duty with me. Extra company and extra protection. No wonder my cat enjoyed the company of Pegasus, who protected him during fights with other "Toms."

In early 1970 an unexpected political movement swept the country. When it found its way out here into the wilderness of Jiangsu, the authorities targeted the conservatory students. They complained about our singing "Our Home by the Huangpu River." They criticized our long-standing joke about the "wind toilet." Most seriously, they brought up charges about the foreign character and the hidden messages in our song "The Carriage Driver." "Beautiful Russian polyphony rather than simple Chinese monophony. Worrisome!" Hidden beneath the music, they discovered in the lyrics our cryptic criticism of Chinese Communism. The correspondences in our code were clear. Who was the carriage driver? The students. Who was the carriage owner? The CCP. And what did the horse typify? Knowledge. Once the clever cryptologists decoded our lyrics, they revealed our subterfuge. Not only did we claim that the Communist Party destroys knowledge, but we also maintained that the government had sent us to the farm where we didn't need such knowledge. Amazing. And also unbelievable. We had never imagined anything of the sort. We had learned and enjoyed this Russian song years ago, during our high school days. We endured these charges and more, as others spoke out against us in one of those famed political criticism meetings. But we also refused to confess to this cryptic nonsense. As for the other matters, we confessed, but only in a limited way. We admitted that we felt homesick when we sang about the Hunngpu River, and we agreed that our joke about the "wind toilet" was in poor taste. No more.

When the authorities cast their net more widely, they trapped and exposed others who opposed Chinese Communism. In particular, they punished one of my friends because he had made a mistake in writing a character while he transcribed the deliberations from one of their meetings. Their evidence was clear: while my friend wrote, he missed a tiny part of one character. This in turn changed the meaning of the word. The military punished him appropriately for his carelessness. They labeled him an "anti-revolutionary" and they took away his political rights. Although the authorities might have sent him off to another prison, this was unnecessary. In the daytime, the poor man worked on the dikes, and at nighttime he sat on his bed, confessed his errors, and wore his anti-revolutionary cap. Others suffered similarly, some for as much as two years. Fortunately, this short-lived political movement disappeared and things settled down. No more victims, at least for the moment.

When spring set in, we returned to our fields. A familiar routine. We tilled our soil and we sowed our seed. This year we took care of additional acreage, for the absence of the military meant more vacant land. Still, a tiring routine. Fifty-two days, bending over, cultivating our rice. Toward the end of each day we groaned in our traditional litany: "Oh, my poor back. I think it must be broken."

During these days the letters we received from student farmers from elsewhere in China suggested that they would be returning to Shanghai. Such rumors proved true, but not quite yet, at least for us. The authorities needed us to tend to planting. Frustrating. Irritating. Aggravating. More waiting before we could return home.

At last the day arrived. We packed our bags, boarded one boat and then another, until we came to a small village. Here in the backwoods we saw a postman, riding the first bike the villagers had ever seen. We chugged on ahead, safely past another town, this one suffering under a perennial flood. We made no lengthy stops until we pulled into Wuxi. Here too the rains poured down upon us. For some reason I looked at the water on the pavement. How could it be so bright and so clear? Civilization. Real roads. Back in Liyang County in Jiangsu Province, back on the farm in Hekou, they had only dirt paths. There, we knew only muddied puddles. No sparkle in such waters. A metaphor for the survivors of unforgettable hardships. Now, as we returned home, we had little time to reminisce. The Wuxi to Shanghai train was ready to take us home. Mother met me at the station. A wonderful welcome—even though I had to register at school before I returned to my real home. Done. Thereafter, we visited. So much to talk about. So much to think about. I still reflect on my eighteen long months in the country. And I still understand my determination never to return to the farm where Mao had seen to my re-education.

9

Political Realities and the Birth of a Child

1970–1974

In April 1969, Mao Zedong called his comrades together for the Ninth Party Congress. There they approved a new Party constitution. This document praised Mao's thought and named Lin Biao as Mao's successor, while also leashing the Red Guard. Deng Xiaoping, who now worked in a tractor factory in an outlying province, couldn't complain. Afterwards, the violence of the Cultural Revolution abated, though former high-level officials like Liu Shaoqi and Lin Biao faced early deaths. Most people, including Nettie and her young family, appreciated the return to normalcy, even if it included food shortages, restrictions of family size, and occasional foolish demotions.

We Chinese suffered through three years of chaos before Mao and other important Communist officials met secretly in April 1969 at the Ninth Congress of the CCP. During these deliberations, they decided to moderate the recent radicalism and to initiate a return to near normalcy. Unfortunately, their decisions and their moderation failed to extend immediately to my friends and me: we built our dikes and we prepared for our first spring planting on our military farm. Within several years, however, these leaders had established a more subdued version of the Cultural Revolution—it finally ended in 1976 with Mao's death. The good news after the Congress? The authorities permanently leashed the Red Guard and began to subordinate the Army to the Party once again. The bad news? They sentenced millions more Chinese youth to a rural re-education and required many returnees to work in factories. But not us at the Shanghai Conservatory. Jiang Qing, Mao's wife and the person in charge of fine arts during the Cultural Revolution, left us alone. For the time being, then, we enjoyed our leisure and reflected on current events. Although I worked hard to make sense of the confusing dialectic of the class struggle as it applied to the Party mandarins, I had little success.

Liu Shaoqi bore impeccable credentials: peasant origins; early member of the Communist Party; member of the Politburo; president of the People's Republic of China, early heir-apparent to Mao; and more. In the end, it did him no good. We heard, but only in pieces, the story of this surprising victim of the Cultural Revolution. He died in disgrace on November 12, 1969.

So strange that our President could be "China's Khrushchev," a traitor, and a "capitalist roader." I had thought of Liu as a man of great stature, a person who had helped Mao win and consolidate the Revolution. Now, Liu's enemies, enlightened by the concept of class struggle, had turned him into an animal. "Class struggle!" A principle that encouraged good people to abandon their normal human affections of kindness. A fierce and cruel strategy designed to destroy rather than save China. A poison to an entire generation. If they could do this to Liu, how safe was anyone else?

Lin Biao's superb credentials may even have surpassed Liu's: Whampoa Military Academy; survivor of the Long March; impressive military victories against the Japanese during the Pacific War, and once more against the GMD during the Civil War; member of the Politburo's Standing Committee; Minister of Defense; as of 1969, the most recent heir-apparent to Mao; and more. In the end it did him no good. We learned about Lin's fall in 1972, when the Party made his puzzling story public. They told us about a traitor who had turned against Mao. Strange.

He tried to escape to the Soviet Union, but his effort to escape failed when his plane crashed over Mongolia.

What were to make of all of this? Lin had been a hero. But now that Mao had condemned this conspirator, we too were expected to criticize him. We felt little regard for this sinister and ruthless man; but still, he seemed right in his conclusions. How could we resolve this particular dialectic, this tension between Lin's and Mao's judgments? Just maybe, the chairman himself was wrong.

Xu and I took advantage of the leisure we "fine arts musicians" enjoyed. Since he and I lived only four hours apart by train, we visited frequently. So good to be together, to enjoy the luxury of a commuting marriage. God answered my prayers in this and also in my discovery that I was pregnant. *We're going to have a baby!* Unfortunately, expectant mothers in China, whatever the period of time, faced serious problems in finding good medical care. During the Cultural Revolution we had treated most of our doctors shamefully: criticized, excluded from hospitals, and assigned to humble work. Young nurses and graduate students now represented the medical establishment. The physician who examined me for my regular checkup was no exception. Her conclusions were either self-evident or worrisome. "You've got a very big stomach." *Indeed!* "It looks to me like you're going to have twins." *Whoa!* "I have felt many limbs, precisely what one would expect with two babies. But I've heard only one heart." *Oh dear!* "You must get a lot of rest to conserve your strength. Here's a certificate that will excuse you from unnecessary meetings." *I'll do my best to take it easy.*

I took my doctor's report and my worries to my mother. "What you need, Nettie, is a second opinion. Your father has a good, old physician friend who is prohibited from working in a hospital. I think you ought to pay him a visit." Mother called and he invited us over.

After this experienced doctor examined me, he eased my concerns. "No need to worry, Nettie. You've only got one baby in your belly. Normally, children turn their faces toward their mothers' backs. But this one is turned around and faces your naval. Your inexperienced physician confused the baby's bottom with a second head. In short, everything is normal. No twins this time." *What a relief and extra rest to boot.*

But not for too long. Three weeks before my baby was due, I started bleeding. I needed expert advice, and perhaps more than that. No better place to go in such a predicament than to the famed Shanghai International Peace Hospital. Mother accompanied me, but only until we arrived at the elevator inside the building. Then she had to go. After the doctor checked my "twins," she assured me that delivery was hardly imminent. She gave me a shot, probably to calm the "babies" down, and told me that I would soon go home. For the present, however, probably as a precaution, she suggested that I rest here at the hospital. It sounded like a good idea to me. So they took me to a large room that offered intensive care and temporary housing for thirty pregnant women—all lined up neatly in two rows. *Rest. That's what I need.* Unfortunately, it didn't happen. I felt so strange.

For good reason. Soon thereafter, my water broke. I called out for the nurse: "Come quickly! I can't wait any longer!" She responded to my call and helped me into the delivery room. There, I saw ten women and two beds. Most of the expectant mothers were lying on the floor. Not me. I got special treatment, for my time had come. Or so we thought. But then nothing happened. A false alarm? Whatever the diagnosis, they moved me down to the floor where I joined the other dawdlers.

My doctor, a friend of one of my father's students, gave me special care throughout my first night in the hospital. By morning, she insisted that I get on with it: "If you don't give birth soon, your babies may suffer injury from oxygen deprivation."

February 2, 1972. An unforgettable date. An awful morning. A wonderful morning. The doctor decided that the "babies" had fallen asleep from yesterday's shot. Since I would get no help from the inside, they would help from the outside. They reached up into the birth canal and found, not two, but only one very large baby girl. Almost 10 pounds. The doctor reflected on the original prediction of a double birth: "If there had been two babies here, the other one would have been dead—not enough room in the womb for two this size." They went ahead and stitched me up even though my afterbirth had not yet come out. A bad idea. Then they re-cut me and went on another fishing expedition, pulled out the placenta and fetal membranes, and sewed me up again. As they finished with this procedure they explained to me what they had done—or not done. "I think we got most of it. But maybe a bit more will come out the next day." Some comfort. Had I been less exhausted, I might have worried. But not now. My weary body needed its rest.

The nurses put me in the observation room and may even have watched me. I couldn't say. I paid them no attention, for I had a more important matter to which I had to tend. I slept. At some point, when I opened my eyes, they moved me back into the large "intensive care" room. Once again I dozed off. Later, when I woke up for good, I wondered when winter had set in. *So cold! For some reason they have covered me with a sheet rather than the usual comforter. So thirsty! I need water, but I lack the strength to help myself.* The stranger in the bed next to me helped out. *So weak! Not even enough energy to sit up or to hold my bowl.* That afternoon, Mother nursed and fed me. Too soon, however, the doctor sent her home with an understandable explanation: "Nettie's blood pressure is unusually high. She needs her rest more than she needs your company."

Alone again? I recuperated while I rested. The next day I learned I had received special attention while I had slept. The janitor, the woman who cleaned our floors, had tended to my needs. But not simply a janitor. In former days, when sanity had prevailed, this physician had served as president of the International Peace Hospital. Although she now pushed a broom and carried a mop, she had forgotten none of her medical skills. Somehow, she had found me and recognized the dangers I faced because of my fever. Afterward, she had watched over me throughout the night. The following morning, however, she returned to her janitorial duties. I learned a bit more about my mysterious caregiver from one of the women in our room: "Your unofficial doctor, a Christian woman, has received more than her share of criticism." Indeed. Sadly, I never met this God-sent "minister" to offer her my thanks. But maybe her ears "buzzed" as we talked about her in our room and with the families who visited us.

Three days after our daughter's birth, Xu secured two days off from work and visited our baby and me. We talked as husband and wife and as new parents do on such occasions. He waited until later to tell me about my wan complexion; but he could not wait to see our daughter in the babies' room. After I recuperated for an entire week in the hospital, I returned home. By that time Xu and I had asked my father about what name he recommended for our daughter—it was a Chinese custom for the grandfather to give the child her name. "Grandpa" selected "Hao," the Chinese word for "clear moonlight." My people, who seemed to be walking in darkness, needed a clear light to illuminate their path. As a nickname, Xu chose "Lanlan," a Chinese word that corresponds to the orchid-like cymbidium flower whose fragrance delights our senses.[1] *So good to have a baby! Somehow, Hao restores love and hope to our family during these trying times.*

Soon after I returned home from the hospital, the authorities decided that they would "remodel" our government-owned, two-family apartment. They intended to break it up so that it would provide space for seven families. Since they owned the building, they neither needed nor sought our permission. I spoke with Mother about interim housing, and she suggested that Lana and I move into the apartment that Auntie Bessie and Uncle John shared. My hospitable and accommodating aunt readily agreed: my baby and I could have her bed and my aunt would sleep on the couch.

Lana set her own schedule as I began my apprenticeship at mothering. She slept for eight hours straight through the day. We could not wake her up to feed her or to change her diaper. But the middle of the night was another story. Then, she woke up and wanted to eat and play; then, she allowed us to give her a clean "nappy." This meant that I needed to grab my thirty winks whenever I could.

Lana and I could have returned to our recently-remodeled apartment a month after we had left, for the government completed its "partitioning" project on schedule. But this would mean that I, like other new mothers in China, would have to take up all my former obligations after only a thirty-day "leave-of-absence." My mother gave me another option: "You and Lana should stay and live with us. I will take care of all the housework for another month." I wasn't about to refuse Mother's generous offer.

The local resident cadres cared little about the personal concerns and privacy of Shanghai residents. Soon after I returned home, they paid us a visit. They explained that the government's population program restricted family size: "Couples may have no more than two children; and, they must ensure that siblings are not too close to one another in age."[2] I explained that they lacked jurisdiction in our case, for I was registered in Hangzhou, not Shanghai. That didn't deflect them from their mission. "What kind of effective birth control are you and your husband using?" *Why won't they let us be? These people have no business intruding into our private lives!* Before my unwelcome visitors left, they understood my anger. After they left, I had to sort through complex problems of parenting and getting situated. This irritating episode was simple, however, when compared to other stories we heard or experienced for ourselves.

Between spring 1972 and spring 1973, Xu and I enjoyed frequent commutes but lived separately. During this year, after Mother's generous care and my maternity leave had ended, I returned to my obligations at the conservatory. They paid me a salary and, as my part in the Cultural Revolution, I attended meetings. A neighborhood friend and I walked to school together each day—we could make it in thirty minutes if we stepped briskly. Like me, she too had a baby; unlike me, she majored in piano. As new mothers and accomplished musicians, we exchanged advice and compared notes. In addition to motherhood and music, we shared a common faith. Even so, my friend surprised me one day when she interrupted our conversation and showed me her special "writings." This resourceful woman had copied selections from Scripture at a time when Bibles had still been tolerated. Such a treasure! I borrowed her notebook and made my own copies. *Thy word is a light unto my path and a lamp unto my feet.*

That an atheist regime would prohibit Scripture during a period like the Cultural Revolution made sense. But the authorities apparently also saw some threat from musicians who practiced their instruments. How could anyone understand a regime that banned such seemingly innocent behavior? Some musicians skirted such silly proscriptions. The pianists wrapped cloth around their instruments' "internal hammers" and did their keyboard exercises noiselessly. Betty, a cousin of mine, taught her son this way. "As you practice your pieces each day, you must also put your imagination to work. So, you must ask yourself what would this Beethoven composition sound like without a mute instrument?" She must have given good advice to her son, for he is now an accomplished conductor in Shanghai.

I got my first real job opportunity in spring 1973. Xu's orchestra, which had no harpist, succeeded in "borrowing" me temporarily from the conservatory. But by joining my husband in Hangzhou, I left my daughter and my home in Shanghai. So hard! Whenever we practiced, the tears flowed. I missed Lana! Friends both scolded and comforted me. "You're just being silly," they said. "In time, you'll get used to the separation," they said. *Impossible!*

With me, the real mother, in Hangzhou, Grandma alone looked after our little girl. Grandpa could do nothing to help, for at this point he lived and worked in the country, at a May 7th Cadre School. There, he cared for the cows while his friend, the chair of the voice department, minded the chickens. Meanwhile, back in Shanghai, Mother had one single "imprinted chick": little Lana followed her grandmother about during all of their waking hours. That worked well, but only until the day when Mother left Lana outside the bathroom. "You wait here for a few minutes and I'll be right back. Okay?"

Not okay. When Mother returned, she found her granddaughter lying on the floor with a bloodied forehead. She rushed Lana to the hospital and then waited while strangers gave their wounded patient three stitches above her eye.

When my father learned about what had happened, he came to the rescue. "I'll sell my coat and you can use the money to buy Lana a walker. That'll prevent any future accidents."

Mama would have none of this. "That's fine for now. But what will you do when winter comes and the cold sets in?"

Daddy's answer won the day. "I don't need that coat for now. And later, I'll just wear a sweater."

So no more bloodied foreheads. Daddy sold that coat and bought the walker. Thereafter, it proved near impossible for a one-year-old to injure herself as she rolled around in such a contraption.

In fall 1973, the government allowed members of my graduating class to take on permanent jobs that officials had secured for us. I started out as a harpist at the Shanghai Opera House but soon persuaded the authorities to allow me to move to Hangzhou and join Xu. For the present, Xu and I lived in a dormitory. Too tiny; we had no room for visitors from Shanghai. So we approached the housing authorities and requested an apartment.

The unresponsive, low-level bureaucrats ignored us. Thus, I decided that I needed to speak to a higher-level official; he, however, kept his distance. Again and again, I set up appointments. He never showed up. Finally, I came to his office and asked to see him. His secretary stonewalled it: "I'm sorry. He can't speak with you. He's in a meeting."

"I'm in no rush," I replied. "I'll just sit here and wait until he gets out."

"That won't work. He's liable to be very late."

"No problem. I've got plenty of time."

My patience paid off. He gave me an audience and listened as I described our housing needs. He thought for a while before he came up with a promising idea. "One member of the Zhejiang Province Dance and Singing Ensemble in Hangzhou City is too old to dance, so he works in a factory. Moreover, his entire family lives in Shanghai. If we can convince him to vacate his second-floor apartment, then you and your husband can have his place."

This bureaucrat exercised real power. Within a month, the ex-dancer received permission to return to Shanghai and joined his family.

Voila! Xu and I left our dormitory and moved into the recently-vacated second-floor apartment. Huge! Two and one-half rooms, set together like a train, with no hallway to separate them. Or maybe it resembled a "lopsided train," for our dormer-like roof slanted downward as it approached the outside wall. In addition to our own place, we enjoyed more than adequate accoutrements on the ground level! A kitchen that served as a modest dining room on occasions when we didn't return upstairs to eat. A communal sink, situated in the apartment complex courtyard. Here, we washed our clothes and our dishes; and here, we visited with our neighbors. A bathroom and a shower, set off to the side of the courtyard. It came equipped with a simple and functional "toilet." No stools. Just a concrete gutter over which one squatted as she did her business. No flushing mechanism. Instead, water ran periodically through the gutter and washed most of the excrement out. No communal toilet paper—we brought our own. Definitely upscale living for us!

So many ordinary Chinese people put up with a lot worse. Xu's friend, for example, a man who worked for the Shanghai-Guangzhou Railroad and lived in Shanghai, described his apartment to me. He and his family—three generations of them—shared one large room on the top floor of their apartment building.

"How in the world can you manage?" I inquired. "Do you have a dormitory or a barracks?"

"We use curtains at night to partition our room," he explained. "My mother and my father-in-law get one room; my brother and my sister-in-law and their children get the second one; and my family gets the third one. As you can see, we get a little nighttime privacy in our tiny, temporary cubicles."

"Even with this arrangement," the friend continued, "we have too few beds. Let me explain to you how we sort this out. When I work, my daughter and my wife sleep in the bottom bunk and our young son sleeps up above them. When I'm off work, I sleep on the bottom bunk with my wife and our daughter moves in with the grandparents. Crowded, but we make do."

Most Chinese people would have shrugged their shoulders at this all-too-common story.

Although Xu and I enjoyed life together in our fine Hangzhou apartment, we missed our daughter. Lana remained in Shanghai with my parents. Father had returned to work at the conservatory in fall 1973, but the situation there was still highly politicized: the professors taught and the students criticized. When, for example, Professor Ma explained singing and deep breathing to his students, they complained about his use of the image of a rose. "Bad illustration! Western! You should have chosen a plant native to China to make your point! Why not rice or vegetables?"

Indeed. Clearly, politics undermined the teachers' authority, and without that they could not teach effectively. Thus, the instructors, intent on avoiding trouble, focused on skills and neglected the finer points of musicianship. "Grandpa" actually appreciated the extra hours the circumstances at work created. This gave him more time to spend with his granddaughter. Each month he and my mother took Lana to the park. While on these outings, they took pictures of our toddler and posted them our way—I still treasure these photos. In this way—mostly at a distance—

we enjoyed our daughter. But twice a year, my folks and Lana visited us in our spacious Hangzhou apartment. Such good occasions!

Chinese politicians had used and abused those in the fine arts well before Mao had initiated the Cultural Revolution. In those earlier days, the authorities had arranged for twenty-six artists from the Zhejiang Province Dance and Singing Ensemble to accompany high Communist Party officials, when they were in Hangzhou, to cultural performances. Only a few of these artists were men—they sometimes played with the performing orchestra or ensemble. The women provided companionship for the male mandarins who ran China. Ye, a beautiful teenage singer and one of the select twenty-six, enjoyed an intimate relationship with Chairman Mao. She and her fellow artists came from worker and peasant families before they took up their special political tasks. They all understood that they had received an extraordinary privilege to be allowed to serve Party officials in this way. They also understood that they had to keep their kind of work secret.

Periodically, women from the "special twenty-six" were asked to share their favors with important dignitaries. On such an occasion, a military officer attended a performance and the Party asked one of the dance girls to serve him. All went well, until her movie-star husband took offense when he discovered that his wife was indisposed. Angry because of her dutiful absence, he returned immediately to Shanghai. The authorities, fearful that the wife had disclosed her secret activities to her aggrieved husband, exiled the two of them far away, to Sichuan Province.

This particular episode caused no problems for the normal "companionship" arrangement. But that too unraveled soon after a male instrumental accompanist from the twenty-six became incensed because of the special assignments that the girls were given. You had only to see his face to understand his anger. Because he had caused a problem, the authorities treated him as an anti-revolutionary. Shortly thereafter, the twenty-six artists "disappeared." During the early phase of the Cultural Revolution, these "unemployed" people migrated to military sites where they sought special protection. Ye, for example, married a pilot and eventually returned to Hangzhou.

During summer 1973, our Zhejiang Province Dance and Singing Ensemble received a signal honor. We were invited to perform at the Guangzhou fall trade fair, a festive occasion that, in former days, foreigners had been invited to attend. The Cultural Revolution had temporarily put a stop to these festivities and the foreign visitors. But now the regime reversed itself, renewed the fair, and gave us our invitation. As we prepared to go, we faced important, unanswered questions. What sort of clothes should we wear? Performers frequently donned dark dress as a symbol of the Revolution. However, if we dressed properly, it would break with the tradition of Zhejiang Province, which was famous for its light music and dance. Or, what sort of problems will it cause when Ye, Mao's former "friend" and now a folk singer in our ensemble, performs with us in Guangzhou?

When our ensemble arrived in Guangzhou, we discovered that another dance and singing ensemble from Shanxi was also scheduled to perform at the fair. In tune with the times, these folks sang heavy music and wore dark clothes. In contrast to them, our routine took up the traditional tone of Zhejiang entertainment. A pretty stage and a colorful background set the mood for our "operetta." As the curtain opened, the light deliberately caught a single woman's extraordinary eyes. We had invited this accomplished movie star and Beijing opera-actress to perform with us. The audience, stunned by what they saw, applauded immediately. Only then did they settle down to enjoy the show. On stage, they witnessed a familiar story about women who picked tea leaves and knitted fishing nets while the village fishermen put out to sea. We wore beautiful silk dresses and treated those in attendance to an evening of light dance and delicate music. A resounding success! They praised us, and those who ran the Guangzhou Fair got lots of business. Our questions were answered. We had done well.

Not so poor Wei, a friend of mine from school. Hers was a sad and troubling story. Early on, her father had divorced his wife and abandoned his family. Then, during the early phase of the Cultural Revolution, her movie-star mother had committed suicide. From this low point, things went further downhill. When Wei and I had worked together on the military farm, her boyfriend had supposedly taken his own life. This made no sense to us. Everything had been normal the day before the reported event, and the boyfriend had been a strong man. Some of us wondered whether his death had really been self-inflicted. Poor Wei. I listened as she recounted her sorrows. "Everyone has left me. My father. My mother, who said she loved me. And now my boyfriend." What could I say? When we returned to school, the authorities picked up where others had left off. They put Wei in isolation and demanded a full confession from her. More questions; more puzzles. *Why are they picking on her? What in the world is going on? Wei lacks the strength to be a counter-revolutionary. Maybe she just has capitalist ideas.*

When the rest of us got real jobs in fall 1973, Wei got nothing. On one occasion she came by to talk with me and explain her way of life. "I know what people say about me. But the rest of you have it easy. The government has secured positions for you; these allow you to make a decent living. But what about me? They have left me unemployed. What else is there for me to do? So I go out and stay with someone, at least temporarily." I understood only too well her shabby treatment. But what could I say about such private matters? The conversation ended there.

Wei's fortunes seemed to change when her aunt, the wife of a high Communist Party official in Zhejiang Province, helped her out: Wei secured a position with the Zhejiang Ensemble. I celebrated the good news when I learned that she would be my colleague. Assuming that what others had said was true, Wei was happy to have a real job. Unfortunately, it didn't last. As she was riding her bike on a busy street—apparently she was making a trip to say good-bye to her friend—Wei had her last accident. A military truck drove too close to her, caught hold of her skirt, and dragged her along for several blocks. Dead! A result of what some called a "tragic accident."

Much later, well after I had moved to the United States, I learned that Wei's mother had been one of Mao's mistresses. Perhaps Wei's death had been accidental; but maybe not, for Wei knew something about her mother's relationship to Mao. Now I understood why they had interrogated this poor girl in the isolation room at our school. They had wanted to find out what she knew about the chairman's personal life.

Although such horror stories may have become less common toward the end of the Cultural Revolution, shortages still continued, even into 1975 and 1976. Thus, we stood in lines at the hospital as we waited for medical care. On a good day, however, those with friends on the inside might occasionally discover shortcuts. When, for example, I lined up to see a physician, an acquaintance signaled, waved me forward, and invited me in to see the doctor well ahead of "schedule." Or when it came to entertainment, one could stand in line for an entire day to get tickets. Even then there were too few to go around. In extraordinary situations, insiders secured and passed along their "extras." Ordinary people were out of luck.

Attempts to secure food proved equally difficult, probably because of low production on the farms and in the factories. A person could hunt all afternoon in the market to find a single cabbage. It did little good to stand in line, for when we reached the front, the vendor had nothing to sell. We stood a better chance of striking a deal with the farmers when they came to the city, for they were willing to exchange their food for our rice ration-coupons. Although the authorities outlawed such exchanges, virtually everyone skirted that law. Given these shortages, my daily routine was highly predictable. I practiced the harp in the mornings and I spent my afternoons trying to get food for our table. Except, of course, for those biannual occasions when my parents brought Lana for a visit. As I prepared for their visit, my highest priority was to find enough good food for my entire family.

10

The Last Train

1974–1980

The Old Guard, current Communist leaders who had assumed leadership roles since the early days of the Party, faced familiar domestic problems one last time in these years. Zhou Enlai won the day on pragmatic economic policies. China retained centralized planning and its leaders pushed for material incentives. Zhou also secured the rehabilitation of fellow moderates, like Deng Xiaoping. Pragmatists and their leftist opponents both recognized the need to limit size. Jiao Qing, Mao's wife, and others on the left opposed Zhou, who, like Mao, was terminally ill. Zhou and Mao both died in 1976. Suprisingly, those leftist hopefuls, soon called "The Gang of Four," found themselves under arrest.

The Old Guard ameliorated or abandoned much of the radical domestic program and xenophobic foreign policies of the Cultural Revolution, and then passed on from the scene. Zhou and Mao could not live forever, and the Gang of Four would not prevail. Of course food shortages would continue, at least until China increased its agricultural productivity or decreased its population growth. Still, we Chinese no longer suffered from the intrinsic terrors of our short-lived dystopia. For the present, we had only to face the routine difficulties and dangers of a pragmatic Marxist regime. So my family and I lived cautious but near-normal lives, even after I gave birth to my second daughter.

In 1970, China abandoned its longstanding policy of hostility toward the United States. Soon, China successfully cultivated a promising friendship with the United States. Who deserved credit for these remarkable shifts in policy? Although Zhou credited Mao with these accomplishments, we were more inclined to attribute them to Zhou.

Events associated with our professional music trip to the capital led me to suspect that Mao would continue his old practices and add new, intrusive policies on top of them. The trip possibility came to our attention rather innocently when, in 1975, the authorities invited our Zhejiang Ensemble to perform in Beijing for National Day. Why not? It isn't every day that a provincial music group gets such a special opportunity. Before we headed north, our hosts gave us an extended "working holiday" at a Zhejiang hotel. For two entire months we practiced our music and enjoyed gourmet food. Since Lana had stayed at home with her grandparents, Xu and I could take it easy. No parenting obligations for us. Not so other couples, whose children came with them. They had their hands full.

When our ensemble arrived in Beijing, our Marxist benefactors treated us royally. They housed us in a special hotel and fed us tasty and nutritious meals. We, or perhaps I should say Mao, had company during these days. Singer Ye remained Mao's "special friend." She visited with Mao and, thanks to the generosity of Mao's nurse, returned as the proud owner of an expensive watch. Some remarked on the apparent exchange: "a treasure for which anyone would willingly sacrifice herself." The rest of us kept silent about these matters, even after our well-received performance.

Upon our return from Beijing I heard a worrisome word about the new, intrusive policies the Party planned to implement. My informant friend, a Communist Party leader who worked on matters related to marriage and population management, spoke frankly to me about the impending change. "The government will soon restrict families to only one child. If you want a second child, you and Xu had better get started. It's time now to catch the last train."

When I awoke on the morning of January 8, 1976, I heard the radio playing a funeral melody. Word spread quickly. "Premier Zhou Enlai has died." Zhou's death came as no surprise. He was in his late seventies, and he had suffered from cancer for the past several years. Mao had remained visibly distant during his comrade's last few months. Even so, most Chinese people held Zhou in high regard. This sensible man had slowed down the chairman in his revolutionary efforts. Now, what would happen? With no one to steady the course and to care for the people, what crazy program would the radicals initiate?

Many wept and wore black armbands as they mourned Zhou's death. Not the authorities. They rejected the idea of celebrating and honoring the dead premier. "No crying! No black armbands! No memorial service!" Still, they allowed state funeral ceremonies at the Great Hall of the People. Mao, however, was visibly absent from the ceremonies. As Deng Xiaoping delivered the eulogy, he honored his comrade, a Party man of integrity who valued the masses. "His example should serve us well!" Closer to home, in Hangzhou, some factory workers took to the streets and set up a large flower wreath in honor of Zhou. I observed the unofficial memorial service firsthand while I was riding my bicycle. I slowed down, got off my bike, and joined the demonstrators. I had so much to think about. *Why does this regime refuse to honor Premier Zhou? Something is wrong with a government and a Party that fails to see and celebrate his good work.*

I needed to talk in confidence to someone about these matters to make sense of them. Xu, ever cautious and sensible, warned that such a conversation would endanger my family and me. "Best to keep quiet about these things." Good advice, but I couldn't follow it. So I got together with a neighbor woman whose husband, the Communist Party Supervisor in charge of the personnel division, kept a watch out for us. We were fortunate to have the man who kept all the personnel records as our friend. Like Xu, he refused to talk with his wife about public affairs. Still, neither of our husbands' fine examples failed to silence two silly women. On one occasion I started our rice supper and then ran over to my neighbor's house to talk about Mao, Jiang, and more. I became so engrossed in this conversation that I neglected the rice. Too much gab and too much fire. Xu didn't fancy burned rice, so I cooked supper again.

Our Zhejiang Ensemble soon had its own private dispute with the Beijing officials. As in previous years, we were invited to many places in Zhejiang Province to perform for the military in celebration of the Chinese New Year. When the authorities saw our unauthorized black armbands, they ordered us to take them off. What else was there to do but follow their orders? Outwardly we complied, but inwardly we failed to understand their opposition to this token memorial for our departed premier.

The authorities faced less compliant opposition when, in early April, thousands of people gathered in Tiananmen Square for the Qingming Festival. Soon, violence erupted. By the time this ugly episode was over, people in Beijing had witnessed two full days of violence, bloodshed, and arrests; many other cities, including Shanghai, experienced violence on a lesser scale. But since such events were not reported to the outside world, they heard little about these remarkable days.

Although the Tiananmen Square demonstrators had been crushed for the moment, the authorities had failed to eliminate continuing, quiet opposition. We simply went underground as we copied the poems and speeches that had been made. When my parents visited us, I showed my father one of these poems. I didn't know whether he copied it, but I was certain that he enjoyed its contents.

This poem eventually got me in hot water. Two secret service men had discovered some underground poems in the home of a Shanghai pastor whom they had arrested. My father provided the crucial connection to me, for he had passed my poem on to his friend. These sleuths visited the Communist Party Personnel leader to check out my file. Then, as they followed the trail to Hangzhou, the leader's wife—and my confidante—alerted me to the investigation and urged me to be careful. Indeed. As I recalled my earlier scribal efforts, I remembered that I had copied the poem from a man from our dance ensemble. How many would be implicated if I were not careful? By early fall 1976, these government agents were hot on my trail. Surprisingly, we had difficulty linking up. The first day, they visited my home after I had gone to work with the ensemble. The second day, the tables were turned. They visited my workplace when I was at home. This comedy lasted an entire week. But then they found and interrogated me—and the man from whom I had copied the poem. The secret service men spoke almost apologetically about what they were doing. "We understand only too well the hard times and the difficulties of the Chinese people. Still, this is our job. We're only following orders." Such sympathetic words would have been impossible in less hospitable times. Nothing much came of this interrogation, for although the secret service men stayed in Hangzhou, they left me alone. Still, I proceeded with caution, for a second friend warned me that another man was watching me and would report on everything I did.

Caution required less than absolute silence. During these same days, our ensemble performed at the "Moon Festival," a holiday also known as the "Chinese August"; the lunar calendar set the celebratory days for late summer or early fall. On this good occasion some close friends from our neighborhood met together. We shared a little wine and a small cake and talked, mostly about Mao's wife. What continuing influence would she have, especially after her husband passed away? This was not idle speculation about an old but healthy man. In fact, Mao had suffered serious physical infirmities. By 1976 the end was in sight. If Jiang came to power, what kind of future would China face? Our conversation continued well beyond midnight, after which we all returned home. The next morning, September 9, we awoke, once again to the sounds of funeral music. Mao had died.

Xu and I were in Hangzhou when we heard the news. Like most people, we could not predict what the chairman's death might mean for Chinese politics. Here at home, a friend once again warned me to be careful. "Your name is on the black list. So you can be sure that your reactions to Mao's death will be reported to the higher-ups." All over China, groups got together and watched the funeral ceremonies on television. The memorial in Hangzhou differed little from that which occurred in the other big cities. We wore the black armbands the authorities gave us and we attended the public memorial service. As we approached Mao's picture, we were required to bow three times. A friend instructed me to cry, even as I had done at Zhou's death. I protested that I lacked the skills of an actress. My friend ignored my protestations and insisted that I start crying. Impossible for me to mourn this man's death! So I covered my face with my hands. Hopefully, the "watchers" took this to mean that I was broken-hearted.

My parents stayed at home and watched the memorial service on the new 9-inch black and white television set my father had recently bought. Given the extreme heat during these days, and given my parents' age, they found it easier to mourn in the comfort of their apartment. Lana, now a kindergartner, also had to attend a memorial service at her school. My mother worried about how well children, and especially her own granddaughter, would behave on such a solemn public occasion. Not one to leave things to chance, Mother gave a stern voice to her worries. "Lana," she said, "you must be serious at the funeral. Absolutely no laughing! I have been a friendly Grandma thus far. But if I hear you even smiled at the service, I will spank you. And after that, I will take away your toys. If, however, I hear that you were sad at the service, I will reward you when you return home."

It worked. The teacher reported that little Lana had kept her head bowed, and then, when she saw Mao's picture, she had cried. "So well behaved!"

Lana told a similar story but with a different twist. "Sure, I cried, but out of fear, not because I felt sad."

One kindergartner laughed at the service, and the story about his improper demeanor was passed on to the authorities. Since, however, he came from the proletariat, neither he nor his family got into any trouble.

High drama continued in Chinese politics because Mao's death brought no clear or immediate resolution to the "succession" question. We knew little, however, about these secret struggles, for the press failed to promptly inform its public about the intrigue that originated in and emanated from Beijing. This was just as well with me, for during these same months I faced my own "low drama" in Hangzhou and Shanghai. Soon after Mao's death, my heart rate increased unexpectedly and I began to lose weight. My parents learned about my condition when they brought Lana to Hangzhou for her usual visit on National Day.

"What in the world could be wrong with you, Nettie?" they asked.

"I guess my worries about the political situation have taken their toll on my health." My reply was not convincing.

"Perhaps," they continued. "But we suspect that something else is wrong. You must go see a doctor!"

So I visited a Hangzhou doctor, who, after looking me over, said he thought everything seemed normal. "If you continue to lose weight," he noted, "you must come back for a more thorough investigation. It could be a tumor or cancer."

Assuring words, but the symptoms continued. My heart beat away—a reading of 108 per minute was not uncommon—and my energy level declined.

My parents suggested that I return to Shanghai for testing. "We've got better physicians here, and some of them are family friends."

In the end, my parents made the medical arrangements, which included a blood test and a heart test. My doctor's diagnosis confirmed their suspicions. "Nettie," he explained, you've got two things "wrong" with you. First, you've got thyroid problems; we can eliminate these with the proper medications. Second, you're pregnant; you should be able to take care of that in due time."

Indeed! The government announced its new population policy in December 1976. "Hereafter, only one child per family. If a woman becomes pregnant a second time, she will have to undergo a compulsory abortion." Not me. I had boarded the "last train" before the regulation went into effect. In spring 1977 I would give birth to a second daughter.

I stayed in Shanghai for an entire month and watched my physical condition return to near normal. In early October, Xu came for a visit. At 10 P.M. on the night of October 6, a close friend knocked at our door. We invited her in and listened to her news. "It is said that four top-level politicians have been arrested." This was high drama!

Elated, we told my mother the good news. Ever cautious, she insisted that we should say nothing to celebrate the arrests. "You never know," she said, "the rumors may not be true."

My friend insisted that she had given us accurate information. At the same time, we heard the fireworks outside. Were others already beginning their celebrations?

By the following morning the unofficial word had spread all over Shanghai. Many people congregated in the market where they tried to confirm the rumors and where they made special purchases. They bought crabs—three males and one female—in hope that they could enjoy a festive dinner. The government remained silent until, in late October, it announced the smashing of the Gang of Four. The next day the newspapers published editorials in support of the "Great Historic Victory." *It's too good to be true. Jiang Qing and her cohorts are out.* I returned to Hangzhou and work in late fall.

Our Zhejiang Ensemble had its own low drama, a near disaster, when my father came, at their invitation, to help us rehearse. As professional musicians who were scheduled to perform for the military in the near future, we knew the value of expert instruction. Unfortunately, few Chinese conductors, Professor Ma excepted, possessed extraordinary experience and training. Fortunately, Daddy agreed to help us out. As we made our way to the rehearsal hall, my father, Xu, and the other members of our ensemble piled into the back of a large truck. Since I was pregnant, they allowed me to sit up front in the passenger's seat. Soon after we got started, the "retaining walls" on the back of the truck burst. Too many people and too much pressure. Everyone tumbled out onto the street. Daddy suffered no injuries because others unintentionally cushioned his fall. Only those who had been standing toward the outside of the truck bed got hurt. One friend hit her head on the ground and suffered dizzy spells for two months. But I had few complaints. The driver and his plump passenger had escaped injury.

This plump passenger, the one who had boarded the last train on time, returned to Shanghai in April 1977 to prepare for the birth of her second child. Government regulations required prospective patients to register at the hospital in their particular geographical district. Five years earlier, as a student in Shanghai, I had registered in the Conservatory District. There, in that district's hospital, I had given birth to Lana. On this occasion, however, I signed up at the hospital in Jiangan, my parents' home district. The Jiangan Medical Center was a good place in which some of my father's students' friends worked. A good place to visit, but only when one needs medical attention. Until that time, I sat at home and waited for things to happen. At last, on the morning of May 14, two weeks before my due date, I knew I was ready to get on with the delivery. My mother accompanied me to the Medical Center and then returned home. I stayed while one of those special friends from the hospital helped me get situated.

Soon after I checked in, a doctor friend informed me that the second child usually comes quickly. That would be fine with me, as long as I could keep my new baby with me in the delivery room. At lunchtime, all of the attending physicians except my doctor went to the cafeteria to eat. She would not take her meal with the others because she had promised that she would take care of me. So she had me lie down on the bed and then instructed me to take it easy. Once I got comfortable, she stepped out of my room to read. But not for long. Too soon, she heard me call out: "Come quickly, the baby is coming right now!"

The predictions about second children proved true. Our daughter "Mary" must have been anxious to get started. A gentle soul, she gave me little trouble as she found her way into her new world. A small child—eight pounds—at least when compared to her older sister. My doctor set my newborn on my leg and then she tended to another woman who was giving birth. The doctor tried to slow that baby down by using a towel. At the same time the doctor yelled for help. A nurse who just happened to be walking past the delivery room looked after the poor woman stuffed with the towel. This allowed my attending physician to care for Mary and me.

Four days after the delivery, we checked out of the hospital and into my parents' apartment. There, I regained my strength; there, I waited for Xu and his father to come to Shanghai and see the newest member of our family. What would they think? I understood only too well that most Chinese preferred little boys to little girls. And then, with that knowledge, I had produced a second daughter. My mother and my Auntie Bessie assured me that they and my father loved little Mary. They also predicted everything would be fine with my husband and my father-in-law. Still, I waited and I worried. Few visitors came by during my first days at home. Moreover, I received no congratulatory cards or celebration notes from Xu's family. *It's so hard not to have my husband present or to have his father's approval.* In fact, these disappointed men remained in Hangzhou and went to the park every morning. They did not like Mary. At last, when our daughter was a month old, Xu and his father came for their first visit. Mother had prepared me for this occasion. "You just watch their eyes, Nettie. You will see there the signs that they love your baby." My worries were unnecessary. All went well.[1] My husband in particular loved (and in time spoiled) his new daughter. At my father's suggestion we named our little girl "Yu," the Chinese word for "bright sunshine." We still needed to have our path illuminated in these dark times. As a nickname, Xu chose "Mei-mei," the Chinese word for "rose," my mother's favorite flower and, in its Anglicized form of "Mary," my grandmother's name.

Everyone loved and cared for our special baby. Who could complain? She slept when we slept and she caused us little trouble. I nursed Mary for a month and then, when Mother reminded me that I must get ready to return to work, I weaned my special baby. Henceforth, she would get the bottle rather than the breast.

Grandpa volunteered to get up at midnight and feed his new granddaughter. That first night when he stood "baby duty," Mother and I got up to watch. As Daddy held and fed Mary, she laughed loudly. We didn't know what to make of such precocious behavior, but we knew with a certainty that Mary had won Grandpa's heart.

It was Grandma, however, who discovered Mary's new bad habit. In the mornings, when my mother took Lana to kindergarten, our baby was still sleeping. But in the afternoons, when they returned from school, they often found an alert little girl with her thumb in her mouth. We tried several remedies—a glove on her hand and spice on her thumb. Mary voiced her objections to each and cried.

My aunt visited us regularly each afternoon at 4 P.M. Mary got so excited as she anticipated her visitor: our special baby started rocking on her stomach. Since my auntie gave all of her attention and care to her niece, my mother found time to tend to her own things.

We also employed a woman to work for us on weekday mornings. Our hired helper cooked, cleaned, washed clothes, and shopped for us at the market.

Even Lana did well by her little sister. On one occasion we heard a neighbor lady teasing our older daughter. "Now that you have a younger sister," she said, "your mother will need to give her more attention than she gives you."

Many siblings would have taken the bait and gotten jealous. Not Lana. She countered in a most surprising and pleasing way. "I'm glad that Mother and Grandma will love Mary because she is my little sister."

The new, self-designated mandarins of our country, now the leaders of a post-Maoist and post-Cultural Revolutionary China, soon discovered that the path toward normalcy was neither clear nor trouble-free. And Xu and I, now the parents of two daughters rather than just one, made similar discoveries about normalcy in family life. For the most part, the Party left my family alone. It was only on rare occasions that the authorities or their underlings intruded into our lives. Surprisingly, we welcomed some of their intrusions.

I returned to work in Hangzhou two months after Mary's birth. Xu and I would have found it hard to care for our two children, for travel and nighttime performances kept us busy. Fortunately, my parents provided us with full-time childcare in Shanghai. During these days, our routine alternated between our professional obligations and our frequent trips to visit the girls.

At about this same time, the government again felt sorry for the way they had mistreated my father. Equally important, they made their sorrow tangible. They returned my mother's jewelry and the books and pictures they had taken. They also reimbursed Father for the money they had unjustly taken from his salary, and they restored the savings account they had wrongly appropriated. Not bad, even though the authorities failed to include the interest Daddy would have earned on his money had they just left him alone. Still, my folks' financial situation improved considerably. My parents, ever generous with their material possessions, shared some of their newfound "wealth" with us. We spent the money for basic necessities: furniture and a reel-to-reel tape recorder. Soon thereafter we copied many records onto tapes and invited friends over to our apartment where we all listened to the works of such great artists as Mozart, Debussy, and Beethoven.

Our circumstances changed when, in 1978, my parents brought the girls to Hangzhou for one of their regular visits. On that occasion, Mother confessed to us that she lacked the energy to care for two small children. Since we knew Grandma's age, we understood her reluctant confession. After talking about the situation, we decided to keep Mary with us and to send Lana "home" with her grandparents. Xu and I hoped we would be able to hire a woman from the country to help us out.

Toward the beginning of another parental visit to Hangzhou, my father told us that he had to return to the conservatory to teach. He assured us that he would come back in two weeks, pick up Lana and Grandma, and return with them to Shanghai. Since we had no phone, we couldn't keep in touch with Daddy during his absence. And then we got an unexpected telegram from Shanghai. "Surprise! We've got a new apartment. The government feels sorry for us. Daddy." Mother and Lana hopped on the Shanghai train right away. Xu and I stayed behind and thought about how we might help out. Given our ensemble's flexible hours during those times when we had no scheduled performances, we suspected that one of us might be able get away and lend my parents a hand with the move. It worked. Xu got several days off, joined my folks, and "moved away." Once Mother and Father and Lana got situated, they still needed to respond to the Communist Party's request for a formal "thank you" for its generosity. My father told them he would have preferred to have his old house back—the one the Communists had confiscated. That's the only word of thanks he could manage.

"A good woman is hard to find"—so we discovered in our repeated attempts to hire domestic help. Many rural women hoped to find just this sort of work. Most of these people were young, perhaps between the ages of thirteen and fourteen. Their families sent them out because they couldn't afford to feed them. When these girls found a job, they lived with their new employer and tried to save a little money for their wedding. In the end, unlike many of my friends who took on such youngsters, we hired an older widow lady. This single woman would serve as our live-in babysitter for an agreed-upon monthly salary. Later, we got to know our babysitter a bit better. She had a son who had disappeared some time ago. During his absence, she had lived in the country by herself for a number of years. She also indicated to us that she was a Christian. Things went well at first, especially in terms of the good care the lady provided for Mary. Then one day we noticed that our widow woman had a nosebleed. When we asked her what was wrong, she told us we shouldn't worry. As we talked further, she admitted that she had stolen and then taken some of our ginseng medicine.[2] She must have gotten the kind of ginseng that raises rather than lowers a person's blood pressure. That self-prescribed medicine had made her dizzy and had caused her nosebleed. Our domestic helper concluded her confession in embarrassment as she acknowledged her moral failure. Soon thereafter, she left us, with an understandable explanation: "I've got to return home."

Next, we hired a retired worker who lived across the street from our apartment. She looked after Mary's normal needs and also took care of some household chores. That still left me with my toddler's special needs. Every ten days or so Mary developed a fever. It seemed like she was always sick. In time, we brought her to a hospital for a checkup. After the doctors' initial diagnosis, they tried to give her an IV. This was not an easy task, for their patient refused to cooperate. The only way that they could get the needle into her vein was to strap her to the table. Then, as they looked Mary over more carefully, they determined that she would need regular, intravenous medication. That might help, but I worried about hospital hygiene, for I knew that they reused their needles. As an alternative, I learned to give shots and bought clean syringes for home use.

Our retired worker stayed with us until we moved into a brand new apartment building. Our ensemble had approved the construction project, which involved the reconstruction of our entire dormitory. In the end, the government built two complexes—three units per floor and five floors—close by our former place. Our new apartment, with a living room, a dining room, a bedroom, a kitchen, and a bath, gave us plenty of space. Our only problem was that the entire complex lacked an elevator. That was okay by us, but Mary's nurse complained that she couldn't manage so many steps. She resigned.[3]

The third person we hired as a domestic helper, another woman from the country, proved the American baseball aphorism "three strikes and you're out." At first she seemed quite nice. When, for example, Mary dawdled over her food and we had professional obligations, we found ourselves in a quandary. If we tried to hurry our daughter, she refused to eat. But if we took our time, we might not meet our other commitments. Fortunately, on those occasions when we were in a hurry, our patient nursemaid volunteered to feed Mary at a pace that our dawdler could manage. Just the kind of person we needed! Or so I thought. But only until one day after I left home and I discovered that I had forgotten something. I returned unexpectedly to the apartment and found our nice, patient woman searching through my drawers. When I made a quick check of my valuables, I realized that some items were missing. I didn't have to look hard to find the culprit. And I didn't have to wait long until I fired her.

Since we no longer employed a live-in nurse, I checked out a daycare center. It looked promising, especially when I learned that Mary's class would have its own teacher. No need to delay getting started. We signed our little girl up. All went well, but only until the day when I heard a familiar cry as I walked by this center. I stopped and looked inside. My Mary was making all the noise and shedding not a few tears. When I asked her what was wrong, she responded with a worrisome story. "I was thirsty and wanted to get a drink. When I asked permission from the teacher, she spanked me."

I asked the substitute—the regular teacher was absent that day—to explain what had happened. Her explanation made perfect sense—to her. "If I get water for one child then I'll have to get water for all of them. That will make me too busy to do my job. But if I spank one, the others who think they are thirsty will be less likely to bother me. So your daughter got the paddle."

Nonsense! I won't put up with it! I took Mary out of this day-care center and never returned. Unfortunately, that decision meant that I had returned to square one. How would I care for our daughter?

While I sought a sensible solution to this personal, domestic problem, Xu faced his own political difficulties at work. The origin of his difficulties involved intractable tensions between the two different groups of people who worked in cultural activities. One group, graduates of universities and conservatories, excelled at their muse. The other group, demobilized soldiers, had limited professional training. The latter, however, believed for political reasons that they ought to be given the most prestigious positions. Unfortunately, when we had tryouts for the principal positions in our orchestra, the military came out second best. They could not play well. And when sensible orchestral assignments were made, these amateurs resented their being required to play second fiddle. So these jealous and envious malcontents turned their anger against Xu, a conservatory graduate and the person who most frequently conducted our orchestra.

They lashed out verbally by calling him and his associates "the stinking ninth."[4] They also decided "to give him small shoes," a Chinese colloquialism which meant that they would regularly make trouble and give him pain.

Xu was unwilling to wear shoes that didn't fit. So he consulted a friend who helped him find another job in another location. A television station in Zhejiang Province hired my husband and placed him in charge of their music. Xu, a professional committed to excellence, worked energetically at his new position. Understandable. Unfortunately, his attempt to excel at work didn't help our childcare problems. Normally, Xu worked nights and stayed home mornings with our daughter. That suited us fine, but only when I had no evening rehearsals or performances. When each of us had evening obligations, I took Mary—by bicycle—with me. When it snowed or rained, I set her on the seat and walked beside her. She and I moved along at our snail's pace, but at least we avoided any injuries. One way or the other, we would reach our destination. When I joined the orchestra and played the harp, friends backstage baby-sat for me. In all of this, our competing schedules and Mary's persistent fragile health complicated our lives. Still, we managed, but just barely. We did not have to continue this frenetic pace forever, however, for in time a series of interrelated events pointed me in a much different direction.

11

Open Door to the United States

1980–1984

Mao's death and the end of the Cultural Revolution set China on a slow, promising, and ultimately incomplete course toward greater openness. The discredited and pragmatic Deng Xiaoping found his way back into Chinese politics, successfully prosecuted the Gang of Four, and outmaneuvered Hua Guofeng for Party leadership. China established diplomatic relations with the United States in January 1979 and, after the Soviet invasion of Afghanistan later that same year, distanced itself even more from the Soviet Union. By the early 1980s, the new openness in China made study in America possible.

During these promising days, my father's situation changed from night to day. In 1980 the government expressed sorrow to him for all the injustices he had suffered over the past thirty years. Equally important, they transferred me back to Shanghai—Xu remained in Hangzhou. Professionally, I started work at the Music Research Institute at the Shanghai Conservatory. I collected music, scores, and tapes and organized these materials for the library. In my spare time, I focused my research on Asian music. But the real reason I was sent home concerned Daddy: at last, I could help care for him. I moved in with my parents when the authorities failed to provide me with housing. Our cramped quarters required us to devise new sleeping arrangements. Grandpa took the study, while Grandma, Lana, Mary, and I "spread out" in my parents' former "bedroom." When Xu came for visits, he got the living room sofa.

China's improved relations with the United States made it possible for my father to accept a 1981 invitation to attend the American Choral Directors Association in New Orleans. So exciting, for him to be able to leave the country again! And that was only a beginning, for his friends in New Orleans arranged for Professor Ma to speak at colleges and universities throughout the United States. His junket took him to so many special places: Westminster Choir College, Harvard, the University of Oklahoma, Brown University, Wartburg College, Oberlin College, and Southwestern Baptist Theological Seminary.[1] What a trip! During my father's absence, I helped Mother at home.

Shortly after Father left Shanghai for the United States, the conservatory gave Mother and me this strangely addressed letter: "To Music Professor Ma; Shanghai, China." Since the envelope bore no return address to allow us to identify the sender, we opened it to see what we had. Dr. Clifton Tennison, my father's former roommate at Southwestern Baptist Theological Seminary, had penned the mystery letter. We read his simple, moving words: "I've written to you every year, for more than thirty years now, and I have never received a reply. I have no idea whether you are alive or dead. But my wife and I are determined to find out. We're on our way to China. I remember your telling me that you have a daughter. So if we can't find you, we'll try to find her." Amazing that we got the letter! In earlier days the officials at the conservatory would have destroyed it.

We might have written our familial friend had we known where to send it. But since that option was ruled out, we mailed the letter to my father. He took it from there. He secured the Tennisons' address from the people at Southwestern and then got in touch with his former roommate. As Daddy talked with Dr. Tennison, his American friend understood why Geshun had left the States so suddenly back in the late 1940s. Dr. Tennison also understood why he and his wife had failed to find Geshun during the Cultural Revolution. After the Chinese government had refused the

Tennisons admission to China, they had visited Hong Kong. Moreover, during their time in Hong Kong they had repeatedly asked mainlanders whether they had any information about Ma Geshun. No luck. At that time the authorities had sequestered the music professor away in one of their infamous "cowsheds," their inhospitable, makeshift prisons. At this point the Tennisons had no choice but to return home. But now the timing of their conversation was perfect, for my father's persistent friends were preparing for another trip to China. With this in mind, my father told us that these folks would be visiting Shanghai and instructed us to meet them at a particular Shanghai hotel at a given time and date.

When we met our persistent foreign friends at the hotel, Mrs. Tennison gave each of my girls a doll. Rather than visit in this fancy but impersonal hotel, we invited our company to our cozy apartment.

Later, when Dr. Tennison and his wife returned home, they were able to attend a special replacement graduation ceremony for Mr. Ma—Daddy had missed out on the first one when, in the late forties, he had dashed back to China. As the two friends enjoyed their reunion, Dr. Tennison asked my father what he could do for him.

"That's easy," my father replied. "Could you see to it that my daughter Nettie gets a good education?"

"Not so easy, and thus no promises," his American friend replied. "Still, I'll do my best."

Before Daddy returned to Shanghai in 1981, he received several other honors. Westminster Choir College, the school he had attended so many years ago, organized a grand ceremony and gave their distinguished alum an honorary fellowship. Not to be outdone, Oklahoma City bestowed honorary city citizenship on their special visitor. Such a good trip, and so pleased to return to China with so many honors. When Daddy returned to Shanghai, he brought us each gifts. My special present, one that friends had asked him to get for me, was a purse. I opened it up, pulled out the paper stuffing, and found a small Bible hidden inside. I felt happy to own such a treasure. But Daddy mused about other matters. "Now, Nettie," he said, "if only we can locate and contact your uncles in America. It would be wonderful to have them visit China and join us in a family reunion." *Impossible to dream in the darkness of the Cultural Revolution. But now that the sun has begun to peak above the horizon, some dreams might just come true. Surprising that I now have a friend in the United States!*

At some point before he left for the United States, my busy father had prayed to God. "Please, dear Lord, give me three years in which I can serve you. This might in some small way make up for the thirty years I lost during the Communist oppression." Now that the regime had allowed the churches to reopen, Daddy's prayer could be answered in a special way. Soon after Daddy returned from the States, the churches decided to prepare a hymnal; they asked Professor Ma to serve as its editor. He accepted their assignment and, ever the teacher, considered how he might contribute to the hymnal's success. He eventually decided to assemble an excellent choir and have them sing and record songs from the hymnal. He hoped congregations would use these recordings to help them learn the new music quickly and well.

Unfortunately, at the same time that Daddy's situation improved dramatically, Mama's condition deteriorated: she grew physically weak, and her energy level declined proportionately. Given our circumstances, we decided to lighten her workload by sending Mary to a boarding nursery.[2] Grandmother, who felt badly about our decision, apologized to her granddaughter. Mary never complained, even though this new situation, coupled with her frequent poor health, could have given her plenty to grump about. On those common occasions when Mary got sick, we went to school before the end of the day, picked her up, and brought her home. On weekends, when Mary lived with us, Grandma always gave her special treats.

During these same promising days, I began my apprenticeship, admittedly lackadaisically, in the English language. Several years after Mao's death, my Auntie Bessie had begun teaching private English lessons as a way of making a little additional money. This is not to say she was impoverished, for my uncle, C. H. Sheng, who had already visited us from the United States, now supported his sister by sending her money every three months. Early on, my auntie recruited me as one of her students. "Nettie, pay attention to me. You too must study English." There was method in her madness, for she hoped I might eventually go to America.

Although I too had my dreams, they didn't extend to such impossibilities. Still, I humored my auntie and I agreed to visit her weekly in her home; there I would start my study of a new language. As we began, I tried, for I thought that if I complemented my knowledge of Russian with English it would serve me well in my work at the institute. As we began, I tried, but not too hard.

Still, the two of us made a beginning and established a routine. My slow progress suited me just fine. We had plenty of time, or so I thought. I learned otherwise on the day Mother called me from one of our daily political meetings at school. Her clear words gave me a new mission. "Nettie, we took your Aunt Bessie to the clinic yesterday and they observed that she had a fever. When they offered to give her a shot, she refused their treatment. She claimed that their needles were unclean. Now you and I may need to become her nurses. I can't pay her my customary visit today. So could you to go to the drug store and buy a syringe and other paraphernalia that she might need? Then could you look in on her and see how she's doing?"

I stopped by the pharmacy, made my purchases, and went to see Auntie Bessie. She watched me clean and prepare the syringe, and she made no objections when I gave her a shot. I also noticed that the color of her skin didn't look right. "Auntie," I asked, "could you lie down on the bed and let me take a closer look at how you're doing?" She cooperated and I turned on the lights. I looked into her eyes and noted their yellow cast; I also observed her sallow skin. I spoke solemnly as I offered my imprecise diagnosis: "Auntie, you've got a big problem. Is anything else wrong?" Only then did she tell me about her stomach pains.

I called Uncle John, who lived in the next room in the same apartment, and my cousin, who resided in the neighborhood, and asked them to come by right away. The three of us talked with Auntie Bessie and consulted together. Afterward, I offered our prescription to our patient: "There's no doubt about it. You need to go to the hospital!"

Her response came as no surprise: "Never!"

Not one to give up easily, I countered. "You must go. Something is seriously wrong with you. If our judgment is wrong, I promise that you may return home." With these insistent words I eventually won the day.

Since my auntie was too weak to walk, we called an ambulance. The doctors at the hospital examined her and confirmed our suspicions. "It's your gall bladder. You need surgery immediately. This can't wait!"

Although my aunt was weak, she still had sufficient strength to complain: "I don't want you to take out a part of my body and throw it away." Had Bessie known how to articulate it, she might also have mentioned her old-fashioned concerns: she felt modest around male physicians. We understood and we heard her unvoiced worries.

Meanwhile, we waited, for the bureaucrats needed a signature before the surgeons could make my auntie better. Uncle John could have signed, but he wouldn't. So we called Mother and asked her to sign, but she too refused to assume legal responsibility for the operation. It looked like Bessie's simple solution—"You just pray for me"—might carry the day.

We did pray, but we also complemented Bessie's simple approach to providence with a more promising alternative. "Sometimes," we argued, "God works through a doctor." We also strengthened our argument with an appeal to Bessie's concern for others. "You must consider the needs of these surgeons. If they have no work to do, they will lose their jobs."

Still no signature and no surgery. We waited with Bessie in the hospital for one night and two days. At last, my father decided we could wait no longer. He talked with the doctor, who agreed that it was past time to end the delay. With that agreement, Daddy signed the consent paper. Now that someone had taken the lead, my uncle also gave in to the doctor's request and authorized the operation.

Unfortunately, when the doctors began their surgery, they discovered that it was already too late. Infection had set in. As they studied the situation, they saw a strange liquid that covered the insides of their sick patient's abdomen. The attending physician attempted to clean up poor Bessie's innards, but he did so only imperfectly. That's all he could do. Still, we hoped my auntie would recover, especially if she rested in bed for several months. During the daytime, my cousins and I took turns sitting beside our auntie's bedside. During the nighttime, a special nurse whom we had hired tended to the patient's needs. Xu, who visited me during these days, took his turn at this long, last watch. In short, we watched and we hoped. In vain. Nothing we did helped Auntie Bessie recover. Her time had come and she died.

After Auntie Bessie's death, we discovered that she had set aside some savings for her old age. Since she no longer needed earthly treasures, the family council decided that my three cousins and I would share the inheritance. We mailed Yvonne's portion to her—she lived in Anhui Province; how she spent it, we never heard. One cousin who lived nearby bought a color television and a second purchased a hi-fi system. Not me. I held on tightly to my unexpected treasure, for I remembered my auntie had always wanted me to get an education. No pottage for me. My thoughts turned to my future. *Maybe I can use my Auntie Bessie's special gift to further my schooling. . . .*

This dream began to materialize when American friends talked with my Uncle John and me about possibilities and arrangements. Early on, we considered the University of Illinois in Champaign-Urbana. At the same time, Dr. Tennison, my father's friend from their Texas seminary days, wrote my father and said that he too would assist me. He contacted the people at North Texas State University, an institution with a good reputation for its music program, and asked about harp scholarships. Hopefully, one of these schools would serve as my sponsor and sign my I-20 form. Otherwise, I would not be able to get a student visa.

But before any graduate school would admit me, I needed to demonstrate my language proficiency on the "Test of English as a Foreign Language" (TOEFL). My deceased auntie had taught me the English alphabet, but I hadn't learned much more than that from her. Hardly enough for proficiency! Eventually, one of my friend's mothers agreed to teach me English and prepare me for the test. We met weekly for ten months while I attempted to understand and assimilate as much as possible. This, combined with my other responsibilities, gave me an unenviable schedule. I worked full-time; I was a weekend mother; and I studied at night. Fortunately, I had a good instructor. She researched the TOEFL and showed me how to answer questions even when, as the Americans would say, "it looks like Chinese to me." It worked. I scored over 400, which was close to passing. Bureaucratically, that was what I needed; this meant that those in power approved my application for a passport visa. Substantively, however, I understood my linguistic deficiencies; I hardly knew the language in which I hoped to pursue graduate studies. For the present, that small matter would have to wait. I had done my best.

Now I needed to select a school. Should I choose Illinois or North Texas State? An uncle lived in Chicago, but that was some distance from Champaign-Urbana. How could I be secure in the center of Illinois if no one lived close by to help me find my way in an unknown land? Texas seemed more appealing on this score. Dr. Tennison was already helping me out, not because of obligations that stemmed from his friendship with my father, but because he knew and cared for me. This was a matter of the heart. My father chimed in and agreed that I should go to school in Texas. He trusted his former roommate to serve as an adoptive uncle to his little girl. He also thought that his longtime friends at Southwestern Seminary might be able to do me some good.

Everything was falling into place. The Shanghai Jiao Tong University, an engineering school that was beginning a fine arts program, invited my husband to join their faculty. Xu accepted the invitation and moved from Hangzhou to Shanghai. My auntie's bequest—I considered it a gift from God—provided me with enough money to buy my plane ticket and thus get started on my studies. The advice from Dr. Tennison and Daddy made good sense. I would attend North Texas State. My entire family accompanied me to the airport. Mama cried. I promised her I would return home in two years. I still remember her reply. "I'm sure you are a woman of your word, Nettie. But I'm less sure that I will be alive to welcome you back. Still, I understand that you must go." After repeated good-byes and hugs, I boarded my plane.

The first leg of my trip started out like a Chinese opera but ended up as a sweet and sensible song. Before I left China, my father had arranged for one of his former choir members to look after me when my flight landed in San Francisco. She would meet me in the airport, help me buy my plane tickets to Louisiana, and let me stay with her for several days while I adjusted as best I could to the changes. Also, again before I had left China, Pastor "J" had called his wife and older son, now residents of California, and told them about my impending visit. The boy, now a man, had been my close friend since childhood.

Now, while I was on the plane, the son called his father and got the name, the address, and the phone number of the woman who was to pick me up at the airport. Also, while I was still on the plane, the son called my prospective hostess and modified our arrival plans. The two of them would both meet me at the airport. Then he would pick me up, take me to his home in Fresno, and, in due course, return me to San Francisco for my visit with my prospective hostess. There was, of course, no way that I could know about the new plans.

When I landed, my original hostess and I connected quickly, probably because we had pictures of each other. The second connection, the one with Pastor J's son, did not go so smoothly. My friend and I waited outside an airport door for thirty minutes and studied faces. Eventually we gave up and drove to her home. At that point, we received a call from Pastor J's son. Although he had been in the airport all this time, he had never recognized me. After talking, we agreed that he should come to my hostess's home and pick me up. When he arrived, I recognized him from the airport, but not from my childhood. He had changed too much.

Thereafter, he took me to Fresno to meet his mother. The three of us spent Saturday together; on Sunday, I joined them at their church. Finally, we returned to San Francisco, where I enjoyed my originally scheduled visit. *Such an exciting time, and this is only the beginning!*

Afterward, I took the bus back to San Francisco and caught a plane to my final destination. I avoided talking with people during the flight, for I understood virtually nothing of what they could have said. At last, our plane set down in Louisiana. Dr. Tennison's wife and several older ladies met me at the airport. She offered an explanation and apologies for her husband's absence: he was busy at a Southern Baptist board meeting. Afterward, we got in her car and drove to West Monroe. I expected America to be rich and fascinating, with its cars, its highways, its fast-paced life, and more. But expectations and realities are never the same. As I took in all the new sights, I felt like I was an actress in the movies.

I woke up my second morning in Louisiana to the sounds of discordant yet sweet music. The birds, oblivious to my presence, were heralding in the day. Such a strange chorus for a Chinese woman! Back in my country, where we caught and ate these poor creatures, a city girl like me rarely heard such serenades. The wonders continued when I walked into my hosts' dining room and looked out their big window and into their yard. There, I saw the rabbits as they nibbled on the grass and the squirrels as they chattered away. I had much to learn about this alien yet inviting new country.

Even before we got settled at home, Mrs. Tennison treated me as if I were her own daughter. She took me with her to visit with her friends and she brought me to every church meeting. Her husband returned home, as she predicted, within a few days after my arrival. Together, they asked me to call them "uncle" and "aunt," a custom that accorded with the Chinese tradition of respect. Their church organized a back-to-school party for me and gave me pencils, paper, and much more. One church member, a woman who owned a dress shop, gave me an entire wardrobe. This included seasonal ware, outfits for special occasions, and even undergarments. In short, these hospitable people virtually adopted me. How could I reciprocate to all those who cared for me in so many ways? I felt deeply indebted and undeserving. When I explained my feelings to Dr. Tennison, he responded as only an uncle might speak. "God has been gracious to me. My two children have graduated from college. I have no pressing needs. And I have more than enough money. Normally, I give 10 percent of my earnings to the church as a tithe, and another 10 percent as a love offering. Now, you're just like my child. I want to use some of God's gifts to help provide for you." I had no answer to his generosity or to that of others in his congregation who contributed to "my fund."

After I had stayed with Dr. and Mrs. Tennison for several weeks, my adoptive aunt and uncle drove me to North Texas State University. A special late August for me. I watched the fascinating sights as we drove through Shreveport and then on through Dallas. Shortly thereafter we stopped, rented two motel rooms, and spent the night. The second day of our trip we drove on to Denton. I expected the American university, like its Chinese counterpart, to be surrounded by walls. Those who belonged would be admitted through the gate; all others would be prohibited from trespassing on what was essentially "private" property. When we drove onto the campus, I asked my "uncle" where the wall was. He explained that these were not needed.

As my first steps in getting started, I had to check in at the admissions office and take an English proficiency test. This time my TOEFL tricks didn't help me: I failed. *Now everyone knows about my linguistic deficiencies. Embarrassing and worrisome. What will I do?* As a sensible response to my score, the university required me to take an intensive course in the language school at the outset my work. Hesitatingly, I told my uncle about my unexpected additional costs of $1400 per semester. "Don't you worry, Nettie," he replied. "God looks after our needs. Yesterday, an out-of-state man visited our church. He wrote a big check and gave me his permission to use it as I saw fit. So I put his $1400 check into your church fund." Words could not express my gratitude to God and his generous messenger for their care.

Soon, I discovered that I had problems with my I-20 form. It looked like I would have to attend the University of Illinois for a semester and then transfer to North Texas State. Fortunately, some school officials in Denton came to my rescue. They would help me deal with the demands of the Immigration Office. They showed me how to fill out the appropriate forms, including a request to change my sponsoring university. Done. Now they told me to stay here in Denton until they heard from the Immigration Office. While all of this was going on, North Texas State offered me a harp scholarship. This meant that they would count me as a resident and I would only have to pay in-state fees.

My course schedule for fall semester 1982 seemed manageable. Each morning I studied English at the language school. Each afternoon I attended two classes. Once a week I took my harp lesson. That would leave me with large blocks of time for study and for practice.

We still had to find me a place to live. The International Students' Office had warned Dr. Tennison against having me share a room with Chinese students. "If you place her with people from her country," they had explained, "the group will resort to their native tongue. If Nettie ends up in such a situation, her English proficiency will never improve." Sage advice. We sought housing recommendations at the First Baptist Church of Denton and at the Baptist Student Union. They came up with three possibilities. The first place, the home of an eighty-two-year-old woman who was a member of First Baptist, was located right across from the university. Dr. Tennison went with me as we knocked on Mrs. Campbell's door. I visited with her, looked her room over, and decided that this was the place for me. On the matter of food, they worked out a special deal. She would feed me and then report her total monthly food expenses to Dr. Tennison. He would divide that figure in half and pay for my board.

Dr. Tennison also took me to the Baptist Student Union and introduced me to some of the people in that organization. A wise move on the part of my uncle, for he rightly anticipated my need for friendship and spiritual support when he and his wife returned to Louisiana. "This will be like a home for you, Nettie," he assured me. "These good people will provide you with anything you need." During uncle's introductions, several of these kind Baptists, including the director himself, extended their warm welcomes to me. Later, I would benefit from their hospitality and generosity.

Now that everything was in order, the Tennisons left Denton for West Monroe. Although I knew some people in Denton, I still felt lonesome. Mrs. Campbell tried to help out as she graciously invited me to call her "grandmother." Unfortunately, I couldn't understand this grandmother very well. She talked too fast and she spoke with a Texas accent. Before the tears came, I sought the solitude of my room. *I'm so lonely, even though I know that God is with me.* After a good cry I decided that I would make the best of my two years in Texas. I would study diligently, and I would get to know God and the Bible better. I concluded that evening with a short word of commitment and supplication. "Dear Lord," I prayed, "I will do the best that I can on my studies. As a loving Father, I ask You to take care of me."

My second day in Denton I had little trouble in finding my way to the University School of Music. But later, when I tried to retrace my steps, the route home eluded me. Alone and also lost. Shame prevented me from asking directions from strangers. So I wandered around and around until, in time, I found my way back to Grandmother's house.

When I took the placement test at the language school, my scores spoke for themselves. "Linguistically challenged." They started me out at level three in hopes that I would progress all the way through level six. For all practical purposes, then, I was little better than mute. But with the help of teachers and in the company of friends, I slowly began to understand this strange western language. Within a month, I was promoted to level four at school. These studies bore fruit at home when I realized one morning that I could understand what Grandmother was saying to me. There the two of us sat, eating breakfast together in the family room or, less frequently, on the patio. There we watched the news on television. Similarly, my breakthrough on television came in about a month. Amazing! I could understand the broadcasters' lingo. When I came home for noon lunches, Grandmother turned the TV to "All My Children." What a fun story! And even better than such simple "fun," I was no longer linguistically challenged. My landlord friend had helped me so much. I reciprocated in small ways—including washing our dirty dishes.

Although I was far from being a native speaker, I could at least communicate with my new friends. This served me well when Mrs. Campbell's entire family—her two daughters and her son, his wife, and their three children—came for a visit. Since some of the son's children were married and had their own families, we had four generations present together in a single place. Here, in our home, these hospitable folk made me feel comfortable. It was almost as if they accepted me as a close member of their clan.

Apart from the Campbells, new friends from several churches welcomed and nurtured me as a member of their communities. At the weekly BSU meetings, I came to love the prayer, the Bible study, and the fellowship. Soon, my BSU friends invited me to visit First Baptist, their home church. I readily accepted their invitation, for I hoped to participate in worship and learn more about the Scriptures. For a short while, I attended three Sunday services in three different churches. I started at 8 A.M., when one of my English teachers picked me up and brought me to a Bible study class at her Bible Church. Afterward, she dropped me off at the First Baptist Church for my 9:30 A.M. Sunday school. And for a month or so, I participated in the 11 A.M. worship hour. In time, I discovered that Grace Baptist Church hosted a group of Chinese students. At that point, I sometimes skipped worship at First Baptist and walked quickly over to Grace. Here, I enjoyed the company of my fellow countrymen. In all of this, transportation was no problem. Sometimes I walked home; at other times I caught a ride.

One fall day the heavy rain and the drop in temperature signaled a more permanent change in the weather. When I walked home from school that day, Dr. and Mrs. Tennison met me outside my front door. I invited them inside, and they explained the reason for their unannounced visit. "We checked the weather reports and bought you a pair of warm shoes." Special care comes in small packages. How could I express my thanks? Before my uncle and aunt left, they checked in at the university and made sure that all was going well.

Central to my visit to the States was my study at the university. Ultimately, that's why I was here in Denton. When I talked with my advisors about graduate classes, they asked me what I wanted to learn. *So different from China, where our teachers decide what they want to teach their students. Something to write home about!* When I signed up for harp lessons, my instructor repeated the same question—"What is it, Nettie, that you want to learn?"—and offered me good advice. "Nettie, let me encourage you to set yourself some clear goals as you begin and progress in your studies." I followed through on that advice and started setting myself lots of goals. *This new approach to schooling is good. I couldn't have made a better choice!*

It was also a demanding program, even for those who spoke English fluently. Given my limited facility with the English language, I had to work doubly hard. Since I understood only bits and pieces of what went on in class, with the professor's permission I recorded the lectures. Also, fellow students let me copy their notes. I relied heavily upon my dictionary as I compared what they had written, what I had on tape, and what I read in the text. It probably took me two to three hours to work my way through a text that others could read in half an hour. Snails might have moved more quickly than me through this review process. After this review, I moved on to my music and my English language homework. No one could have envied my study schedule. I hit the books until midnight and rose at 6 A.M. for breakfast. After eating, I walked to the Music School where I practiced my harp until I began my 8 A.M. English lessons. I ate my lunch at noon and then I attended my two music classes. When I had the time in the late afternoons and early evenings, I practiced my harp. At last, when the clock struck seven, I left campus and walked home.

Grandma and I ate our supper together and chatted. Then it was back to the books. No grass grew under my feet.

Still, I took a short break during the Thanksgiving vacation. The Tennisons, suspecting that I might be lonesome, sent me a plane ticket so that I could spend the holiday in West Monroe with them. Just what I needed! Refreshed, I returned to Denton for the final weeks of school, exams, and "judgment." I received straight "A's" at the Music School. I also took and passed the TOEFL. The instructors at the language school recognized my progress, skipped me up two levels, and then let me graduate. As icing on the cake, the Immigration Office said I could stay at North Texas State. God had answered my prayers and cared for me.

Christmas vacation proved to be special. Once again the Tennisons invited me to their home; once again my uncle paid for my plane ticket. Such a Christmas! Blinking lights, colored lights, holly, decorations everywhere. So exciting! And then the Tennisons' daughter Carol and her two children came for the holidays. For the present, we enjoyed one another's company. In the future, we would become near sisters. On Christmas Eve we all attended the music program at our church. The following morning we opened gifts. Hanging on the mantel over the fireplace, I discovered a "Nettie stocking" that a church member had made. Under the tree I found one present after another, beautifully wrapped, for me. My "aunt," Carol, and church friends spoiled me with their generosity.

After the Tennisons and I enjoyed a few sedentary Christmas vacation days together in Louisiana, we hit the road. We started out with a Tennison reunion in West Texas. So many relatives! The clan welcomed me and treated me as if we had shared the same blood.

After the reunion, we drove to Wichita, Texas, Mrs. Tennison's hometown. The grandparents and grandchildren took one car and Carol and I rode in the other. She and I took advantage of the quiet to get better acquainted and to deepen our friendship. I told her stories about my life in response to her many questions. Then I took on the role of questioner. But only temporarily, for the decorations and lights in Wichita captured my attention: they resembled a winter wonderland. Wonderful! They had arranged their parks to tell the tales of Hansel and Gretel, Cinderella, and more.

On the way back to Dallas, a heavy snow created hazardous road conditions. My chauffeur, recognizing the dangers, made a reasonable request. "We better watch out, Nettie. Slick streets will increase our chances of having an accident. For safety's sake, I recommend that you lie down on the back seat." A sensible recommendation, but not for me. This was the first big snow I had ever seen. I had to sit up and watch. Fortunately, we made it safely to Denton, where I dropped my presents off at Grandmother's house and then continued on to the Dallas Airport.

My itinerary called for yet one more trip, a visit with Uncle John and his family in Chicago. This would be my first time to meet Auntie Christina and my cousins Evelyn and Philip. Apart from one important conversation, this proved to be a pleasant and uneventful trip. In that conversation, my uncle stressed the importance of computers. "Maybe, Nettie," he said, "you should combine computers and music education. Then, when you return to China, you will be prepared for a brand new era." With this wise counsel Uncle John clearly anticipated the computer revolution.

I brought Uncle John's idea back with me to Denton where I began my second semester of school. Since I had successfully completed my basic language studies, I was now qualified for graduate school. At this point I needed to declare my specialties. I considered majoring in harp, but in the end I thought better of it. Instead, I chose a music education major and a computer minor. Education was important in China. And with the right kind of education, one in which my people could discover what was best for themselves, we might reverse our pattern of blindly following the leader.

Before classes began, I took a series of diagnostic tests. I passed ear training, sight singing, and the fundamentals of theory. So far, so good. Then I moved on to the music history exam, which was divided into pre-baroque, baroque to the twentieth century, and contemporary music. I scored well on the baroque, but failed the other two sections. These failures meant I had to take a heavy course load.

I registered for classes in music history and computers, and for English 401 (which would not count toward my degree). Although I had graduated from language school, my English was still far from perfect. So I limped along slowly, relying upon my dictionary for the definition of almost every word—or that's what it seemed like. Whereas the study of music drew at least partially upon the imagination, computers depended upon a flawless scientific logic. I could work for three hours on a single program and then it wouldn't work. Somewhere along the way I had misspelled a single word. But which one? If only I could find someone to help me. This semester proved to be even more demanding than the previous one. I worked so hard and so long that I frequently got only four hours of sleep at night. One Saturday, however, I got an unplanned break. While I was studying in the library, I became engrossed with all of the fascinating things. When I came to my senses and checked the time, it was 9 P.M. *No more of this! I can't afford such luxuries in the future.*

Unless it's spring break and someone else picks up the bill. Mr. and Mrs. Hestekind, people whom I knew in the Seattle area, bought me a plane ticket and invited me to spend my holiday with them. Years ago, in association with my grandfather's church, they had worked as missionaries in China. In the end, they had been among the last to be expelled from my country. It seemed at the time that we would never see them again. But now, more than thirty years after their expulsion, they welcomed the woman they had known as "Little Nettie" into their home. Later, they showed me around their island, brought me to church with them, and took me to visit an Indian reservation. I left the American northwest with a deep appreciation for its beauty and my friends' hospitality.

Even though Dr. Tennison paid my tuition and my room and board, and even though I now worked part-time in the library, my finances remained tight. On one occasion I had only ten dollars to see me through the month. After I bought stamps and envelopes—I had to write home—I had only seven dollars left. When I went to church on Sunday, I wondered whether I should give an offering. *I've got so little to get by on. Surely God doesn't expect me to become a beggar. On the other hand, I know that God expects generosity, not miserliness, from his people.* Such a struggle! In the end, I put my tenth in the offering plate. An odd way to gain a sense of release. The next day, I received a hundred-dollar gift in the mail. This was more than pocket money.

Mary Walker[1] and her husband also helped me out. Years ago, they and my father had been classmates at Southwestern Seminary. After graduation, this couple had accepted an appointment as missionaries to Japan. Now, as their current furlough came to a close, we arranged a time when we could get together in Denton. Unfortunately, we had to postpone our visit because Mr. Walker had unexpected open-heart surgery. Eventually, however, we got together just before my friends had to leave for their Asian home. Before we parted, they emptied their pockets and gave me all of their American money. When I protested, they explained that they had no need for useless currency in Japan. In the end, I accepted their explanation and their generous gift. In these special ways my father's friends, members of my larger Christian family, served as God's agents in caring for me.

I enjoyed my company and my trips, but I still had to pass my courses. The pre-baroque period in my music history class was especially difficult. I knew nothing about Roman Catholicism or the Mass, the form of Christian faith and worship that dominated the music of the period. So I took extra measures to make sure I could understand the material. With permission, I copied the notes of the woman who sat next to me and I recorded the lectures. Outside of class, I showed up regularly in the library and listened to the appropriate music. Before our first exam, our instructor reviewed the material with us. In addition to that, a friend who studied with me helped me in important ways. Then we faced judgment: the exam. As our instructor returned our exams, she noted that only three of fifty students had earned an "A." She also insisted that those who had earned a "B" had done quite well. "I just want you all to know," she concluded, "that Nettie Ma received an 'A.'" The friend with whom I had studied noted that she had only earned a "B." Our professor, who knew about our preparation together, playfully explained my superior grade: "It must have been that Nettie took her notes in Chinese." By the end of the spring semester, when final grades were distributed, I had done "very well" and earned a "B" in this course.

To complicate matters, I felt my thyroid problem coming on again. The doctor at the university medical center gave me a blood test, diagnosed my condition, and prescribed the proper medicines to bring my condition under control. Healthy once again.

After I completed two sessions of summer school, Dr. Tennison bought me a plane ticket to Louisiana. Their place, my home away from home, offered me the rest and relaxation I needed. I was glad to be in West Monroe again, or so I thought. When I learned that my uncle and aunt needed to be away for a week, I moved temporarily into another lady's home. No one expected any trouble, for I had spent a few uneventful days with her on another occasion.

During my temporary visit, this lady drove to Shreveport to pick up her cousin, a woman who couldn't drive because she was afflicted with Alzheimer's. Thereafter, the three of us, my hostess, her cousin, and I, stayed together. Although the cousin's memory was impaired, I expected no trouble. Then one day my hostess called me into her cousin's room and asked me what seemed like an innocent question. "Nettie, we've looked around for my cousin's watch and we can't find it. Did you happen to see it?"

"I'm sorry, but I haven't seen it," I replied.

Then she reframed her question, this time in a way that was hardly innocent. "How much would a watch like that sell for in China, Nettie?"

The implications of that question were clear. I was the chief suspect in the case of the missing watch. Again, I spoke forthrightly. "We don't sell watches like that in China. Moreover, I have a watch of my own that works quite well." The implications of her accusation also brought tears to my eyes, so I returned to my room where I could cry in private.

In time, they found that watch under the cousin's mattress. Vindicated. I was no thief. Even though the cloud of suspicion had disappeared, I found it hard to repair the emotional consequences of that incident. Thus, I anxiously awaited the Tennisons' return and the unquestioning hospitality of their home. Although at first I had wanted to tell them this story, I eventually decided to say nothing about it. I needed to learn forgiveness by myself.

In time my accuser sent me regular gifts and I responded with cards. She was doing what she could to heal our relationship. Even so, my sense of injury has remained.

Despite this unwelcome incident, my summer ended on a high note. When I had first come to the United States, my father's California friends had recommended that I apply for a P.E.O. Scholarship. At last, that application bore fruit. They awarded me the money and honored me with the Mrs. George Anderson Peace Honor Scholarship. The $2000 that accompanied this award, together with my harp scholarship, covered my entire tuition for the next year. I felt pleased to tell Dr. Tennison that I could now take care of these expenses.

I got to know these P.E.O. folks on a Saturday in late August. Three women, Mrs. (Myrtle) W. H. Williams, Mrs. Kathryn Carpenter, and Mrs. Gloria Hall, came from Dallas to visit me in Denton. They represented the branch of P.E.O. that had sponsored me. Later, they invited me and other international students into their homes. Thus, yet another "family" had adopted me. Later, I attended a national P.E.O. meeting where I performed on the harp for them.[2]

My classes for fall 1983 were as demanding as usual. Nothing new here. But as the semester drew to a close, I took a break for a trip to Florida. My sponsor on this occasion was Mrs. Tonnesen, a friend of my father's and a choir director in Daytona Beach. She invited me to give a concert, rented a harp for me, and covered my expenses. Afterward, she showed me some of the sights. This was my first time to see the ocean up close. So nice! I walked along the clean white sand and let the water cascade across my toes. Then the two of us headed inland, to Orlando and its manmade tourist attractions. Surprisingly, I enjoyed Epcot even more than the Magic Kingdom.

After Daytona, I returned to Denton for finals, and then on to Louisiana for sleep. I was exhausted. My second day at the Tennisons', I was supposed to attend a music rehearsal. As a precaution, I set two alarm clocks. Unfortunately, neither of them woke me up. My uncle and aunt let me be, for they realized that I needed my rest more than I needed the rehearsal. Eventually, I opened my eyes and climbed out from under the covers. Noon! Eventually, I caught up on my sleep, and that well before our Christmas celebrations and our annual trip to the Tennison reunion. This holiday brought me just what I needed: good food, happy times, long, sleep-filled nights, and special conversations with Carol. When January came, I returned to Denton for the last leg of my marathon.

This final semester, I hoped to take an overload. Only one clear rule stood in my way: "The maximum course load for a graduate student is twelve hours. Anyone who wants to take additional hours must secure the approval of the Academic Dean and the President of the University." Since I wanted to take sixteen hours, I set up an appointment with these high-level officials to explain my unusual request. During our visit I pointed to my special needs and circumstances. "I'll be returning to China at the end of the semester. In my country, there will be no opportunity for me to study advanced computer courses like those you offer at North Texas State. So while I'm here, I must learn as much as possible so that I can teach my people these important skills." After listening to my convincing speech, they granted me their permission to take the overload.

My heavy load allowed me little time for play or shopping. Still, I did take an occasional break. One Saturday, for example, Grandmother asked me to join her for a berry-picking expedition at her son's farm. She had suggested that we spend the entire day together. I wanted to go, but I also worried about the time commitment. "Maybe for half a day, Grandma. I've just got too much work to do." She understood and readily accepted my alternative. We had such fun that morning as we picked and ate the blueberries. Afterward, I parked in the library and worked on my studies.

On my birthday, I felt especially lonely. *Nobody here knows. Of that I am certain! And I miss my family so much!* I expected no congratulations, no cards, and no calls. But when I returned home from school the phone rang. For me! Alison Martin from the BSU wished me a happy birthday.

"How did you find out that today was my birthday?" I inquired.

"Simple. I checked the BSU records. It's right there. February 3rd: Nettie Ma's birthday. You and I need to do something special together. How about a make-up party?"

Impressive that foreigners would remember me. But what in the world is a "make-up" party?

Alison explained what this entailed—"It's about how to use cosmetics on your face"—and then came over to my apartment and picked me up. Up until this point, I had used nothing other than lipstick. Now, my friend showed me innumerable fine points about how American women beautify their faces. *This is turning out to be a better day than I had expected.*

After we finished our party, Alison made some mysterious phone calls. I had no clue what she was up to. When we stopped the car in front of my house, I noticed that all the apartment lights were out. I assumed that Grandma had gone to bed. Thus, I thought nothing was unusual when Alison walked me to the door. But then I stepped inside, where someone turned on the lights and shouted "Surprise!" I looked around and saw so many people who had come by to celebrate my birthday with me. And to top it off, Vivian had baked a cake. *You have blessed me, O Lord, in so many ways. You have turned my night into morning.*

My father was invited to give a lecture in Chicago at the MENC[3] in March 1984, a time when he was back in the States. He suggested that I fly there to meet him; his friend, Dr. Lawson, offered me accommodations. We both enjoyed the father-daughter reunion. I also listened to Daddy's impressive speech at the convention. When I returned to Denton, I took the GRE. Several Chinese students and I had worked together to prepare for this exam. Fortunately, my high math scores more than compensated for my low language scores. With this hurdle out of the way, it was possible for me to be a graduate student in good standing.

Before my father returned to China, one of his former students invited Daddy and me to come visit him in Toronto. By now I understood the bureaucratic procedures and followed them to the "T." I applied at the Dallas Emigration Office for permission to leave the country. When they gave me the "okay" on that, our Canadian friend bought our tickets. Too late, we discovered that my father's visa would not allow him to make the trip. Thus, I traveled alone to Toronto. I knew, however, that my host would not be a total stranger, for during his student days in China when I had been a little girl we had known each other. When he and I met at the airport, I explained my father's absence. The highlight of this trip came when my host and his wife took me to visit Niagara Falls. Crashing blue water. Mist floating in the air. Spectacular! When it was time for me to return home, my host and his wife dropped me off at the airport. I expected no trouble, but then I learned that I had to go through customs. These officials checked my papers and discovered that I had no financial sponsor. I gave them Dr. Tennison's name, and then Uncle John's name, but neither of these worked. Things seemed hopeless and frightening, for the officials absolutely refused to allow me to return to the States. *"Dear Lord," I prayed, "I really need your help now! I'm stuck!"* At the last minute, just before my plane took off, the customs officers relented and let me climb on board. I looked forward to landing in Dallas and completing my studies in Denton.

I brought my graduate work to a close in May 1984. I had completed fifty-three hours of credit with a 3.57 GPA. North Texas State University nominated me for membership in "Who's Who Among Students in American Universities and Colleges, 1983–84." Before the actual graduation ceremony, many friends and relatives from China called and advised me to stay in the United States. When they learned that I would be coming home, they thought I was stupid for not paying attention to their wise counsel. I was, however, neither stupid nor deaf. I simply wanted to bring back to my people the knowledge and the skills I had learned in America. I had also made a promise to my mother.

But I still had some business to tend to before I walked across the graduation platform and received my degree. My Chinese friends asked me whether I had found time to shop at the Dallas-Denton Mall. They guessed rightly. I had never made a single excursion to this modern Texas landmark. They insisted that I go with one of them and see this expansive and wonderful shopper's delight. I'm glad I did.

I also had an important errand of mercy before I returned to my home in China. Mr. Williams, the husband of my P.E.O. friend, was suffering from a serious bout with cancer. I borrowed a harp from my school while Kathryn, a member of P.E.O., borrowed a van. The two of us drove together to the hospital and stopped by to see our sick friend. There he lay, asleep in his bed, with an oxygen mask over his face. Both the doctor and the nurse reminded us of the rules: "No noise or musical instruments may be played in this room." At this point Mr. Williams woke up. Although he felt weak, he asked me to play for him. "Nettie's harp," he suggested, "will either bring me down to earth or send me on to heaven." So much for the rules. I played familiar songs for thirty minutes. Later, someone told us that a woman who was just being wheeled out of surgery heard my music and thought that she was in heaven. Her comments gave us all a good laugh.

In time, the doctor released Mr. Williams from the hospital and sent him home to recover. Once again I stopped by; this time I stayed for two nights and two days. Mrs. Williams spoke frankly and encouragingly to me about her husband's condition. Before my hospital visit, he had repeatedly cried out in pain. But by the time of my stay at their home, he had stopped his outbursts. Apparently my "harp therapy" had brought him some relief from his suffering. Indeed, he felt well enough for the three of us to attend a service at their church. But on the way home from that tiring trip, we had to stop to rest in a nearby place.[4]

Well before I returned home, the celebrating and ceremonies dominated the days. Before graduation, the president of the university honored the "Who's Who" students with an American tea party. Mrs. Williams attended as my guest. When we finished these preliminaries, we moved on to graduation. What a new and exhilarating experience for a Chinese woman. We lined up, walked onto the stage when they called our names, received our diplomas, and flipped our tassels over to the left side of our caps. After graduation, the BSU, intent on sharing in the good times, threw a huge picnic for all the Baptist graduates of the university. Finally, still in the month of May, Grandma called a family get-together in my honor. Her son and two daughters, husbands, children, grandchildren, and more came to offer me their congratulations. One "granddaughter-in-law" gave me a bracelet on which I recognized the engraved word "Campbell." Then, as a special "extra," she explained the meaning behind the gift. "No matter where you live, Nettie, you will always belong to the Campbell family." I could not forget those words, and the ceremonies, or what the ceremonies represented when I returned home to my family and my country.

Even after graduation I was not quite ready to abandon my tourist avocation. I called, one last time, on Mr. and Mrs. Bratton, a Fort Worth couple with whom I had often visited during my two-year stint in the States. On this occasion I still followed the Chinese tradition of respect: I addressed them as "Uncle Bill" and "Aunt Lucile." After having lived two years in America, I suppose I could have called them by their formal names. But I was not yet thoroughly Americanized. Even more important than this, "Aunt Lucile" had taught my father voice years ago when they were together at Southwestern Seminary. Senior professors deserve respect.

From much further away, Xu's youngest brother and his wife bought me a plane ticket and invited me to visit New York. How could I refuse a trip to this famed city, especially since some of my friends and relatives lived there? I had so much to do and see. I spent an entire day at the Metropolitan Museum and took in a musical play on Broadway. I also secured a standing-room-only ticket for a performance of the opera "War and Peace" and found a seat after the show began. Later, Mrs. Tonnesen, my Florida friend, picked me up in the city and brought me to visit her son at Huntington Station on Long Island.

Toward the end of my New York tour, one of my father's three surviving classmates from Nanjing University invited me to take a side trip to Washington, DC. How could I miss this chance to see the Capitol? I took so many pictures, here and elsewhere. But now my time was running short. I had to return home and present my scheduled lecture for the National Normal School Convention in Fujian.

12

"A Time to Sow, a Time to Weep"

1984–1986

In the mid-1980s, Deng Xiaoping and key political allies faced significant opposition from their more conservative comrades. Even so, Deng and his pragmatist Marxists successfully set a reforming agenda for China. So, for example, China witnessed increased foreign trade and tourism, urban reforms, and a British agreement to return Hong Kong to China. But inflation, a black market, and periodic demonstrations for greater freedom also accompanied these economic reforms.

In an equally important sphere of society, teachers and students appreciated the reformers' attempts to reinvigorate the schools. Here, Chinese leaders encouraged professional societies, research, cooperation with foreign experts, and more. They allowed considerable independence in scholarship, pedagogy, and learning—an independence of which Nettie took full use.

My entire family, Xu, our two daughters, and my parents, welcomed me at the Shanghai airport. There, we celebrated our reunion even as we began the process of getting reacquainted and resettled. The conservatory limousine, really only a van, "chauffeured" us home in style. We stopped first at the tiny apartment the school had provided for me, and, after I left, for Xu. It was a familiar yet strange place. When I had lived in the States, I had become accustomed to good lighting. But now we walked through a dark hall and then up the dark stairs. I felt crowded, and I negotiated my way with difficulty. Still, we avoided accidents. Soon, we set my luggage inside the front door and then headed on to my parents' place. The girls had lived there during my two-year absence.

Home again. It too was familiar and yet strange. Before I had left for China, this familial apartment had seemed so roomy. Somehow, during my two-year absence, it had shrunk. With the exception of the problems of lights, I eventually adjusted to the realities that defined my homeland. Now, as the five of us ate supper together, we had so much to talk about. Those conversations only dimly reflected the excitement we felt. At midnight, we called it a day, and Xu and I returned to our apartment.

Outside and inside, I made do. Xu had fixed up a bicycle for me to use. It gave me just the right kind of transportation for our crowded city. Except for after the sun went down: our streets also had no lights. Apart from our one single bed, our little apartment resembled a storage room. All of my belongings from Hangzhou, together with those pieces of furniture I had "inherited" from Auntie Bessie, took up more than enough space. Amid all this, we stacked five big boxes of books. Dr. McGuire, one of my professors from the States, had asked members of MENC for extras, and then had sent them on to me. In time, I picked out those I wanted and gave the rest to the libraries at the conservatory, Shanghai Jiao Tong University, and the Shanghai Xingzhi Normal School.

The high-level music professionals in the Chinese normal schools paid me a visit on my second day back in the country. Their own importance was indisputable. They reedited the music textbooks and supervised the national music educators' convention in Fujian. However, since their schools offered no graduate education, they wisely knew their own limitations. Now they could remediate their deficiencies and learn from a woman who had studied for two years in the United States (this included my six months of intensive language work), a woman who was the only person in China with a M. Ed. At the upcoming national convention they had scheduled four workshops: one for music appreciation, one for music and politics, one for choirs (my father would lead this), and a yet-unnamed workshop for me. They wanted to hear what I had to say.

After due reflection, I decided that I would speak about comprehensive musicianship and creative teaching methods. Traditional Chinese presuppositions and patterns of instruction in music would provide the backdrop for the new alternative I would commend to them. For decades (or perhaps even longer), we Chinese had equated musical proficiency with technique. Or, to put it another way, we believed technique is the beginning and end of the entire process. In practice, this boiled down to five simple, successive pedagogical steps. First, the teacher organized the class. This included taking attendance and compelling all children to behave. Second, she revised the old lesson. Third, she explained the new lesson. Fourth, she concluded her instruction with the main point of the lesson. And fifth, she assigned homework to her students. Throughout China, this pedagogical "orthodoxy" prevailed. In this, the teacher took the initiative and the student remained passive. The teacher set the criteria for success and then evaluated student learning through exams. If the student performed poorly, too bad; and if the student performed well, so much the better. In contrast to this, I would argue that a comprehensive approach to music education starts differently and advances well beyond technique. From the beginning, I would insist that our students must actively analyze and create music.

I would explain my approach to music education, the one I had learned in the States, in terms of five alternative principles. My presentation would take my listeners in a different direction. First, the instructor should encourage "free exploration." Early on, I would explain, when we teach our students about high and low pitches, we might try the following experiment: Set out drinking glasses with varying degrees of water in them and then let the students tap each one and listen for the differences in pitch. Afterward, the children might sing "high" and "low" for themselves. Second, we should emphasize "guided exploration." For this, we should use the Kodaly Method and we should have our students "play" Orff instruments. As they play, they should listen carefully to the different sounds. Third, we should reinforce our earlier instruction with "exploratory improvisation." In this, the students adopt two or more pitches that they have heard on the Orff instrument and then play musical games. These games will help them incorporate what they have been doing into their thought. Fourth, we should direct our students toward "planned improvisation." In this, we ask our students for reflection and design before they play their instruments. Fifth and finally, we should stress "reinforcement." In this, we must get our students involved in their music. If we succeed in this principle, they will learn pitch by themselves. In my alternative, students take the initiative. A teacher will find instruction more difficult because she must know every student well in order to help them with their work. She uses the five principles, not to determine grades, but to encourage student progress in ability and creativity.

Those who organized the national convention wanted the participants to see how I fleshed out my principles in practice. So they asked me to teach a few classes while others could observe me at work. My workshop went well, even though in age and social composition my students reflected considerable diversity. In short, as the observers watched me at work with thirty to forty children, they developed an enthusiasm for what I was doing. In particular, they picked up on my strategies for involving my temporary charges. In addition to my successes, we heard my father's choir sing at the end of the convention. It was apparent that his workshop had gone equally well.

Soon, the music educators asked me to take on a position of leadership from my home base in Shanghai. In my initial assignment, I worked with three kindergartens, two elementary schools, and one normal school. In each place, I concentrated on the education of children. My friends and a famous doctor followed me around to "test" my students. This was relatively easy because each school divided its students into two groups, each equal in background. In the end, I chose to focus on rural kindergartners who had no musical background.

At this point I started my research program on the relationship between children's intelligence and music education. My traditional counterparts established discipline and the axiom that anything that the teacher says must be right. Unlike them, I began my instruction on the first day with free exploration. As expected, some disorder followed. Indeed, even the principal stopped by my class to hear the noise. That disorder continued during recess. My students didn't stay in a straight line.

As we walked past the trashcans, they banged them to see what kinds of sounds they made.

That first day I also gave my students an unusual homework assignment. "When you go home," I said, "you must discover two different sounds, one high and one low." The next morning many parents came by to find out what the new teacher was up to. When I asked them what had provoked their questions, they remarked that their children were making all sorts of noises at home. I picked up on this as I explained my assignment. "One child," I noted, "told me that when he turns on the water it makes a high pitch." I pressed him to distinguish whether it might have been loud and not high. As I interrogated other children about their experiments, sometimes they were right and other times they were wrong.

As the class progressed, I played my Orff instruments and invited the students to pay close attention to the pitches. "When the notes are high," I charged them, "you must stand. And when the notes are low, you must sit." They listened carefully, compared the sounds, and entered enthusiastically into the fun. They also tried to determine whether there was a pattern to what I was doing. In short, we played musical games. I asked the children to listen for when I came "home" to the "so" pitch, and then to match it with their voices. I asked them to fly balloons that made different sounds. I organized them into competitive groups, a pedagogical strategy that energized them. I let them try out my xylophone and attempt to recognize the "so," "mi," and "la" notes. In the end, most of my students had perfect pitch.

On planned improvisation, we adopted a Chinese version of "I've Got a Secret." One by one, the students devised a plan, whispered their secret in my ear, and played their music. During the solo performance, the others listened attentively, for they knew I would require them to repeat what they had heard. Afterward, I taught them the song "Little Tadpole Finds Its Mommy." Sometimes I said the words to them and played the melody on the Orff instrument. Then I invited them to sing it back to me. We all had such fun together on this exercise.

When it came to conducting the "Tadpole" song, the children had their own ideas. I divided them into three groups and asked them to consider what dynamics they thought should be emphasized in this music. The first group decided that they wanted a big crescendo when the little frog[1] finds its mommy. The second group determined that at the beginning of the song, the little lost frog must cry out loudly for its mommy. In the end, when it found its mommy, they would conduct the music softly. The third group chose to begin loudly, soften the music toward the middle, and as the piece concluded, have a big crescendo. After they made their plans, I allowed each group to conduct the class. Now I was ready to teach my students the techniques of crescendo, diminuendo, and matching pitches. In the end, it all came together perfectly. Those who observed my work were duly impressed. Moreover, I didn't evaluate the students in terms of grades.

In addition to this research, my varied and demanding professional obligations eventually pushed me in directions I had not anticipated. I gave more than thirty lectures and workshops in numerous provinces. I published twenty articles in Chinese periodicals. The authorities asked me to teach in a satellite education program that they called "Western Teaching Methods, American Class." I objected to the incorrect and inappropriate course title, but I still agreed to help out. In this way I participated in the general reform movement as it embraced education.

At the same time, my interactions with foreigners and my reflections on paternal aphoristic wisdom led me, slowly and hesitantly, to consider additional education. These foreigners, professors from Harvard University, were investigating how Chinese students learn. Eventually, they planned to publish (in America) their findings from this Project Zero. When these distinguished visitors showed up in my class, they watched and we talked. Each day, teachers from many different provinces wrote and asked me questions about educational philosophy and psychology. The obvious, my ignorance and my need for further study, stared me in the face. But my heavy workload, which included my research program in Shanghai and my employment by the Research Institute of Shanghai Conservatory, made remediation impossible.

Now I remembered what Daddy had told me years ago. "When you graduate from elementary school, Nettie, you will think that you know everything in the world. When you graduate from high school, you will think that you know almost everything in the world. At this point, you will recognize that you need to develop just a little bit more, so you will go on to college. After college, you will think that within all the knowledge that you have mastered, there is one small part that you don't know well enough. So you will go on to graduate school. After you receive your master's degree, you will realize that you only know a little about all there is to know. Finally, when you earn your Ph.D., you will think that you know well a tiny field from your area of specialization, but you will readily acknowledge the limitations of your knowledge in that area." A wise educator's version of Socratic ignorance.

While I pondered my ignorance, the Chinese authorities recognized my work with a number of awards. I received the "1984 Advanced Woman of the Red Flag Star Award" for Shanghai. I received the "Certificate of Merit" from the Shanghai City government in 1984. And I received the "Outstanding Teacher of the First National Teachers' Day" Award in 1985. Such public honors could not, however, free me from my familial responsibilities.

Our two daughters had aged considerably during my absence. Lana, the older one, attended "high school," while Mary, her younger sister, remained in elementary school. Even after I returned to China, the girls continued to live with their grandparents. Given our limited options, this seemed like the best choice. Xu and I lacked the space in our crowded apartment—still furnished with one single bed—to have our daughters stay with us. Moreover, our careers kept us so busy and required me to be away so often that we would have found it near impossible to care for our children if they had lived with us. Unlike us, Grandpa and Grandma had plenty of time. At their place they could nurture and instruct their granddaughters in important yet informal ways. Even if Xu and I could have resolved these two matters, we still would have faced the "school problem." After the Cultural Revolution, China suffered from a teacher shortage. Although our country had progressed since those days, we still lacked qualified teachers. Only a few post-secondary institutions possessed the facilities and the professors to adequately prepare prospective teachers. Those who studied elsewhere almost wasted their time. This impacted the Shanghai school system in unequal ways. Had the girls gone to school in the district in which Xu and I lived, they would have received a low quality education. On the other hand, the district in which my parents lived was blessed with fine schools. On this score alone the choice of where to house our children would have been clear. All of this settled the girls' residence question. Meanwhile, I compensated as best I could for my absence: I continued to live with my parents during the week and with Xu on the weekends.

On one such day, Mother talked with me about the spiritual development of the girls. While our home influence was distinctly Christian, she worried about the atheistic propaganda that all children received and that most children embraced in the schools. How could our girls swim against the tide when their peers ridiculed anyone who believed in God? This became particularly apparent to Grandma one day when she and her granddaughter talked about God. "Show me God," little Mary said, "so that I can believe in him." This ploy, probably learned in school, served as only one of the many indoctrination tactics Communist teachers used. Churches could do little to counter such nonsense, for children rarely attended worship and we had no Sunday schools. All of this took its toll, particularly on Mary, for she was younger and more impressionable than her sister.

Understandably, I worked both directly and indirectly to point my children to the strong faith that had enriched our family for several generations. Lana and I talked seriously about these matters on numerous occasions. During our after-supper walks together, our conversations frequently turned to spiritual matters. "Tell me, Lana," I asked, "whether you can see the wind."

"Of course, Momma. Just look at the way things blow around."

"But Lana, you don't really see the wind. You recognize its effects when you see the leaves rustling in the treetops, or when you feel the breeze as it gently ruffles your hair. What you see, in fact, is a response to the wind."

"Tell me, Lana," I continued, "whether you can see love."

"Not really, Momma."

"Then are you quite sure that love exists?"

"I'm sure, Momma."

"The Bible tells us, Lana, that God is love. If you feel love, then you see God. Moreover," I continued, "all one has to do is look at nature to determine that there is a creator God."

My words, sown in love and watered by prayer, eventually had their effect. I rejoiced on the day that Lana declared her faith in God to me. Thereafter, even though Chinese policy prohibited children from church attendance, she and I sometimes worshiped together with our fellow believers.

But how could I help my littlest girl? *Each day, O Lord, I pray that you will gently draw Mary into the family of faith. And if it is possible, please use me as an instrument in her spiritual renewal.*

My mother also recommended prayer for "her girls." In Grandma's dreams, she imagined that Lana would have a church wedding with a three-tier wedding cake.

I feared that Mama's funeral might well precede Lana's wedding, for in early winter 1985 I watched Mama become weaker and weaker. A visible part of her deteriorating condition involved her gastronomical system. She found it difficult to swallow; and much of the food that she finally forced down her throat came right back up. Understandably, we sought medical help. When the people at the hospital performed an endoscopy, they found nothing wrong. In my conversation with the doctor I suggested that Mother might have some debilitating nerve condition. He followed up on this lead and sent us to see a neurologist.

This physician offered us a most worrisome diagnosis. At the outset of our visit, when Mother walked through the doctor's door, he made a shocking pronouncement. "I believe, young lady, that our patient has Alzheimer's." Mother sat down and he continued his examination. Then he spoke once again: "I've got more bad news for you. Our patient has Parkinson's disease." These words didn't surprise me, for I knew that this disease ran in our family. "I fear," the doctor continued, "that your mother has a complicated form of Parkinson's. Let me ask you a few questions."

"Is it common for your mother to lose things?"

"Certainly," I replied. "But this is nothing special. I too lose things."

"Indeed," the doctor agreed, "but not because of a particular disease."

By the end of this visit the doctor determined that Mother's nerve problems made it difficult for her to swallow and then prescribed a medicine that was supposed to help.

When we returned home, I did what I could to ease Mama's pains. She complained in particular that her neck hurt. I massaged the aches, but this provided only minor and temporary relief. Sadly, we could do nothing substantive for Mother's deteriorating condition except watch. Surprisingly, Mother refused to become absorbed in her misery. Indeed, she often reminded me that I must see to it that Lana and Mary get a Christian education.

Xu, the girls, and I visited Xu's parents in Guangzhou during the 1985 Chinese New Year. We thought it would be fun to travel by boat, and Lana and Mary were excited at the prospects of viewing the sea from a different perspective. Too soon, however, Lana's face turned pale. Although she didn't complain, I recognized the signs of seasickness. When Lana's stomach settled down, she and I had a good chance to talk. After we all got settled in Guangzhou, many of Xu's relatives came to see us. Indeed, this was the first time we had gotten together with his entire family. We made the most of this relaxing and enjoyable vacation. For when we returned to Shanghai, our spring semester was as busy as usual. Since Mama's condition continued to deteriorate, I lived in her apartment all the time. This way I could care for my daughters and my mother.

At this stage in her disease, Mama demanded considerable care: she could not even walk by herself without help. One night, for example, she woke me up five separate times so that I could take her to the toilet. That night I asked her why she got up so much. Her surprising answer extended beyond nature's call. "Nettie," she explained, "I just want your attention."

"But Mama," I countered, "I need to sleep at night so that I can work during the day. I assure you that I think of you frequently while I am on the job." I could not avoid reflecting on my childhood years when I had wanted my parents' attention. Now, the situation was reversed. *It would be best to keep these thoughts to myself.*

Mother's condition went from bad to worse. Ecclesiastes' Preacher speaks rightly about a "time to weep." In former days, Mary and Grandma played together with her necklaces and beads. Now, however, Mother tried to eat those beads. I had to take them away so that she would not injure herself. We thought Mother might enjoy the sunshine, so we sat her at my father's desk where the bright light shone through our big window. There too she got confused and tried to take my father's medicine. Although she still knew us well, she didn't recognize many of her friends. Indeed, by this stage in her disease Mama needed to be reminded to go to the toilet; and when she got there, she needed help. Eventually, we hired a lady to provide daycare for my mother.

Dr. Tennison, his wife, Carol, and Carol's two children visited us in Shanghai in early summer 1985. They brought with them a special present, a wheelchair, for my mother. This was just what Mama needed, for she could no longer walk at all. At about this same time we hired a lady to move in with us and provide round-the-clock care for Mother. Daddy and I spelled one another at home while the one of us who was free gave lectures and conducted workshops.

Toward the middle of the summer, Daddy and I resolved a number of matters. We would keep Mother at home rather than place her permanently in a hospital, for we knew that in these institutions care for such patients was less than adequate. At the same time, I canceled all my professional commitments so that I could stay with Mama. Daddy, who had an important, long-term assignment in the south, left for Guangzhou. As familial nurse, I changed Mama's undergarments and washed every inch of her skin. As I cleaned her, I put ointment on her bedsores. As familial cook, I prepared a medicinal Chinese ginseng soup that, because of its gravy-like consistency, made it easier for Mama to swallow. Thereafter, I fed her and gave her water, for she needed to get some meat on her bones. Unfortunately, it took the two of us an entire hour to finish off a single bowl. Mostly, Mama remained comatose, except for short periods of time when she would awaken.

Others offered me special help and advice. I called in a doctor to evaluate Mother's condition. This physician reported that my mother's heart was in good shape. I also brought in a Chinese specialist to try acupuncture. After one day with the patient she declared her reluctance to return and try again. Eventually, she agreed to do what she could. I talked with Uncle Silas, who visited us each Sunday after worship. His thoughtful and cautious advise made sense. "Don't call your father yet, Nettie. He would be shocked at what he saw. And if your mother holds on, he may have to return to Guangzhou before she dies. Indeed, if things take a sudden turn for the worse, you shouldn't worry that your father isn't present. I'm here to sign all of the papers and to take care of this business." I appreciated his words of assurance.

Round the clock, night and day, I tended to Mama's needs. Lana taught herself to cook and, when I was preoccupied with other matters, prepared our meals. Since we had no air conditioning, the heat permeated our apartment. We bought ice and placed it under Mama's bed, and we set a fan close by Mama's head. Surely the cool air would do her some good! On one day when the temperature peaked, we propped open the refrigerator door and used a fan to blow its cool air on Mother. Our many visitors spoke appreciatively about the absence of those "awful nursing home smells" that were all too common in the hospitals. If they hadn't seen my mother, they would never have known that we had a sick woman here. When I consulted with yet another doctor, she expressed doubt that she would be able to heal her comatose patient. Indeed, she said that Mother would probably live only a little longer.

When Daddy returned home, he was unprepared to see his emaciated, near-lifeless wife. He and I agreed that we would stop the ginseng medicine and the acupuncture. On the sixth day after Daddy's return, Mama suddenly woke up. She recognized everybody, but despite her efforts, her mouth failed her. She could not speak a word. As an alternative, she nodded and smiled at each of us. Maybe, we hoped, she has turned the corner and will continue this short-term improvement. Late that evening, I encouraged Daddy to get some rest. "I've got a book," I said. "I'll sit up with Mama." Daddy rested until midnight, but that's all. Sleep eluded him. A few hours later, death took my mother. At last, she found rest in her heavenly home. *Blessed are those who die in the Lord.* Later that morning I called the doctor and told him what had happened. After he stopped by, he wrote in his death certificate that this woman had died because of complications from Parkinson's disease.

We designed Mother's funeral service so that it would reflect her lifelong Christian witness. Even under Communist authority, a time when our rulers prohibited us from speaking to people about Jesus except within our church buildings, she had kept the faith. In these days, the only "external" witness one bore was in her life rather than her words. Despite these restrictions, Mother made her way, The Way, known. I remember well the occasion when, in the early 1980s, a Communist journalist interviewed my mother. His first question—"Are you a Christian?"—indicated that Mother's silence spoke clearly about her faith commitment.

Now, in Mother's absence, we would have a memorial church service. There, we would speak those words that could not be said in a public forum. Such a service was unusual in these days. Still, we sent out our letters of invitation. One particular line in those letters provided an excuse for those who feared that attending a church would endanger them: "If it is inconvenient for you to come, we will understand." We also indicated that we would not accept gifts.

On the day of the funeral we expected maybe as many as 100 people to show up. In fact, more than 300 came! Each person brought a flower. I saw one woman who had been a prostitute before the 1949 revolution. Later, the Red Guard had shaved her head as a way of identifying and shaming her. This woman brought tiny Chinese jasmine flowers, woven together around a small metal ring. She placed her gift on the altar, which by this time was covered with flowers. I watched as she prayed and then took her seat. I knew nothing about her relationship with Mother. Another man, one of my mother's former kindergarten students, came all the way from Beijing. He offered these simple words: "My former teacher was important to me." Doctors, engineers, and other professionals came from Wuhan and more distant places. Mother had taught each of them. Many of our guests had never been inside a church. Since the Communists taught that religion was for the weak, they found it difficult to understand what was going on. The pastor delivered a touching sermon titled "From One Room to Another Room." Strange, but many were touched by this unfamiliar Christian message. Afterward, a woman came up to me and said that her spirit had been purified in this church. And a Communist leader asked whether he might have such a memorial service when he dies.

Mother's entire life, both outside and inside the church, testified to her faith in Christ. Her memorial service ended appropriately. The pastor's wife picked roses from the church garden, pulled the petals off, and put the petals from a single rose on Mother's memorial box. Everyone in attendance followed her example. Thus, we buried Mother's remains in fragrant flowers.

After Mother's funeral, I tended to Daddy's needs. Although his emotional recovery could and should not come quickly, he appreciated the strength and the presence of his family. We bought a small plot of land and buried Mama in the Suzhou Cemetery beside my grandmother and my aunt. Later in August, Xu, the girls, and I invited Daddy to accompany us on a short vacation away from the city. We chose to spend our time together at the shore. While there, we found our way to a famous site from which we could watch the huge waves—that's what everyone expected—as they crashed down upon the rocks and sands. A beautiful sight, even if the waves lacked the power and the size the optimists had predicted. We took in the salt smells, the occasional mist, and the soothing sounds. Each brought healing and refreshment to our bodies and our souls. For when we witnessed these simple and telling sights, we also felt the presence of One who, in power and love, made the heavens and the earth.

When we returned to Shanghai, obligations at work awaited each of us. Xu and I decided that, at least for the foreseeable future, I should stay with my father and the girls and care for them. By this time, fall semester 1985 had begun. Once again we found ourselves quite busy.

During this time, my commitments consumed my days and my nights. The pressures I faced as a professional seemed like they would never cease. I went regularly to three kindergartens and two elementary schools. I taught at the Shanghai Xingzhi Normal School. I was employed by the Shanghai Conservatory Music Research Institute (a place where they still required political studies). And I conducted and wrote up my research. That still left community service. I served as a trustee of the Shanghai YWCA, a member of the Chinese Musicians Association, a board member of the Shanghai Music Educator's Association, and an advisor to the Quanzhou Children's Intelligence Development Center.

The new openness in China extended to the Christian community. Not too long ago, the government had closed all of the churches. But now it permitted one open church in each geographical district. The Shanghai International Church from our district asked me to serve as one of its board members. When we talked about this possibility, I explained my reluctance to take on a position of ecclesiastical leadership while I was still only a "baby in Christ." They countered with a pragmatic and political argument. "Some Communist Party members," they observed, "disguise their political and ideological commitments and join the church, sometimes even as pastors. In this way, they become spies, report on board members, and thus corrupt and injure the Christian community. Now that the church is reorganized, we have vacant seats on our board. Even if you are inexperienced, we know that you're not a spy. Even though you may have nothing to offer, at least you can fill the position." When I sought the advice of friends, they suggested that I take the seat. Finally, I agreed to this assignment. At the same time, I hoped to do more for the church than just fill a vacant seat. The question was how? I lacked the time for study, a prerequisite for spiritual maturity. Maybe I could figure that out later. But for the present, as one who had been baptized years earlier, I joined the church. I also registered and signed the paper that made me a board member.

Of course, the responses to the government's new openness varied. Unlike me, some still felt reluctant to join any church; others started underground churches. Whatever people chose to do, they certainly didn't boycott our Shanghai International Church. Even with three services on Sundays, we still lacked space for all who wanted to worship with us. Many lined up outside, at 6 A.M., in hopes of finding seats for the service two hours later. When we opened the doors, the pews and even the aisles were quickly filled. In order to accommodate the crowds, we put microphones in the small adjoining rooms and in the outside gardens. My parents had joined this church before Mother died. Now, I watched my family as they continued in positions of leadership. Uncle Silas conducted the choir, and my father worked on the special music.

I might have continued on at this frenetic pace had not personal health concerns led me to rethink the trajectory of my life. Once in 1985, when I was teaching kindergarten, my heart had protested my pace. That same thing happened a second time, when I had to race to catch my bus on my way to the Shanghai Xingzhi Normal School. I successfully caught the crowded vehicle, but I was utterly exhausted. Indeed, I had pushed myself so hard that I felt my heart stop beating. Understandably anxious, I turned to the deep breathing exercises associated with the martial arts. Maybe, I hoped, that would do the job. Soon, I caught my breath and my heart started beating again. Understandably, this signal forced me to reconsider those commitments that currently shaped and stressed my life. I needed rest. I reflected in particular on my new assignment as the highest leader in the music reform movement. In assigning me to this position, the authorities hoped they could learn and apply my teaching methods to other subject areas. A fine idea! Except that I understood only too well my lack of expertise and my ignorance about so much.

Out of this context, I wrote a letter and explained my situation to Dr. David McGuire, my former professor in Denton. I received his reply during Christmas holiday 1985. He encouraged me to return to the States and study for a Ph.D. He also suggested that once I earned that degree, and the level of expertise it reflected, I could return to China and be more confident and more effective in positions of leadership. He noted that he had already talked with the dean of the school. If I chose this route, they would give me a teaching assistantship and a research assistantship to help cover my expenses.

I talked this possibility and opportunity over with my family. They responded positively and encouraged me to get the degree. Now that Mama had passed away, no pressing family matters demanded my attention. Of course it would have been best for Daddy for me to stay in China. But we all realized that it would be better for me (and for our country and the reform movement) to secure a deeper knowledge of my subject. Following these initial conversations, I worked on bureaucratic matters. When I applied for admission to North Texas State University, they sent me the I-20 form and the application materials. I filled them out and returned them with no difficulty. At this point I began thinking about passport questions. Once again our family talked through our options. It would be simplest for our daughters to stay in China, except that Xu's and Grandpa's busy schedules would give them little time to care for both girls. My father spoke to me about the Christian education Mary could get in the States. We both knew how Chinese education pushed in the opposite direction. In the end, we decided that I would take Mary with me and that Lana could manage for herself and cook for Grandpa. Both Xu and my father suggested that when I return, I might leave Mary in the United States. There, she could avoid the difficult experiences that the three of us knew only too well; there, she could enjoy the good life. But that was a long time away, and circumstances might change. For the present, I applied for passports for Mary and for me.

The authorities rejected my application for Mary's passport. Their reason? "If you take your daughter with you, we don't believe that you will return to China." I persisted by seeking the support of many of the important people whom I had met because of my present positions in China. In time, the government relented and agreed to reconsider our application. This process required them to look into Mary's file. Would they find any bad marks in it related to the Communist Party, or to her teacher, or to her experiences in kindergarten? Their background "check" on our nine-year-old girl took them more than a month. Among other things, they visited Mary's former teacher, who had to sign a paper that endorsed her former student. Eventually, in May 1986, the government approved our passport applications. Next, I applied to the American consulate for a visa. I faced no problems here. Toward the end of this entire process we wrote Dr. Tennison and told him about our plans. He agreed to serve as sponsor for Mary and me. Finally, I looked over our financial situation. I had saved all the money I had made from my lectures, my workshops, and my publications. This constituted much more than my salary. Thus, I could easily afford two plane tickets to the United States.

Before I left for the States, the many journalists who interviewed me asked whether I planned to return to China. "Certainly," I replied. "I am going away to earn my doctorate so that I will be able to help my country with its music education." I also pointed out that Xu, Lana, and my father would remain in China. I did not say, however, that I would bring Mary back. In all of this, I spoke the truth. I really believed that I would find my way home.

The night before my departure, Daddy spoke to me once again about the future. "You must do all you can, Nettie, to encourage Mary in matters of faith and her knowledge of God. On a more practical note, you must see to it that Mary learns good English. If she is genuinely bilingual, it will serve her well in the future, even if you can't leave her in the States." *Leave her in the States? In my mind, I still thought she might return to China with me. Whatever the case, she would learn English and enjoy the support of a nurturing community of faith.*

I had one last errand to run before I left. I went to the Suzhou Cemetery and stood alongside of Mama's grave. I missed her! She needed no promises from me this time. When I had completed that mission, we all headed to the airport. After sad good-byes, Mary and I boarded our plane. Down below, Xu, Lana, and Daddy watched as we took off into the sky. We both wondered what our adventure in America would bring to us.

13

Adoption or Expatriation

1986–1990

Deng Xiaoping continued his foreign policy of openness toward other countries well beyond 1985. China pursued diplomatic relations with Indonesia, a Portugese promise to return Macao, a meeting with Soviet President Gorbachev, and more. In economic policy, Deng continued his pragmatic approach to productivity. Young people hoped for even more. Students took the lead in urging democraticization and greater personal freedoms. In December 1986 they demonstrated in Hefei, in Shanghai, and in a dozen other cities. Conservative Communist leaders blamed General Secretary Hu Yaobang for the uprisings and, in January 1987, forced his resignation. Students protested once again in the spring of 1988.

In April 1989 this unresolved conflict between China's intractable leaders and its persistent young people escalated when students in Beijing boycotted classes, demonstrated openly, and called for democracy and a free press. Two days laters, Shanghai students took up the torch.

In May, Gorbachev, a man who had witnessed his own share of discontent in the Soviet Union, conducted his scheduled meeting with Deng, right in the midst of China's troubled days. Others supported and joined the students. Eventually over a million demonstrators gathered in Beijing. Martial law. The protestors wouldn't budge. Government arrests. The battle was joined. In early June, soldiers in Tiananmen Square opened fire and the world took notice. As a graduate student in Texas, Nettie, like so many Americans around her, witnessed the bullets and the bloodshed on television.

After an uneventful flight and an airport mix-up, Mary and I eventually enjoyed the hospitality of our California relatives. Our flight manifesto had indicated a destination of San Francisco. From there, we planned to go through customs and then meet up with my Uncle John, a recent transplant from Chicago, Illinois, to Milpitas, California. Unfortunately, airport realities didn't quite match our expectations. For some reason our plane was diverted to Los Angeles. After we went through L.A. customs, the airline flew us north to San Francisco. Easy enough, except that my Uncle John failed to find us at the airport. So I called Aunt Christina while Mary guarded our four big suitcases and kept an eye out for our missing relative. Eventually, we found Uncle John. Thereafter, Mary and I stayed with these relatives for a week. They took us to Stanford University, to the Golden Gate Bridge, to Fisherman's Wharf, and to other nearby sights. Mary managed all this, despite the wearing effects of the trip. But she clearly wasn't up to snuff. She still felt weak, and she had no appetite. My aunt tried to feed her poor niece more food, but little Mary simply couldn't stomach it.

After our short west-coast tour and another plane flight, the Tennisons met us in West Monroe, Louisiana. Mary and I quickly adopted the fitting forms of address: I continued to use the terms "uncle" and "aunt," and Mary called our hosts "grandpa" and "grandma." She chose appropriately, for these good friends treated her like their own granddaughter. Among other things, they bought her clothes and took her to Sunday school and church. Finally, in late August, we all headed toward Denton. The four of us spent the night with Carol in Plano, Texas, the town to which she and her family had moved. This simple get-together was like a reunion for me. The following day we arrived at North Texas State University and I registered for my classes.

Thereafter, we scouted around to find a suitable place for Mary and me to live. I wanted to visit with "Grandma" Campbell right away. During the past two years in China, she and I had corresponded. She had kept me posted on how her family was doing, and she had kept me current on the story line in our favorite soap opera "All My Children." Although she knew I was returning to the States, she had no idea exactly when I might pop in. Unfortunately, "now" turned out to be bad timing. Grandma was on a fishing trip in Alaska. So we checked in with her "granddaughter-in-law," a woman who ran a nearby flower shop. When we talked with her about accommodations, she reminded us of Mrs. Campbell's increasing age and suggested that it would be better if we could find another place to live. I remembered back to 1982, when Grandma had returned from her stay in the hospital with a broken hip. I had enjoyed caring for her, but I had also found my nursing responsibilities time-consuming. I doubted whether I would now have the time to care for an aging friend and for my own daughter. Eventually, Mary and I rented a well-situated apartment—close to the university—from a Chinese man. Once again, the Tennisons paid all the fees.

We also made schooling arrangements for Mary. With regard to transportation, Sharon, Mrs. Campbell's granddaughter-in-law, agreed to drive Mary to school while Dr. Tennison agreed to pay for her gas. Mrs. McGuire helped us with matters related to Mary's school registration and immunizations. In China, Mary was supposed to be in the third grade. But the Texas school officials, recognizing Mary's language deficiencies, recommended that we put her in the second grade. I understood their position, but I also came from a country where we preferred not to hold our children back. I suggested that we try the third grade and see how it worked out. At the same time, we enrolled Mary in an "English as a Second Language Class," and also hoped that a Taiwanese girl from her third-grade class would help Mary in her studies. After registration, we turned to the issue of immunizations. On this, the Chinese system differed greatly from the American one. In practical terms, this meant bad news for poor Mary: they required her to get countless shots.

My school jobs proved to be easier than my homework. At the university, I divided my time between assisting music theory students in the computer lab and helping my professor find materials for a book she was writing. In this, I managed my language problems satisfactorily. At home, however, it was a different story. I disregarded the advice that I speak only English with Mary, for I wanted my daughter to retain fluency in her native tongue. In fact, we spoke Chinese all the time. That was easy enough. But her homework nearly killed the two of us. During Mary's first semester in school, she understood virtually nothing. So I helped her with her homework, but I needed my dictionary. When, for example, they studied the solar system, I had no clue as to the meaning of the terms "Jupiter," "Mars," or "Mercury." I knew the names of the planets in Chinese, but not in English. Thus, I looked up every word, ever so slowly, in the dictionary. In fact, at this stage in Mary's schooling I did the homework. My evenings took on a familiar pattern. I cooked for Mary, put her to bed, did her homework, and then turned to my assignments. In the mornings, I prepared breakfast and then waited with her for her ride to school.

Larry Campbell (Grandma's grandson) and his wife Sharon lived close enough to provide what care Mary needed during this first semester. This was important, for Mary's frequent illnesses meant that she stayed home a lot. Although I checked in on her from the university, I could not guarantee her safety. So I warned her never to open the front door for anyone. When the mailman came, she climbed up to the window to see who was there. But she didn't need to let him in, for our door had a mail slot that he could use. As to Mary's health, I secured Chinese medicine for her and gave her shots. Slowly, she regained her strength. Understandably, we both celebrated the time when, after two days of rain, Mary enjoyed sustained good health and could stay at school. It looked like we might succeed in this foreign land. Indeed, even Mary's ESL classes seemed to be doing her some good.

Although we no longer lived with Grandma, I by no means wrote her out of the picture. Indeed, I consulted this smart and wise woman whenever I needed advice. And on Sundays, Mary and I made church a regular part of our routine. Early on, she and I walked from our apartment to the First Baptist Church of Denton. Given Mary's slow pace, it took us thirty minutes to get there. In time, a Sunday school teacher gave us a ride. At First Baptist, Mary attended the children's Bible study and I went to an adult Bible class. Afterward, we hiked another fifteen or twenty minutes to get to Grace Baptist for services in Chinese. There, I joined the adults for worship and Mary participated in a children's Bible study. I was pleased that our time together in church reinforced our dependence upon God in prayer. Whenever we faced problems, Mary and I joined hands and directed our concerns to our heavenly Father. In this simple practice we learned the reality of the biblical promises: "Ask, and it will be given you; seek, and you will find; knock, and it will be opened to you."

Even though we prayed, I hardly expected the extraordinary opportunity that came my way. One day after practicing my harp, I noticed a poster on the graduate school bulletin board. "Anyone interested in applying for an AAUW Scholarship should contact 'Ms. Smith' in the administration building." *Why not?* Shortly before 5 P.M., I popped in and caught "Ms. Smith." We talked in general terms, and then she asked me about the specifics of my situation. I appreciated her interest, especially after she said they offered a $10,000 grant for the degree. I returned home that day with the application forms. After I told Mary about the possibilities, we joined together in prayer. *Thy will be done.* Then, I turned to the forms. I noted one condition in particular for receiving the scholarship: the graduate student must agree to return home and serve her country for at least two years. In this narrative section of the form I explained why I had come to the United States to earn my Ph.D. "I hope to learn about music education and then return home to China and take on a leadership position in the reform movement. If I had intended to stay in the United States, I would have changed my major. I understand only too well that foreigners with a doctorate in music education find it hard to secure employment in the States. Those who plan to stay emphasize nursing, computers, and accounting." Once I completed the form, I mailed it to the AAUW Scholarship Committee and waited.

Special holiday fun and celebration introduced high points into our fall studying. During my earlier days in Denton, I had for the most part ignored the holidays. But not now. I bought Mary a mask and then took her out to collect Halloween candy. We had such a good time with this. At Thanksgiving, Dr. Arnold, the former assistant to the president of North Texas State, invited us out for a visit. Free plane tickets; the opportunity to see Waco and the Baptist school at which Dr. Arnold now taught; and the chance to renew a good friendship. Who could turn this down? In December, Carol drove to our apartment, picked us up, and took us to her parents' house for Christmas.

By this time, Mary understood English reasonably well. That put her at about the halfway mark on her way toward English proficiency. For the present, she remained hesitant to speak the foreign tongue; in fact, she resorted to her own self-designed sign language as a way of signifying "yes" or "no." During our visit with the Tennisons, I spoke with Mary about her faith. As a result of this conversation, she committed her life to Christ as Savior. We were both delighted. Soon, I talked with Dr. Tennison about having Mary make a public profession of her faith. Believer's baptism. I knew we would find it difficult to secure a Christian education for her after I completed my degree and we returned to China. Understandably, I felt pressed to do as much as possible now. We needed to get on with baptism, membership in a church, and instruction in the Christian faith. But "Grandpa" Tennison wanted to ensure that his "granddaughter" understood her faith commitment. "Baptism would be premature," he explained, "if Mary doesn't comprehend what she is doing, or if she is merely acting to please her mother." So he counseled and questioned Mary. I translated. Sometimes, however, Mary responded in her sign language. *Bring the little children unto me and forbid them not, for of such is the kingdom of heaven.* On December 21, 1986, Mary was baptized in the First Baptist Church of West Monroe, Louisiana. How appropriate to bring in the Christmas season this way, and in Dr. Tennison's home church. Thereafter, our celebrations continued, with gifts, a tree, a reunion with the Tennison clan, and more.

When Mary and I returned to Denton, Dr. McGuire, my graduate school advisor, told me he planned to retire in spring 1987. Given this impending change in his status, I would need to change my major professor. Disturbing, even shocking news! Dr. McGuire had taught me how to study. We had already agreed upon my dissertation topic, a comparison of Chinese and American music education today. All that was gone. Well, not quite "all." He indicated that he would be around to help, but he also made it clear that Dr. Hildegard Froehlich would be my new advisor. Since I had taken classes from Dr. Froehlich, our new relationship had at least something upon which it could build. When, however, she and I talked, she asked me to change my dissertation subject. Eventually, we agreed that I would consider the "Curriculum Content of Elementary Music in China Between 1912 and 1982." This meant that I would analyze the influence of the many political changes from this period upon music education. It also meant that I would have to gather many new materials and conduct much new research.

Old and new associates helped me establish connections with highly regarded music educators in the United States. During fall semester 1986 I received a letter from Dr. Howard Gardner, a psychology professor at Harvard University. He told me that he knew of my work through the Project Zero study his colleagues were conducting in China. More importantly, he asked me whether I would be willing to give a lecture at Harvard and participate in visits he would arrange at other schools. A flattering and a frightening invitation! I talked with Dr. McGuire, who said I must go. When I raised the question of who would care for Mary during my ten-day absence, Mrs. McGuire volunteered to child-sit. "That would be wonderful," I countered, "except that my daughter can't speak any English." Eventually, I set aside my objections and accepted the invitations.

On February 1, 1987, Dr. and Mrs. McGuire took me to the Dallas airport, the starting point for my northern expedition. I stopped first at Northwestern, where I met Dr. Bennett Reimer, the professor who coordinated this lecture. After my presentation, faculty and students questioned me. I felt encouraged when Dr. Reimer spoke positively about the evening's activities. I also recognized the importance of practice before my appearance at Harvard. After my short stint in Evanston, I visited the New England Conservatory of Music. There, I worked with Professor Lyle Davidson and visited classes. One professor suggested intriguing problem-solving activities to me. Finally, after considerable practice on my lecture, I arrived at Harvard. Apparently the practice helped: my lecture went well. Afterward, I met with Joe Walters, Lenny Scripp, and Joan Mayaard, members of the research staff of Project Zero. From Cambridge, I moved on to MIT and Yale—visits, not lectures—and Boston University. At this last school I met with Lucie Lawrence. I observed how she taught harp, and she gave me several lessons.

In the end, my frightening northern expedition proved profitable in many ways. My hosts and I benefited as we exchanged teaching ideas. In a broad sense, I introduced Chinese music education to leading American academicians and those whom they taught. Surprisingly, they had a special interest in my students' drawings. As for me, I listened attentively to all that I heard. Now that China had initiated a reform period, we could learn much from the West. I was particularly intrigued with western problem-solving strategies. When all of this was over, I was pleased to learn that the Harvard Graduate School of Education placed my picture in their 1987–1988 catalogue. Back home, I wondered how Mrs. McGuire and Mary had managed. When I returned, I learned that each night this generous woman had read a story to my daughter. And most surprising, after ten days away from Mama, Mary spoke fluent English. A profitable trip indeed!

Later that same month I gave a lecture at the Texas Music Educators Association in San Antonio. Earlier in the year, Dr. Froehlich had invited me to make this presentation; now, she drove me in her own car to the convention. While in San Antonio, I stayed with Vivian, a BSU friend whom I had met at North Texas State when I had studied for my master's degree.

Well before this, Wartburg College had arranged to give my father an honorary degree. When Daddy had applied for his passport, he had also asked for permission to travel in Texas. Our prayers were answered when, during the 1987 spring break, he visited us. During part of that break, the three of us took a bus up to the University of Oklahoma to see my father's friend who taught there. When we returned to Denton, we continued to enjoy one another's company. Daddy cooked the dinners, which meant less work for me. Since his English was better than mine, he could help me with the language as I brought my spring semester studies to a successful end.

When May arrived, Daddy, Mary, and I traveled north to Iowa. My Uncle John and my Uncle Silas joined us at Wartburg to witness and celebrate Daddy's receiving an honorary degree. The excitement of the occasion made it difficult for the celebrated Professor Ma to sleep. On his special day, we attended all the ceremonial events. For at least this short period of time, Daddy reigned, "King for the Day." But as we prepared to board the plane for our return trip to Texas, our economy tickets reminded us that normalcy would be the order for most of our days. Then, much to our surprise, they "bumped us up" to first class. Elizabeth Dole, the Secretary of Transportation and a fellow recipient with my father of a Wartburg honorary degree, had treated us to our first "royal" flight.

Mary and I moved to a less-expensive, recently-vacated "apartment" during the summer. The Honeycutts, our new landlords, were remarkable women. These good ladies had seen much of life. Olive, at age eighty-six, ran the household. Katherine, who had quit her job because of periodic bouts with depression, depended upon the care of her older sister. Their small dog, Scotty, brought his own kind of cheer to the household. These big-hearted women's generosity exceeded their limited means. As a way of raising money to support their church, they started a recycling project. They collected pop cans at the university campus and stored them in their backyard. In time, folks from the church picked up this unusual treasure and cashed it in. When the Honeycutt sisters completed this project, they put more than 100 hard-earned dollars into the offering plate. As an ongoing project, they crocheted and quilted for their church. On a more personal level, they looked in regularly on Mrs. Pessy, a woman from the neighborhood who suffered from Alzheimer's. They cooked for her, walked with her, and visited her when she was sick. Even closer to home than all this, they cared for Mary when I was away. Their gentle, consistent, undramatic example provided a wonderful model for my young daughter. We had made a good move.

A few other surprises punctuated our summer routine. Over the past year I had corresponded and renewed my friendship with Rebecca Zhang,[1] a classmate of mine from our elementary school days in China. In our letters, we learned to talk about more than the mundane. Now, fortunately, we were near neighbors. Rebecca and her husband lived in nearby Fort Worth, where he attended seminary. One day in June my good friend stopped by for a long, face-to-face visit.

About this same time, I finally received my long-awaited letter from the AAUW. Wonderful news! They had approved my application for an International Fellowship for 1987–1988. Moreover, they asked me to attend their national convention in Houston on June 23 and even offered to pay for my plane ticket. This was an offer I couldn't refuse. I called Dr. Tennison and told him my good news. "You know that my assistantship takes care of my school expenses," I reminded him. "Now," I continued, "this fellowship will easily cover our housing costs. You will no longer have to pay rent for your impoverished 'niece.'" Unfortunately, it didn't turn out to be quite that easy. The AAUW prohibited recipients of this fellowship from working. In doing so, they hoped people like me would be able to focus exclusively on their studies. But that just wouldn't work for me. So I wrote and explained my situation. "Much of my outside work is connected to my studies, and my computer job at the library is rarely busy. Furthermore, if I resign from my job, I will lose my resident status at NTSU and my school expenses will go up. Finally, you must understand that my youngest daughter lives with me here in Denton; children cost money. Given all of these complicating factors, I hope that you will be able to waive your 'no-work' rule for me." The AAUW scheduled a meeting in which they considered and approved my special request.

The Tennisons and I got together twice during this summer. Carol brought her parents by for a visit before they took off on their scheduled China trip. As I talked with the Tennisons, I asked them whether they could bring back a violin for Mary. I explained that we wanted her to take Suzuki lessons and join an orchestra. They listened and they left. When they returned from China, gift in hand, I had completed summer school. At last, time to relax in Louisiana. Carol picked us up in Denton and drove us to her parents' house. As usual, she and I started catching up on things as soon as we hit the road. Not much happened in West Monroe, except that Mary got her new violin. Now, instrument in hand, she was ready to join the orchestra in the fall. She also decided to take ballet lessons.

My father and I talked one more time about Mary before he had to return to Shanghai. He was pleased that his granddaughter was receiving a good education in the United States, and he celebrated her recent commitment to Christ. But he also worried about what might happen to her. Would our personal stories of persecution become hers if she accompanied me back to China? While Daddy appreciated recent reforms in our homeland, he doubted that they would be permanent. Indeed, his analysis of policy patterns worried me. "When the economy is weak," he observed, "the Communists give some people freedom. But when the economy prospers," he warned, "they find a greater number of enemies." "As for Mary's future," he concluded, "Xu and I both agree that Mary should remain in the States." *Good advice, but so hard to imagine abandoning my daughter.* When I consulted Grandma and asked for her opinion, she asked me to give her time to think about it.

While we all thought about Mary's future, the demands of the new school year were upon us. Travels, professional and personal, remained important in our lives. Dr. Richard Swenson and his wife, my father's friends, invited me for a five-day visit to the University of Wisconsin at River Falls. My itinerary there reflected their joint appointment as administrators of cultural affairs, and her membership in AAUW. I lectured at the Wisconsin State University, and I spoke before public school teachers and the AAUW. When I returned to Texas, Southwestern Baptist Theological Seminary invited me to deliver a lecture. Thereafter, Mary and I periodically visited Fort Worth. On those occasions, we often called upon Mrs. Bratton, my father's former voice teacher, and her husband. While I followed the Chinese form of address and called them Auntie Locile and Uncle Bill, my Americanized daughter rejected our custom of calling them "grandma" and "grandpa" and used the same terms I used. During this same fall semester Mrs. Tonneson asked me to give another concert in Florida. This time, she bought plane tickets for both my daughter and me. So Mary and I toured Disney World and, as usual, enjoyed one another's company.

Mary came into her own when she won first place in a drawing competition at her elementary school. Back in China, she had "failed" because she had refused to follow every suggestion the teacher had made. Thereafter, she simply had given up. Even though she now studied in a new country,[2] she still felt reluctant to enter her school contest. In time, however, her friends persuaded her to do so. We were surprised and pleased when we learned that her "Sunset" drawing took first place. Later on, she won another first place in the citywide competition in Denton. This recognition of her talent and her promise meant much to her. Indeed, she eventually chose art as her college major.

In mid-December, Carol chauffeured us to Louisiana so we could spend the holiday with her parents. This year, Dr. Tennison decided they needed a family portrait. When the photographer showed up, Mary and I stepped aside and watched. The Tennisons would have none of this. They asked Mary and me to join everyone else—Carol and her brother Cliff had brought their entire families. This small gesture touched me deeply and permanently. Indeed, I still keep that picture as a reminder that I am a part of the Tennison family.

When we returned home to Denton, Grandma told me that she had talked with her family about the possibility of Mary's remaining in the States when I went back to China. They understood only too well my dilemma. My love for Mary pulled me in one direction, while our unpromising future pushed me the other way. Her granddaughter Sharon and her husband would have liked to adopt Mary, but their house had only two bedrooms. This wouldn't work. But Grandma's oldest grandson had plenty of space: Bobby and his wife Carla owned a large farmhouse in Ballinger, Texas. They also had two sons, five years apart in age, but no daughters. Mary would fit in perfectly between the two. With all this in mind, they agreed to adopt my daughter.

It might have been the perfect decision, but the tears still flowed freely. Grandma offered her words of consolation, but they didn't help. *Abandon my daughter and still love her? Impossible!* Mary and I talked, but it did no good. "Surely, Mama, I too will be able to survive whatever persecution I face in China!" Then she took another tack. "Look at me. I'm so young. You can't just throw me away!" When I tried to explain the proposed adoption in other ways, she cried. Like me, she simply couldn't face the prospect of permanent separation. We prayed together and I explored every angle. If matters of faith had been inconsequential, I could have considered taking Mary back to China with me. But we were followers of Christ. I had experienced propaganda and persecution. The first undermined faith or marginalized the stalwart; the second destroyed faith or martyred the stalwart. As I prayed every night, my thoughts turned to Abraham's sacrifice of Isaac. Unlike this great patriarch, I lacked the strength to sacrifice my own offspring. *But adoption is not a sacrifice. I will be helping, not hurting, my daughter. Dear Lord, I pray that your blessing may rest upon my Mary.* While I sorted through my impossible possibilities, Larry, Sharon, and I visited with the lawyer whom they had hired. This was so hard. I saw a baby on television and I cried; I saw a picture of a mother changing a diaper and I cried.

On February 3, 1988, I had plenty to occupy my mind. Slouching toward Moriah. Hoping for a ram. Preoccupied. Until I opened our apartment door and I discovered a surprise birthday party for me! Mary had worked it out. The Chinese tradition called for noodles and a cake. Mary improvised. I got spaghetti and, with Catherine's help, a cake. Just the right kind of cake, too. Mary remembered last fall, when the doctors had discovered that I was diabetic. Sugar-free. What a special eleven-year-old.

With one significant exception, school and the impending adoption dominated my thoughts during spring and summer 1988. The Music School scheduled my graduate recital for April of that year. I wanted to get this out of the way as soon as possible and then get on with my dissertation. My preparation and performance went well, even though I was preoccupied with our personal concerns. In recognition of my success in school, the U.S. Achievement Academy honored me with their 1988 Scholastic All-American Award. In June, Grandma drove us to Ballinger, Texas. While there, I tried to imagine this farm as Mary's home and these people as Mary's parents. But Mary's position remained firm: "I don't like this at all!" I reminded her that these were good people, but she wouldn't budge. After this trip, Mary and I flew to Evanston, Illinois, to see Margaret Lawson. Her husband, now dead, had been my father's good friend. At the time of her husband's death I had been unable to attend his funeral. At last, I paid my respects at his gravesite.

When we returned from our usual post-summer school vacation in Louisiana, I hoped to solve my transportation problem. Up to this point I had relied on the offers of generous friends. Now, when I talked with the Brattons about my problem, they recommended that I learn how to drive. Moreover, their proffered help extended well beyond words. Uncle Bill, a retired airplane engineer, offered to give me his well-kept 1967 Camaro. A vintage year, and Chevrolet's answer to the Ford Mustang. Auntie Locile, not to be outdone, offered to pay the $100 tuition for driving school. They both agreed that professional instruction would teach me to drive properly and thus reduce my chances of having an accident.

So in fall 1988 I signed up for a driving course at the university. At the same time, I prevailed upon others to let me practice with them. Andrea, a BSU friend, Dr. Black, my English instructor, and Dr. McGuire; they all helped out. Everything went well, except for parallel parking. I failed that part of the exam twice. Embarrassing! Especially since I had never failed at anything before this. My harp teacher consoled and encouraged me by telling me her own story. "Unlike you, Nettie, I'm an American. I've been around our cars and our rules all my life. But like you, Nettie, I had more than my share of difficulties with that driving exam. Don't worry, and don't give up. You'll pass."

Her prediction proved true, the third time around. So I inherited Uncle Bill's Camaro. And Dr. Tennison's disapproval. He remembered well the car wreck my father had when he was a student in the States. "I'm your American sponsor," he reminded me. "I need to return you to China in one piece. I'll pay for your transportation. You shouldn't drive."

"I appreciate your sensible advice," I replied, "but I really do need my own car. It's just too inconvenient for me to get rides from others." That settled that.

Now, I needed to focus on my dissertation. If I had been permitted to write it in Chinese, I would have done just fine. Unfortunately, the university required me to write in English. When Dr. Froehlich and I talked about my progress, she liked my ideas and my research, but she worried about my facility and my speed in a foreign language. Although I had hoped to finish up after three years in the States, she doubted whether I would succeed—unless I got special help. In the end, she suggested that I hire people to edit the separate sections of my dissertation. I secured a volunteer from among my friends at the Dallas AAUW. When, however, this woman took on other commitments, I slowed down too much. Mrs. McGuire also did what she could. But what I really needed was regular, professional help. The Dallas AAUW, recognizing my needs, met and asked each member to donate $1. They collected $1000 and hired a Denton woman to be my editor. This woman contacted me right away and we started together on our joint project. Afterward, Dr. Froehlich was pleased with my progress.

But not without a break. Betty Pope, the Librarian at NTSU and a friend from First Baptist, Denton, invited me to her Mississippi home over Thanksgiving. Soon, on Thanksgiving Day itself, we headed back home; this allowed us time on our way back to Texas to visit with the Tennisons. At the beginning of the Christmas break, I drove to Plano. Carol was proud that I had managed to do this with no trouble. I didn't want to push it too far, however, so I let Carol drive Mary and me back home to Louisiana. I too was pleased with my progress.

While I worked on my research, politics in China reshaped our lives in unexpected ways. In spring 1989 I put all of my energies into my dissertation. At the same time, I learned from a Chinese newspaper about the possibility of domestic demonstrations back home. The reporter suggested that many reform-minded young people were headed toward Beijing. Once they reached the capital, they hoped to discuss strategies for creating a strong and rich China. Understandably, this made the central government nervous. I followed this story and these events closely, for my heart remained in my homeland. As the situation in China escalated, Chinese students in Denton met to discuss these matters. In addition to all this, our local television station interviewed me because they knew I had been a teacher in China. They got right to the point. "We hear that the soldiers have already mobilized. Do you expect the government to crush the democracy movement?" I guessed that the soldiers would warn rather than kill the students. After all, the students had no weapons. I suggested that they simply wanted to talk with their leaders. It turned out, however, that like me, the well-organized students were naïve in their hopes for peaceful reform.

In nearby Dallas, Chinese students gathered for a peaceful march on the main street. Before we started our walk, one student warned me not to allow the television cameras to catch my face. I never even thought about this. I just wanted to show my support for those brave demonstrators in China. Because of my naiveté, everyone who watched the national news on ABC and CBS saw my face. I didn't make too much of this at the time. Meanwhile, my friends and I continued our meetings and tried to keep current on what was going on at home. We paid special attention to *Night Line,* because they broadcast everything that American journalists in China reported. We also received personal internet letters about the situation in China.

On June 4, 1989, we witnessed the recent violence in Tiananmen Square. We cried as we watched the tanks take on the poorly armed opposition. Earlier, we Chinese students in Denton had collected money to assist our compatriots at home. At that time, Mary and I had dug deeply into our pockets. Afterward, our group had elected a member to take the money to Beijing. He flew home, met the leader of the student demonstrators, and offered them our money. The leader refused our gift and asked us to deposit the money in a new account in America. "This way," he explained, "you will be able to provide us with financial help when we need it." So our Denton representative in China returned to Texas just before the Chinese government crushed its critics. Now, as the crisis unfolded, we weren't sure what we should do.

Soon after these events, friends and relatives in China wrote and told us more about what was happening there. In the letter I received from Xu, he encouraged me to stay in America. He noted that some people in China were already criticizing me. They claimed that I had brought democracy from America when I had taught in China between 1982 and 1984. They also remembered that my name had been on a 1976 black list in relationship to a political movement in our area. Even more worrisome than this, Xu reported that the Chinese security system, in its routine collection of television broadcasts from America, had seen my face on TV. He minced no words in his conclusion: "It would be dangerous, Nettie, for you to return home."

I've always planned to return home. But now, with these very real dangers, what should I do? What should we do? I passed my written comprehensives this spring. Now, I must concentrate on my dissertation and finish my education. But before that, I may need to take advantage of the good health care that is available in the States. I had good reason to worry about my health, for I had felt especially tired during the demonstrations. I had also experienced some unusual bleeding. When the doctor examined me, he discovered a nonmalignant tumor. Still, he recommended surgery. I followed his advice and had a hysterectomy. Fortunately, my student health insurance paid for everything except the 200-dollar deductible.

I never realized that I had so many friends. Xu would have come and cared for me had not the authorities refused his visa application. As it was, Dr. and Mrs. Tennison and Carol came to Denton and stayed with me through the surgery. Afterward, friends and acquaintances from our three church homes showered me with gifts. They filled my room with flowers and food. Although Catherine and Olive volunteered to cook for Mary and me, we didn't even need their help. After my quick recovery from my surgery, I returned to my work on the dissertation.

Although I made excellent progress with my education, I still wrestled with the issue of repatriation. I passed my oral defense of the dissertation in fall 1989. Thereafter, I had a few bureaucratic formalities to tend to, but that was basically it. My father and I were pleased to learn that his visa application to attend my graduation was approved. I was so happy when Daddy arrived safely. But Xu's letter, delivered by my father, gave me pause. "If China were to repeat its history from 1949," he said, "it would mean that our doors would be closed for another forty years. Even if you and I can't see each other later, you must still stay in America. You keep safe and look after Mary. I will take good care of Lana. Love, Xu."

My heart and my mind tugged in different directions as I reflected once again on our future. *The Tiananmen Square events prove that the Chinese government remains committed to class struggle. Indeed, I expect to see several similar episodes in my country's future. So sad! Maybe, after an appropriate waiting period, peace and calm will be restored. At that point, I will be able to return to China and will be given a position of leadership in music education. But until that time, I must steer clear of the class struggle method. If only Mary and Lana lived in the United States. Here, they can get a good education; here, they can develop into good Christians. Both are important to their futures. Although the 1989 Reform Movement brings many benefits to our economy, it creates other serious problems for our young people. I guess that settles it. At least for the present, we will stay in America.*

For the present, I orchestrated what I hoped would be a smooth transition from the certainties of being a graduate student to the uncertainties of the job market. My efforts brought mixed results. Prior to graduation, Gloria Hall, Kathryn Carpenter, and Mrs. Williams held a graduate reception in my honor. These final celebrations were exciting. Afterward, I wrote two important letters. In the first one, I told Carla and Bobby Campbell about my decision to stay in the States. "This decision must reverse our plans for Mary's adoption. She and I will stay together." Carla responded immediately. She and her husband had agreed to the adoption to help us out as we faced difficult circumstances. But now, she agreed that it was only right that a daughter and her mother stay together. I sent the second letter to the AAUW. I reviewed our relationship and my commitments, and expressed my hopes that they could be accommodating. "Earlier, I had promised you that I would return to China and teach for two years. But now," I explained, "if I follow through on my promise, I will endanger myself. In short," I concluded, "I must stay in the United States." I could not have hoped for a more understanding response. They sympathized with my situation and understood that it was hardly unique to me. Given my unusual case, they released me from my two-year commitment.

The American government also supported those of us who were stranded in the States: they gave us special permission to work. (I would have to wait several years, however, before I got my green card.) Now I had to find a job. Before my father had returned to China, he and I had talked with Dr. Jimmy Allen and Dr. Russell Dilday, the president of Southwestern Theological Seminary. Both men had indicated that they wanted to help me. Dr. Dilday thought he might be able to find me a job at the seminary. Dr. Allen suggested that I leave Denton, a city in which jobs were scarce, and that I move to Fort Worth.

I took their advice and moved to the "big" city. Unfortunately, neither of these men found me a job. At this point, my cash reserves were meager and our prospects were slim. But then a woman from AAUW came to my rescue. She hired me to deliver tickets for her travel agency. I dressed up for work, and she let me drive a company car. Before she sent me out, she urged me to be careful: "Remember, Nettie, these tickets are the same as money to me."

Two neighborhoods in Fort Worth reminded me of my need to be careful. As I set out to deliver tickets in a rundown neighborhood, I kept my eye out for trouble. Somehow, I unknowingly missed the exit I should have taken. Unaware of my error, I got off the highway, slowed down, and looked at street signs. As I crept by one intersection, I saw a group of people standing in their street. They stared at me in a fearsome way, so I took off. They followed, fast and slow, slow and fast. I had no idea where I wanted to go; I knew, however, that I needed to escape from real danger. Eventually, I found and reentered my highway. At that point my pursuers gave up the chase. Afterward, I found a gas station and called the travel agency. "You'd better be careful there, Nettie. You're right in the middle of a drug area." Careful indeed!

They then gave me directions to the place where I was supposed to deliver the tickets. This time I made no navigational mistakes. I suppose I should have felt relieved when I arrived in this new neighborhood, but it had its own set of problems. The backside of the building where I parked looked rundown. Undaunted, I entered the building, knocked on the door, and waited. A man from inside the room opened up just a crack and asked what I wanted. When I told him my business, he let me in. Inside, I saw boxes everywhere. I climbed around these obstacles, handed the tickets to a man and got his signature as surety that he had received the "merchandise." In fact, these people turned out to be okay. But they still scared me when they warned me to avoid driving on the street behind their building. I was super careful.

Soon, I tried my hand at another trade. I found a position as a hostess at a restaurant and quit my work for the travel agency. In addition to this, acquaintances from the Arlington Chinese Church put me in touch with two young piano students. This gave me a promising yet modest way to supplement my income. While I worked, Mary, a seventh grader, applied for admission at the William James College Readiness Academy. The leaders of this school, believing that their students were the future of America, used selective entrance examinations. We were pleased when Mary won admission into this fine institution.[3] But we worried because it was located so far away from our apartment.

Mary and I organized much of our lives around her transportation needs. I woke up at 5 A.M. to prepare breakfast and then drive Mary to the station for her six o'clock bus. In the afternoons, Mary had to transfer from the school bus to a public bus to get home. She spent the hour-long afternoon ride doing her homework. When she got off the public bus, she headed over to a Taco Bell. There, she bought what she could with her twenty-five-cent daily snack money. At first, she couldn't buy much with her quarter. But after the workers got to know Mary, they were more generous with their food. At this time, I was out teaching piano (and later, harp) lessons. So, Mary came home to an empty apartment. Here, my lonesome daughter turned on all the lights, the radio, and the television, and then napped, but only until her mother came home and fixed our supper. After supper, she finished the little homework she had left and hit the sack. Each weekday morning we repeated this taxing routine.

Many friends suggested that I follow my profession as a harpist and play at churches and weddings. They were right. I could supplement my income in this way, but only if I owned a harp. Mrs. Monica White from the AAUW located a young woman in Austin who offered to help me. This girl had bought a harp, taken lessons for a month, and then given up on that project. For the last four years she had kept her harp in her living room. Now, as a voice major in college, she wanted to sell the harp, but only to the right person. She rejected the idea of selling the instrument she still loved to some jazz band player who wouldn't care for it. The AAUW explained my situation to this woman, and then, on a Monday, I drove to meet her in Austin. We talked, and she agreed to sell me her harp—on excellent terms, too. She required no down payment. And she would charge me what she had paid for the instrument: $13,000. This was $3000 less than the current market price. Most importantly, we worked out a manageable arrangement: I could pay her off, interest free, at $200 per month. Five and one-half years later, I made my last payment. Meanwhile, I earned extra money by following my friends' suggestion.

I periodically sought the help of Dallas lawyers on emigration matters. Their advice? "Find an employer who will help you take care of the case. Or wait until the political matters related to Tiananmen Square are resolved." Not much help here. Others gave me more promising suggestions with regard to Lana's situation. "Get her a student visa and minimize your relationship to her." With the help of friends, I located San Marcos Baptist Academy, a boarding school in Texas. Afterward, I secured an I-20 form from this school and sent it on to Lana. Unfortunately, her application for a visa was turned down. So I tried an alternate route and wrote my congressman from Texas. A good letter, but we still remained stuck. In all of these legal matters, I only succeeded in getting my work permit extended. In the afternoons, I turned from my frustrating inquiries in the legal world to my simpler work as a restaurant hostess. Afterward, I drove to Arlington, where I taught my six music students. Despite our busy schedule, Mary and I seemed to be happy.

Since money was tight, we lived a simple life. On those occasions when I took Mary to the Waterburg Restaurant, I bought her a chicken fajita. Scrumptious, that's what she thought. The best food in the world! Since money was tight, I got only a glass of water for myself. Still, I enjoyed watching Mary eat while I drank.

I also tried to ensure that our difficult situation would not adversely affect Mary's schooling. Although her school was deliberately located in an impoverished area of town, it differed in quality and kind from its counterparts. In addition to the excellent instruction they provided, they also took their children on field trips. On these occasions, they rented regular buses and charged their pupils a small fee to cover the expenses. I remember well the field trip to San Antonio that the teachers planned. I worried about finding the extra money to cover Mary's fee. In the end, I discovered a way to cut down on my expenses. I parked my car in the free lot next to the train station and took public transportation into the city. From there, I walked to work. By doing this, I saved the five-dollar daily parking fee I normally paid in the city. The money I saved went for Mary's field trips.

Much later, I learned from Mary that our Fort Worth days had been hard for her. I was too busy just coping. This left my little daughter with the task of doing the best she could in handling the many changes she faced. A long trip each day; always lonesome; sometimes scared. *If only I could find a professional position, a job, that would draw upon my training as a musician and an educator. If only Xu and Lana could join us. If only we could all put down our stakes in a welcoming community.*

14

Green Pastures

1990–1991

China witnessed few surprises in the early 1990s. While the government ended martial law in January 1990, it persisted in its crackdown policies on dissidents. The following January, officials conducted their first trials of leaders of the 1989 democracy movement. They sentenced seven people to two to four years. Understandably, Li Peng continued to defend the government's forcible suppression of the demonstrators in Tiananmen Square. Continuing its openness in foreign policy, China established diplomatic relations with Saudi Arabia and Singapore. In the economy, China's leaders slowed down Deng's reform program and tackled corruption. None of these policies reached as far as Liberty, Missouri, the city in which Nettie and her daughter Mary lived and hoped the rest of the family might join them.

Mary and I attended a Chinese church during our Fort Worth days. There, in that church, we found friends who understood and helped us. There, in the Sunday services and in the Wednesday evening prayer meetings, we found spiritual sustenance for our souls. While my daughter and I continued our difficult work and our school routines, Dr. Tennison continued to help out from behind the scenes. In early spring 1990, he sent letters to virtually all of the Baptist colleges in the United States; he still hoped he could find me a job. Surprisingly, he received only one response to his inquiries. Dr. J. Gordon Kingsley, president of William Jewell College in Liberty, Missouri, answered by letter. He sympathized with me about my situation and, more importantly, he said he would do what he could to help.

In May 1990 Dr. Kingsley invited me to William Jewell College for a job interview. The Tennisons drove me up to Liberty, where Dr. Brown, chair of the Music Department, Dr. Tanner, provost of the college, and Dr. Kingsley met with me. The interview went well, so much so that they decided to create a position for me: I would serve on the Jewell faculty until I could get a green card. Such good news! More than I could have hoped for! When I returned, I shared my excitement with our friends at our Chinese church. Of course they celebrated with me. Then, at a Wednesday evening prayer meeting, they gave me a formal commissioning. This wonderful act of blessing, more common for the ordaining of deacons and missionaries than for sending music teachers to Missouri, prepared me in a special way for my new calling. That night they laid their hands on me and prayed to God for Mary and me.

A promising commission, but most of my practical problems remained unresolved. I could rent a Ryder truck, but what would I do after that? Who would help me pack and who would load my truck? How would Mary and I manage by ourselves on such a trip? I looked at a map and imagined a straight but long line between Fort Worth and Liberty. Another question: how would I, a woman who had never driven a truck, negotiate the traffic in such a huge vehicle? My desperation drove me to my knees. "Dear God," I prayed on a hot August day, "please let all the traffic get out of my way on the day when we make this impossible trip. I really need your help!"

That day I received a call from Reverend Chen, the young pastor of another Chinese church. He and I had enjoyed a friendship long before this stage of my wanderings. When, in 1983, my father had come to Texas to deliver a lecture at Southwestern Seminary, school officials had asked Mr. Chen, a graduate student at the seminary, to pick my father up in Denton. During their visit together, Mr. Chen had developed a profound respect for my father. Some years later, when Reverend Chen learned that

I was living in Fort Worth, he had called and we had talked several times. Now I received his special call: "I'm moving west, to California," Pastor Chen told me. "It's time for us to say good-bye to one another."

"Good-bye, indeed! I'm moving north, to Missouri," I replied. When Rev. Chen asked how I planned to move our belongings, I told him my thoughts about renting the Ryder truck.

"Maybe you could use a little help," he suggested. I quickly agreed, for I needed as much help as I could get. "I have some discount coupons," Rev. Chen continued. "They should reduce your costs substantially. And I think I can find a couple of young men who have the time and the muscle that we will need."

Before we left Texas, I contacted Joan Lawrence, Dr. Kingsley's assistant. She had located an apartment on Kansas Street; a five-minute walk and I would be sitting in my own office. She had also talked with Dr. Carl Hunkler, a former missionary to China who offered to meet me at the Brother's Conoco Station when we arrived in Liberty. She had also given Dr. Hunkler our apartment key, and he had agreed to help us get situated. Pastor Chen, who had high regards for Dr. Hunkler, knew we would be in good hands.

And if this were not enough, my friends from my Chinese church in Texas gave me an old car, a vehicle that one of their members had given to them. Afterward, I called Uncle Bill and told him that his Camaro would be staying in Texas; then I arranged to return his car.

Mary and I got moved from Texas and settled in Missouri in a single weekend. Fortunately, we had lots of help. Church friends volunteered and loaded most of my goods—on a Thursday evening. That meant we could get an early start the next morning. Rev. Chen and his two young volunteers drove the Ryder truck and my old car while Mary and I enjoyed the ride. Since that car had no air conditioner, we opened the windows so that we could survive the August heat. We also turned on the heater as a way of cooling off the engine—at least that's the explanation my driver offered. Along the way, we took occasional breaks, including a lunch stop when we ate the noodles my Chinese church friends had prepared for us.

At the end of the day, when we arrived in Liberty, Missouri, Dr. Hunkler met us at the Brothers Conoco Station. He led us a mile and a half down Kansas Street to our apartment; there, we parked the rental truck and my car. Next, Dr. Hunkler took us to Kentucky Fried Chicken, where he treated us to some of the world's best Southern cooking. After supper, we returned to our apartment and unloaded our goods. When I opened the refrigerator, I was surprised to find food. Don and Dorothy McClain, our neighbors just to the south of us, had provided for our needs. And when I stepped into the bathroom, I discovered that another generous soul had helped us. Joan Lawrence had stocked the cupboard with the basic necessities. Such a good Friday and such a long day!

On Saturday, Oz and Mary Quick, former missionaries to China, came to visit us. They drove us around Liberty, pointed out the grocery store, and gave us church information. On Sunday morning, the Quicks took us to their Chinese church in Gladstone, Missouri. Even though the church was small, it was big-hearted: all the members welcomed us with a fine party. At the end of the day I realized that we had actually made it, but not by ourselves. What a tiring and exciting weekend!

So much left to do in late August! I visited Jewell and got situated in my office. Dub Steincross, the pastor of Second Baptist in Liberty, stopped by, welcomed us into the community, and invited us to attend his church. Mike Lassiter, Second's youth pastor, assisted us with practical matters. He helped me with Mary's registration at the junior high school. He also helped me contact the Immigration Office—they had raised questions about Mary's residence in the United States. Among other things, they insisted that Mary be immunized again. Poor child.

By the end of August we had still not decided on a church home. Dr. Hunkler invited us to his Chinese church, a wonderful, large, Chinese congregation in Olathe, Kansas. This would have been a fine place for me had it not been a 70-mile roundtrip drive. But there was also Mary and her spiritual needs; I knew these must be primary. Second Baptist was only a five-minute walk down the street. Even more important than Second's convenient location was its terrific youth program. Soon, we joined this community of faith.

School started in September 1990. Mary seemed to manage well: she walked less than a mile to the junior high, and she had her own key to our apartment. At the same time, I began my teaching assignments at William Jewell. Soon, Jerry Cain, vice president for Religious Affairs at Jewell, helped me. He began by asking me to play my harp at the chapel services. Thereafter, he recommended me to the many Baptist churches in Missouri. They responded to Jerry's recommendation by regularly inviting me to speak and play my harp. So I was officially employed and working, maybe even too much.

During these same days I talked with a lawyer who helped me on immigration matters. I needed to get a label certificate and to switch my classification from a J-1 "visiting professor" visa to an H-1 "employed professor" visa. After a month's wait, the Immigration Office approved me for my H-1 card. Now I applied for a green card and listed Jewell as my employer. Maybe, if things continued to go well, my husband and my older daughter would be able to immigrate to the United States and join me in Liberty.

I tried to raise Mary, my teenage daughter, in a culture that, in filial relationships, was more alien to me than it was to her. In China, children rarely challenged parental authority. On those few occasions when I had questioned my own mother's wisdom, she had easily convinced me that I needed to listen to her. "I have eaten more salt than you have eaten rice," she said, "and thus I clearly know from experience much more than you do." She was right, and that was that! But now I had an Americanized daughter who, like her peers, took a different tack. "Why, Mom, must I make my bed? Why can't I stay up late?" "I'm not going to do my homework when I get home!" What to do, especially since Xu was far away and could not help me lay down the law?

Back in China, we talked about the need for both spouses to work together in order to raise their children properly. "When one parent sings a red face," we said, "the other needs to sing a white face; and when one sings a white face, the other should sing a red." This aphorism drew its imagery from Chinese opera; here, the character with red makeup always sang roughly, and the character with white makeup always sang smoothly. The aphorism suggests that both parents play a crucial role in raising a child. But I, a single parent, found it nearly impossible to "sing both faces." When, for example, Mary and I argued, she knew she was wrong. But like most young people, she found it difficult to admit her mistake. What she needed was another parent, one who could "sing a white face." This would have given her enough space to change her position without suffering undue humiliation. Unfortunately, in our situation, and with only one parental singer, it didn't work well, especially when my temper got the best of me. On these occasions I sang with only a "red face," and Mary was slow to embrace my parental counsel. If Xu had been here to "sing a white face," I could have found space to calm down. More importantly, the conflict between Mary and me would have been solved more easily. Chinese wisdom was right: I found it most difficult to sing with a red face and a white face at the same time; and that meant Mary and I were not getting the space we needed at home. I learned from experience the difficulties of being a single parent.

I also faced new difficulties when my old jalopy refused to cooperate on my frequent "deputation trips" to nearby Baptist churches. Too often, "she" made it to the outskirts of Liberty and then quit. Only a good mechanic could patch her up and persuade her to try it again. Even on those occasions when she ran well, she was still too tiny for my big harp. I was in a pickle. Shank's Mare could get me up to the College, but she lacked the energy to go much further.

Fortunately, good and generous friends from Texas recognized my needs and came to the rescue. Dr. McGuire and his fellow church members at First Methodist in Denton decided that they would raise enough money to find me a replacement vehicle. Fortunately, they didn't have to look far. Dr. McGuire discovered that a member of his own congregation was willing to sell his reliable old station wagon for 1,000 dollars. A done deal. My Methodist friends completed the paperwork, and Gloria and Kathryn, friends from P.E.O., drove my "new" car up to Liberty and delivered it to my doorstep. Now, my harp and I successfully completed our many trips to the Missouri churches that supported me. Once again I recognized God's care, a gift that extends beyond the birds of the air and the lilies of the field and includes his own children.

About the same time that I was working on changing cars, Xu faced a series of hard choices. In China, he held several high positions: assistant professor of art and literature at Shanghai Jiao Tong University, director of China University Education Council, and general secretary of University Music Education. Would the Chinese government let him emigrate? Could he abandon such a successful career for an unknown and maybe even less promising future in the United States? Would our daughter Lana be able to come with him?

My own recent success with the Immigration Office should have made it easier for Xu and Lana to come to the States. Indeed, they had no difficulty when they applied for H-2 cards. They were approved. But this was only a first step. It offered no guarantees of further success; more paperwork required more persistence.

They took a second step when they applied for their immigration visas. Two months later, in December 1990, they received the results: Xu alone was approved. If he had known that only one of the two of them would receive permission to immigrate, he would have chosen his daughter Lana; unfortunately, this choice was not his. But another one was.

Xu took his third step in January 1991: he boarded his plane for the United States. Once he got settled in our apartment in Liberty, he faced the problem of finding a job. It seemed unlikely that a man with no English would be able to secure a professional position anywhere near the level that he had held in China. Should he stay? Could he learn a new and difficult language? What sacrifices were necessary for freedom and family? Xu, now "Joseph," made his decision when he signed up for English lessons at the Don Bosco Community Center.[1]

We faced even more difficult problems when it came to getting Lana out of China; and without her, Mary, Joseph, and I could only dream about a complete and permanent family reunion in our new home. American friends and strangers sympathized with us and offered what help they could. Jerry Cain told me that Jewell students, young people whom I had never met, gathered together regularly in the college chapel in the early morning hours—between 6 A.M. and 7 A.M.; there, they prayed that Lana might be given a visa. Unfortunately, their prayers did no immediate good. When Lana applied again for that all-important visa, she was turned down; it was spring 1991. How discouraging! Since Lana had little hope of immigrating, she pursued a more realistic alternative: she took the entrance exam to study drama at a school in Shanghai. If she worked hard at that school, she might eventually find a satisfying career as an actress. But I knew that China was the wrong place for our daughter. We needed to have Lana live with us in Liberty, Missouri.

While we struggled with Lana's dilemma, Dub Steincross, our pastor from Second Baptist, showed up at our door for a pastoral visit. He listened attentively as I told him about Lana's being stuck in China. "The situation seems impossible," I explained. "She's been turned down twice, and now she must wait another three months to apply again. If that's not bad enough, Chinese guards surround the American consulate, and they won't even let her in to fill out the paperwork." Dub must have understood the Jewell motto, *Deo Fisus Labora,* "trust in God and work," for he suggested that we pray together; then, he placed a phone call.

Amazing! Dub got through, all the way to the American consulate in Shanghai. "Hello," he said, "I'm George Steincross, pastor of the Second Baptist Church in Liberty, Missouri. I'm wondering whether you could assist me on a matter that one of my parishioners faces?" The stranger on the other end of the phone listened and invited my pastor to continue. "Dr. Nettie Ma, one of our church members and a professor at William Jewell College, has a problem. Her nineteen-year-old daughter, a Chinese citizen by birth, has been unable to get a visa to immigrate to the United States. We'd sure like for this family to be united! I'm wondering whether you could help us?" I was even more amazed when this unknown man, this foreign service officer, readily agreed to "help us out." Dub went on to explain that Chinese guards blocked the way into the consulate. Easy enough. This American official, this stranger on the other side of the Pacific, promised to meet my daughter outside his building and beyond the perimeter of the guards. Afterward, he himself would walk her through the human barrier and into his consulate.

"Tell me Lana's age and size so that I will be able to recognize her. And you tell her that I will meet her tomorrow morning, outside the consulate; I'll take care of this matter from there." That ended this most unexpected and most promising conversation. I immediately phoned my father and asked him to pass the instructions on to Lana. So now Lana faced her own hour of decision. She had already received a reply from the drama college in Shanghai: they had accepted her as one of their students. If she chose to attend this school, she would remain in a world she knew, a China in which she could imagine her future. Should she stay? But she also had the real possibility of leaving China. If she chose to move to the United States, she would face the unknown. She knew little about this country and its language, except that her father and mother and sister wanted her to join them for a permanent family reunion. What should she do? She showed up outside of the consulate the next morning. Thereafter, it went like clockwork. Lana met the American diplomat, and he took her inside and signed her visa. It took only minutes.

A long flight to Kansas City, a short drive to Liberty, and at last, we were all together. Thereafter, with Dub's advice and with the help of the church staff at Second Baptist, we moved into a two-bedroom apartment on Missouri Street—still close to William Jewell and to the junior high. When we had first immigrated to the United States, each of us had needed only two suitcases. Now, we needed a truck and cars. At last, we were set. Our geographical journeying was over.

So many good things, and even more to come. I speak here, but only briefly, about spiritual pilgrimages and a family of faith. In spring 1991, I scheduled an appointment with Mike Lassiter. He listened attentively and talked with me about my worries. He explained that a small-town church youth group can unwittingly set up barriers that make newcomers feel less than welcome. "This summer," he continued, "we're taking a van to Centrifuge to attend a Christian youth camp. Second Baptist has some scholarship money. I sure hope Mary will be able to join us on this trip!"

Soon after my session with Mike, Mary and one of the girls in the youth group developed a close friendship. Then, at the appointed time, all the young people climbed into the van—Mary too—and took off for Centrifuge. There, they experienced Christian commitment, fellowship, and renewal. I sensed that something was different when the bedraggled youth, now back in Liberty, stepped down out of our van and into our church driveway. Mary's relationship with the youth had been deepened and enriched. I watched as they all hugged one another; only then were they ready to head home with their parents. Finally, Mary told me about the Centrifuge sunrise service, a time when she had experienced God's presence in a new and powerful way.

That summer of 1991, Mary requested baptism and joined our church. She was not alone in this, for Lana took the baptismal waters at the same time. Then, a year and a half later, Joseph committed his life to Christ and joined Dr. Hunkler's church. A reunion indeed! *My cup run-*

neth over. Surely goodness and mercy shall follow me all the days of my life: and I will dwell in the house of the LORD for ever.

I think back now to my deceased grandmother's prayers of so many years ago—they had borne fruit. Twenty-three years of geographical and spiritual separation were over. At last, my family was permanently united. We had found our way to our new home in Liberty, Missouri.

Epilogue: Comfortably at Home

At last, my family and I have settled in. We no longer face the high drama that had been central to our stories for so long; instead, we enjoy comparatively calm lives in our new homeland. At last, we can relax a little, even as we celebrate all the good dreams that have come true.

My father remarried and retired after my family settled in Missouri. It's the kind of retirement Daddy needs: part-time teaching at the Shanghai Conservatory and occasional conducting for the Shanghai Philharmonic Symphony Choir and for his church choir. Four generations of former students gathered in Shanghai in December 2003 to honor their Professor Ma at his ninetieth birthday.

Both of our girls have received an excellent education. Mary, who graduated from the Kansas City Art Institute, is a graphic designer for Trozzolo Creative Resources. She married Keith Enright in October 2003. Lana, who graduated from William Jewell College, is a senior marketing director for World Financial Group. She married Jay Chen in 1999; now she and her husband have a little girl named Katelyn. Unimaginable! My husband and I are grandparents. Joseph works as a Chinese cook. I still teach two classes a year at William Jewell College. I also offer instruction in harp and piano at Jewell's Community School of Music, at the

Northland Cathedral, and at home. And since 1996, I have taught Kindermusik, also in our home.

My political dreams came true when, in 1998, I became a United States citizen. I cast my own meaningful vote in the 2000 presidential election. I realize, however, that even the best politicians will fail to create a utopia. My parents taught me long ago that "man does not live by bread alone."

On Sunday mornings I gather together with a community of friends at the Second Baptist Church in Liberty, Missouri. There, we worship the God whose strength is made perfect in weakness, the God who turned the suffering of the cross into a triumphant resurrection. I know only too well that enlightened political leaders with messianic schemes and modern technology have failed to eliminate suffering. So I join my fellow Christians as we look in hope to a time when the nations will learn war no more, when the lion will lie down with the lamb. Like all God's people, we await the "city" whose builder and maker is God. And while we wait, here in our new home, I know that God's love spans oceans, that it has sustained his people in difficult times, and that it has embraced four generations of my own family. Such a beginning!

Notes

Prologue

[1] In this prologue, I will focus my comments about my family on the years between 1912 and 1940. The reader will note that in the main body of my narrative I weave my family's later stories and my own story together. In these footnotes, however, I will also occasionally speak of matters that extend into the 1950s.

[2] Miss Nettie lived with my grandparents during a portion of this period; at other points she lived in one of the more primitive nearby villages. My parents named me after Nettie. When times were difficult for me, Grandmother told me about the sacrifices Nettie had made in order to bring the gospel to China. I do not know what denomination supported Ms. Moomau.

[3] (1) Sheng Zhenwei (Robert Sheng), a lawyer trained at Northwestern Law School in the United States, married Shen Xianying (Rachel Sheng). Shen Minxing, Rachel's father, was a rich official in the Qing dynasty. Robert and Rachel had three children (Betty, Yvonne, and Roberta). (2) Sheng Beisi (Bessie Sheng). She earned her BA and MA degrees in the United States. She served as the President of the McTyeire First Elementary School. Aunt Bessie never married. (3) Sheng Zhenhua (C. H. Sheng). He and his wife Dora have lived in the United States since 1946 or 1947. They had one child (Marie). Dora was 101 years old in 2001. At that point she visited Europe, only one indication that she kept active. (4) Sheng Zhendong (John). (5) Sheng Lude (Ruth), my mother. The two other children (the second and the fifth) died in early childhood.

[4] Her generosity continued even after her husband died and money became tight. In time, Grandma's houseguests would become my extended family.

[5] Both of these good people faced severe tests in the 1950s. The Communists imprisoned their oldest son Zhenwei and their daughter Beisi, who lost her job. Soon, the Communists

arrested my paternal grandfather, one of my maternal grandfather's best friends. In the end, when Grandpa Sheng was blind, the government decided to close down his church. This was too much for him to bear. "God called Grandpa home and thus eased his burdens," or that's the way Grandma put it. But as for Grandma, I never saw her reduced to tears because of her difficult circumstances. Somehow she understood what it meant to trust God in whatever situation she found herself.

[6] A crippled beggar, a man whom people passed by every day, attended the revival with my grandfather. While there, the beggar experienced this "remarkable healing." Like most Pentecostals, my grandfather believed that one of the Holy Spirit's gifts was speaking in tongues. Not surprisingly, he rejected alcoholic beverages. He saw his first movie, a form of entertainment that conservative Christians questioned, at an American Air Force Base. In time, Grandfather mellowed on these social issues.

[7] At this time, Beihai was a part of Guangdong Province. Now, however, it belongs to Guangxi Province.

[8] The children at the home called Mrs. Lawler "Mother" Lawler. I assume they chose this term of endearment because of the affectionate care they received from their substitute mother.

[9] Nathan and Grace gave their children the following (biblical rather than Chinese) names: (1) Ma Geshun (my father). (2) Silas. He and his wife Barbara had one child (Luxia). (3) John. He and his wife Christina had two children (Phil and Eve). They have lived in the United States since 1947 or 1948. (4) David. He and his wife, Ling Binqin, had one child, Wenlei (Christine). (5) Philip, the second of the brothers, died of tuberculosis while he was in college. This last uncle is the only one of the five children whom I have never met.

[10] I understand that this school may have marked the beginnings of a household industry in Nanjing.

[11] It is common to see this name spelled "Soong" Ailing. This spelling reflects the old Wade-Giles system of transliteration. Some modern writers retain the Wade-Giles system for well-known names like Chiang Kai-shek (Jiang Jieshi) or for the "Soong" sisters. We have used the more modern Pinyin transliteration system in this book.

[12] They named this self-supporting church the Nanjing Independent Assembly of God. They moved the orphanage to this same location, on 189 Fengfu Road. Later, a noted Assembly of God missionary, W. W. Simpson, worked with my grandparents at this church.

[13] At one point, the orphanage had nearly 200 residents. Normally, the figure was closer to 100.

[14] One of these women played the most important role in having a church built in Nanjing.

[15] In many places in China, one could rent a donkey for transportation. Readers might see in this an early and primitive version of Western car rental. In the China of my grandfather's day, the donkey's master got the money, and the renter got to go where he wanted. Once the renter reached his destination, the donkey returned home (on its own) to his master.

[16] I used here the word "colored," the currency common in the late forties. I understand at least some of the later shifts in language (e.g., from "black" to "African American" to "people of color").

[17] They gave my grandfather a certificate as a formal award; in this document they designated him the "Bishop of China."

[18] More than 160 centimeters.

[19] Although teaching was Mother's calling, she also tried her hand at politics. In the 1950s she was elected as a local representative of our school district in Shanghai. (In particular, she served as people's representative for the second and third Changning County, and then as fourth, fifth, and sixth for the Jingan County.) In her capacity as people's representative, Mother visited with her constituents to discover their problems and then reported her discoveries to the local "council" of people's representatives. This council met regularly and tried to solve such problems. However well Mother succeeded as a "politician," she excelled as a teacher. In the 1950s the government gave her the most selective and rare rank of "first" among its elementary school teachers. Only four kindergarten teachers in all of China had an equal ranking. One important benefit of this special appointment was an increase in salary. In 1956, the city of Shanghai honored Mother as a "super teacher" and as an "advanced worker" in their city.

[20] She published a book, *More than Twenty Ways to Teach Children to Speak,* to disseminate her research.

[21] My grandfather loved the violin and led hymn singing. At Christmastime he played for the sick in the hospitals. At some point, he heard a recording of himself on a Manila radio station. At another point, he invited Yo-Yo Ma's father to play violin in his (Grandpa's) Nanjing Church.

[22] This choir sang the "Messiah" and the "Creation," but used Chinese rather than English words.

[23] He stayed on at the Zunde Girls' School for two years.

[24] Some foreign journalists took a picture of him as he conducted the choir. This picture would become a significant document in the history of China for these years.

Chapter Two

[1] Later, Mother taught at the first normal school in Shanghai and at a kindergarten associated with that school. It may be that after 1949, when the Communists reorganized the government educational system, Gongbuju became the kindergarten associated with the normal school. Later, in the 1950s, the kindergarten separated from the normal school and took on the name "Nanjing Xilu Kindergarten" and became independent. Thereafter, Mother no longer taught at the normal school. (In this case "Nanjing" was simply the name of a street in Shanghai.) My mother continued teaching there until she retired.)

[2] The Communists expelled foreign missionaries as they "liberated" lands from the GMD. Our missionaries left later than many others because the Communists arrived late in our city.

[3] From what I know, these three missionaries were probably affiliated with the Assembly of God Church.

[4] Rev. Hestekind died in 1998. His wife Grace lives on Camano Island off the coast of Washington State. In 1982–1983 these friends invited me to visit them in their home.

[5] Years later, in 1981, Southwestern Seminary had a special ceremony for my father; at that time he received his diploma and graduated. That same year Westminster Choir College offered him an Honorary Fellowship. In 1987, as I explain in a later chapter, Wartburg College awarded him an honorary doctoral degree.

[6] If we had paid rent, it would have meant that the church was in business to make money; this would have made it a capitalist organization, if you will. That would have caused big problems with the Communists. But a "love offering" was acceptable. The church, which was short on money, would have been even harder pressed than normal if it had offered us free housing.

Chapter Three

[1] Even after 1950, when my grandfather died, I still began my school days with my traditional "good morning," offering all my family a greeting as I prepared to go to school. My Auntie Bessie responded more quickly these days, for she didn't want me to feel badly when Grandpa gave no answer.

[2] Up to 1958, we always had a cat, even though the government didn't like it.

[3] Shunzhu had to leave us when the Cultural Revolution broke out. My parents helped her locate her son, who invited his "rich" mother to move in with him into his village house. Filial love was short-lived. Once the son had spent all of his mother's money, he kicked her out of his house. She returned to Shanghai, but she could not stay with us. So she rented a small room and worked in a city market. She still found time to visit us occasionally. I am

uncertain whatever happened to our former housekeeper, but I expect that she has died by now.

[4] Decades later and thousands of miles away, others heard that Christmas cantata, for choirs in Australia in 1998, and in California in 1997 and 1999, performed my father's "prison musings."

[5] This "Suppress" the Counter-Revolutionaries Campaign, *Zhen Fan Yundon*, lasted from 1950 to 1953. It is sometimes confused with the "Eliminate" the Counter-Revolutionaries Campaign, *Su Fan Yundon*, which began in 1955.

[6] After I came to the United States, my father gave me my own copy of his songbook. These choruses served Chinese Christians well during the Cultural Revolution, a time when the authorities closed the churches and prohibited people from owning Bibles or hymnals. Father's simple tunes and the scriptural texts that accompanied them had become a part of our lives. When the Cultural Revolution ended, many people thanked my father for the songs he had written. "Through your music," they reported, "we were reminded of the comfort and strength that God provides for his people in his Word." "You must," my father countered, "thank those Americans who funded the Lottie Moon Scholarship that allowed me to come to the United States where I learned composition techniques." In this modest response, he also spoke words of appreciation to his generous benefactors in the United States. He had learned his lessons well.

Chapter Four

[1] I.e., the General Line, the Great Leap Forward, and the Peoples' Communes.

[2] This Campaign to "Eliminate" the Counter-Revolutionaries is known in Chinese as *Su Fan Yundon.*

[3] This brand name drug rather than the generic "Rifampin" seems to be the expensive drug that my father secured for me.

Chapter Five

[1] I chose Russian over English.

[2] Although most of these college classmates have left China—some have immigrated to Hong Kong, Australia, and the United States—most of us still keep up with one another. Indeed, I often call these dear people in places all over the world. So it was that in 1998 "W," one of the best of my college friends, came from California to visit me in Missouri.

Chapter Six

[1] This man was also my father's close friend.

[2] In the summer of 1966, Mao tried to incorporate Chinese young people into the Cultural Revolution. He encouraged these adolescents or young adults to learn first-hand from the vanguard of the Revolution, the Beijing university students. Historians use different terms with slightly different emphases to speak of this same episode. "Exchange Revolutionary Experiences" emphasizes sharing stories; "Establish Revolutionary Ties" emphasizes bonding.

Chapter Seven

[1] The American version of this story is slightly different. "When the cross is present we can spell 'life'; without the cross, we must spell 'hell.'"

Chapter Eight

[1] Much later, this would become my room.

[2] Indeed. "H" still suffers because she stayed too long in the water. To this very day, she has serious knee problems and limited but permanent paralysis.

Chapter Nine

[1] In the late 1970s, when my cousin Maria Sheng visited us from America, she suggested that we give Lanlan the English name of "Lana," a word that sounded much like our daughter's Chinese nickname. We accepted her suggestion.

[2] Later, the government limited couples to one child.

Chapter Ten

[1] Although "all went well," we were terribly crowded. My folks, Lana, Mary, and I, all crowded into my parents' bedroom, while Xu and his father slept in a small storage shed out back.

[2] The Chinese call it Renshen.

[3] When Mary and I visited China in 1995, we visited with this woman.

[4] This "stinking ninth" label may go back to 1968, when the authorities classified its enemies into (1) landlords and their associates, (2) rich peasants, (3) counter-revolutionaries, (4) bad elements (i.e., criminals), (5) rightists, (7) capitalist-roaders, (8) reactionary bourgeois academics, and (9) intellectuals with ideological problems (i.e., "the stinking ninth").

Chapter Eleven

[1] Other schools included Roosevelt University, Colgate University, the University of Illinois, West Virginia Institute of Technology, Lamar University, Gustavus Adolphus, the University of Wisconsin, Luther College, Eastman Conservatory, Mount Vernon College, and Augustana University in South Dakota.

[2] At this point, my two daughters and I lived at home. When I went to work, Mother cared for Lana and Mary. Mary came home on the weekends, when I was home.

[3] Dr. Culpepper was her father.

[4] I have, since those days, kept in touch with P.E.O.

[5] The National Association for Music Education.

[6] Much later, after I had returned to Shanghai, Mrs. Williams wrote and told me that her husband had passed away.

Chapter Twelve

[1] The tadpole changes into a frog.

Chapter Thirteen

[1] Her Chinese name was Zhu Chongde.

[2] We must note the differences in the educational systems in China and in the United States. In my home country, the teachers required their students to follow each and every instruction. Experimentation and innovation were taboo. In America, however, teachers encouraged students to develop their own styles. Later on, I used this American pedagogical strategy when I taught music. Like my mentors, I encouraged children to discover what they liked and then to develop their own styles.

[3] She attended this school from December 1989 through August 1990.

Chapter Fourteen

[1] Now that Xu had settled in America, Dr. Tennison refers to him as "Joseph," his American name.